Gardens to V...
2009

Publicity Works • PO Box 32 • Tetbury • Gloucestershire • GL8 8BF

Copyright Tony Russell

Join Tony Russell in 2009 on a superb 'behind the scenes' tour of
The Cotswold's Finest Gardens

The Cotswold landscape is one of the most evocative in England. Gently rolling hills, secluded wooded valleys, clear running streams, Cotswold dry-stone walls and unspoilt villages, all paint a picture of timeless beauty.

Crowning glory of the Cotswolds is its gardens and in 2009 BBC garden writer, broadcaster and former Head Forester of Westonbirt Arboretum, Tony Russell, will be leading a series of unique and exclusive 'behind the scenes' tours of some of the very best gardens including Hidcote Manor, Kiftsgate Court, Abbey House Gardens, Westonbirt Arboretum and the private gardens of His Royal Highness the Prince of Wales at Highgrove House.

Tours take place in May, July and October and last four days with accommodation in the delightful Tortworth Court Hotel – which is set amidst beautiful gardens and has its own pool and spa for guests.

Cotswold garden tours

Exclusive behind the scenes tours of some of Britain's finest gardens in the company of BBC Garden writer and broadcaster Tony Russell

The all inclusive tour cost is just £495 per person. For further information and to receive a Cotswold Garden Tour brochure - please telephone **01453 836730** or email **mail@cotswoldgardentours.co.uk**

Gardens to Visit 2009

Welcome to the seventh annual edition of Gardens to Visit and once again I am delighted to report an increase in the number of gardens featured in the publication, thereby offering you even more interest and diversity when choosing your garden visits for the forthcoming year.

As always, we have your tried and tested favourites for you to enjoy, such as Batsford Arboretum, Portmeirion, the Lost Gardens of Heligan and Savill Gardens Windsor, the RHS gardens at Rosemoor and Harlow Carr, the National Trust's Hidcote Manor and Upton House and private delights like West Green House and Trewithen. Joining them this year are a further 40 new and exciting gardens for you to discover, including London's fascinating Chelsea Physic Garden, Cambridge's spectacular Anglesey Abbey and all four of Scotland's botanical gardens - Edinburgh, Benmore, Logan and Dawyck.

In all, Gardens to Visit 2009 features close on 200 of the very finest British gardens, compiled specifically for your enjoyment and such is their diversity that you will find gardens to visit in literally every month of the year. So, with that in mind, let me wish you an immensely enjoyable and rewarding year of garden visiting in 2009.

Tony Russell
BBC garden writer and broadcaster

Feed the Children's Tree Project

The Saplings project provides saplings, tools, fertiliser and training, giving triple benefits - fruit for nutrition, wood for fuel and confidence building skills.

Help to fund the project by buying special Saplings ribbons at £1 each. Each ribbon green (for leaves) and brown (for roots) represents a sapling. Alternatively donate on-line at www.feedthechildren.org.uk or contact Feed The Children on 0118 932 0095.

There's also going to be a fundraising walk at the wonderful Westonbirt, the National Arboretum, on Sunday 26th April 2009 to raise funds for Feed the Children.

Every tree counts . . . .

Feed the Children's simple questionnaire (at www.feedthechildren.org.uk), reveals that most families in developed countries need to plant more than 200 trees to offset their carbon footprint! We produce 6-7 tonnes of carbon per family and each tree can convert up to 29 kilos of carbon dioxide each year to oxygen. The implication is clear - plant more trees! How? Support the charity's Saplings Project.

Charity chief executive Brian Main explains, "Most of us can't plant 200 trees, but we can reduce our carbon footprint whilst giving life saving resources to others. Some 80% of rural Africans depend on wood for fuel, but trees are coming under pressure due to nomadic habits and growth. Our Saplings project educates children on the importance of trees for their future and gives them trees to cultivate, underlining the message to the whole community."

Typically, a child will be given two saplings - either a fruit tree or one with medicinal properties and another, fast growing tree for cutting for firewood. Learning through songs and poems they take home a simple, powerful message: if you cut down a tree, plant two more!

Gardens to Visit is now online at www.gardenstovisit.net

www.gardenstovisit.net

Stourhead - Wiltshire

Contents

Borde Hill Garden - West Sussex

England

*'I hold the firm belief that the purpose of a garden is to give happiness
and repose of mind, firstly and above all other considerations, and to
give it through the representation of the best kind of pictorial beauty
of flower and foliage that can be combined or invented.'*

Gertrude Jekyll – 1905

A simple statement made over 100 years ago and yet possibly even more pertinent
today, given the need for all of us to be able to 'take time out' from our busy and all too
often pressured lives. Gardens provide us with oasis of tranquillity and beauty,
somewhere calm for reflection and a place to 'recharge our batteries' ready for our
next foray into 21st century life.

In the pages that follow you will discover many such places; from Cornwall
to Northumberland and from Kent to Cumbria, located within our busy
cities and immersed in the countryside. We hope you enjoy our 2009
selection of the very best English gardens.

The Swiss Garden   Bedfordshire

The Swiss Garden was created in the early nineteenth century. It contains picturesque features hidden in an undulating nine-acre landscape. The garden is planted with magnificent trees and ornamental shrubs which are arranged in a series of glades, lawns and winding walks, designed to provide unexpected vistas. The recently refurbished and replanted, subterranean grotto and fernery nestles in the centre. 'The Grand Tour' provided inspiration for the tiny thatched Swiss Cottage. The fashion for 'Swiss" architecture, so popular in the Regency period can be seen all around the Garden. Elegant floral arches and a network of ponds with decorative bridges and delightful islands complete the picture. Peafowl roam freely in the garden. Spring bulbs, rhododendrons and rambling roses are spectacular in season. Benches are located at frequent intervals. There is also an adjacent picnic area and a woodland lakeside walk.

Fact File

Opening Times:	November 1st to March 31st 10am - 4pm, April 1st to October 31st 10am - 5pm
Admission Rates:	Adults £5.00, Senior Citizen £4.00, Accompanied Children Free.
Group Rates:	Minimum group size: 20 but all groups welcome Group Rate £3.50, Accompanied Children Free.
Facilities:	Visitor Centre, Restaurant, Toilets, Gift/Souvenirs and Plant Stall.
Disabled Access:	Yes, Toilet and parking for disabled on site. Wheelchairs on loan, booking advised.
Tours/Events:	Guided Tours and Group Bookings by appointment.
Coach Parking:	Yes.
Length of Visit:	2 hours
Booking Contact:	Karen Wilsher The Swiss Garden, Old Warden Park, Old Warden, Biggleswade, Bedfordshire, SG18 9EP. Telephone: 01767 627924 Fax: 01767 627949
Email:	karen.wilsher@shuttleworth.org
Website:	www.shuttleworth.org
Location:	Approximately 2 miles west of Biggleswade A1 roundabout signposted from A1 and A600.

Please quote this guide when making a booking

Savill Garden - Windsor Great Park Berkshire

The Savill Garden provides a wealth of beauty and interest in all seasons with 35 acres of ornamental gardens and woodland, including National Collections and rare international species.

Spring is heralded by hosts of daffodils, magnolias and wonderful varieties of rhododendrons and azaleas. Summer brings a contrast of colour with the floral vibrancy of the borders and the pastel shades of the Golden Jubilee Garden. The glorious displays and textures in Autumn are fantastic, with the golden hues of the acers and unique native plants in the New Zealand Garden. The Queen Elizabeth Temperate House also showcases original and unusual seasonal plant displays throughout the year.

Plus, visit the environmentally sustainable and award winning Savill Building.

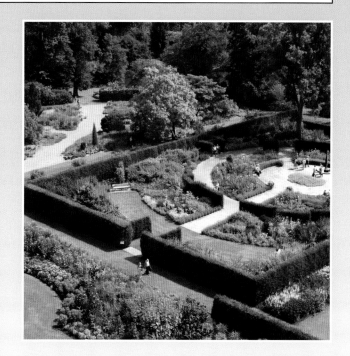

Fact File

Opening Times:	10am - 6pm March - October, 10am - 4.30pm November - February (last admission to the Garden is 30 minutes before closing).
Admission Rates:	Adults £7.50, Senior Citizen £7.00, Child (6 - 16) £3.50, Family £18.50.
Group Rates:	£6.00 per person for groups of 10 or more.
Seasonal Prices:	Prices shown are peak prices, (March 09 - October 09). Please contact The Savill Garden for off peak prices.
Facilities:	Shop, Plant Sales, Teas, Restaurant.
Disabled Access:	Yes. Toilet and Parking for disabled on site. Wheelchairs available to loan.
Tours/Events:	Guided tours are available, (please book your tour two week prior to visit) Ongoing programme of events and exhibitions. Please visit www.theroyallandscape.co.uk or contact The Savill Garden for details.
Coach Parking:	Yes.
Length of Visit:	3 - 4 hours
Booking Contact:	Carla Hall Crown Estate Office, The Great Park, Windsor, Berkshire, SL4 2HT Telephone: 0845 603 6228 Fax: 01753 624107
Email:	enquiries@theroyallandscape.co.uk
Website:	www.theroyallandscape.co.uk

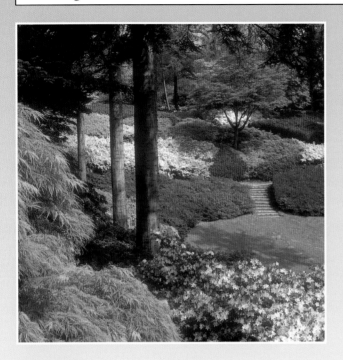

A woodland garden on the grand scale; set beneath the canopies of beautiful mature trees with delightful views to Virginia Water Lake. Over 200 acres of camellias rhododendrons, magnolias and many other flowering trees and shrubs provide visitors with breathtaking displays in March, April and May.

Massed plantings of hydrangeas are the highlight of the summer before a myriad of autumn tints from Japanese maples, birches, sweet gums and tupelos light up the woods.

Winter brings the flowers of witch-hazel and drifts of heathers amongst the dwarf conifers in the Heather Garden before swathes of dwarf daffodils stud the turf in the sweeping Azalea Valley.

Truly a garden for all seasons.

Fact File

Opening times:	Car park open: 8am - 7pm (4pm in winter) or sunset if earlier.
Admission Rates:	Car Park Charges: £6.00
Facilities:	At nearby Savill Garden.
Disabled Access:	Limited. Toilet and parking for disabled on site. Wheelchair trail in the garden.
Tours/Events:	None.
Coach Parking:	Coaches by arrangement on weekdays only (Charge applies).
Length of Visit:	2 - 3 hours
Booking Contact:	Carla Hall
	Crown Estate Office, The Great Park, Windsor, Berkshire, SL4 2HT
	Telephone: 0845 603 6228 Fax: 01753 624107
Email:	enquiries@theroyallandscape.co.uk
Website:	www.theroyallandscape.co.uk
Location:	On the eastern boundary of Windsor Great Park (off A30)
	Access to Valley Gardens car park via Wick Road.

Please quote this guide when making a booking

Waltham Place Organic Farm & Garden Berkshire

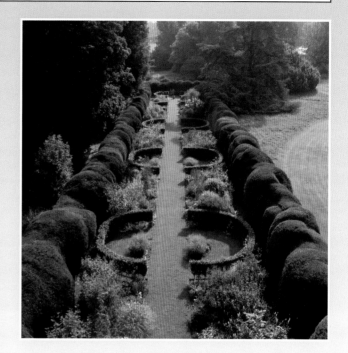

Waltham Place Estate has often been described as "the best kept secret in Berkshire", and what you find here is a little oasis which has much to offer the visitor at all levels. There are beautiful gardens designed by Henk Gerritsen, which explore the boundaries between gardens and nature and are a haven for an array of flora and fauna.
The estate includes a farm, ornamental and kitchen gardens, with a lake and woodlands. It has been managed organically for over 20 years and has matured into a thriving environment.

Visitors can come and enjoy the gardens on their own or on a guided walk. Head Gardener Beatrice Krehl, takes groups around the gardens. She explains the principles of naturalistic planting used here, for example how the plants are allowed to run their natural cycle and therefore support the wealth of insect and bird life.

The Tearoom and Farm Shop sell only produce from the estate and it's a real chance to enjoy local food at its best.

Fact File

Opening Times:	From the beginning of May until end of September. Please refer to website or contact office for confirmation of 2009 opening times. Gardens Open Wednesdays in aid of NGS 10am - 4pm everybody welcome. Fridays' Walk with the Gardener only 11am and 2pm, duration 11/2 - 2 hours. Tuesdays and Thursdays, visits to the garden by appointment only. Tea Room and Farmshop open Tuesdays - Fridays 10am - 4pm, Organic Lunch (Estate produce) served between 12noon and 2pm.
Admission Rates:	Adults £4.00, Senior Citizen £4.00, Child £1.00. Group Packages available.
Facilities:	Organic Farm Shop, Tea Room, Plant Sales, Education & Group Visits.
Disabled Access:	Yes. Toilet and parking for disabled on site.
Tours/Events:	Seasonal walks, group tours by arrangement.
Coach Parking:	Not on site but very close by.
Length of Visit:	2 - 3 hours
Booking Contact:	Estate Office Waltham Place, Church Hill, White Waltham, Berks SL6 3JH Telephone: 01628 825517 Fax: 01628 825045
Email:	estateoffice@walthamplace.com
Website:	www.walthamplace.com
Location:	From M4 junction 8/9 take A404M and follow signs to White Waltham. Turn left to Windsor and Paley Street and St Mary's Church. Estate on left handside.

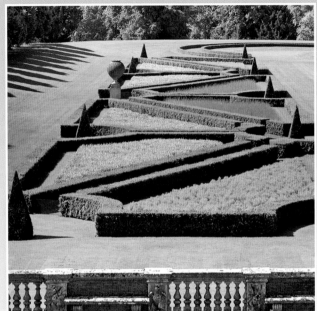

Once the home of the fabulous Astors, Cliveden's Grade I listed garden has recently undergone, and continues to receive, major conservation and restoration works.

The spectacular south-facing parterre originally designed by John Fleming has been completely replanted and offers magnificent views over the Thames Valley and beyond. The Long Garden with its extravagant topiary will be planted for 2009 with 25,000 tulip bulbs for spring followed by a colourful scheme for summer. The lawns to the front of the Italianate mansion are flanked by great herbaceous borders providing summer-long colour.

Lunches and teas are served in the Orangery, with plants and a wide selection of interesting products available in the gift shop.

Fact File

Opening times:	28 February – 25 October – daily, 11 a.m. – 6 p.m.
Admission Rates:	Adults: £8.00, Children: £4.00
	NT Members Free.
Group Rates:	Minimum Group Size: 15 Adults: £6.80 – Not Sundays
Facilities:	Visitor Centre, Shop, Plant Sales, Restaurant, Teas, Audio-visual guide
Disabled Access:	Yes. Wheelchair loan available
Toilets on site:	Yes
Car Parking on site:	Yes
Coach Parking:	Yes
Guided Tours:	Yes, booking required.
Length of Visit:	2 – 3 hours
Booking Contact:	Gill Coop, Cliveden, Taplow, Nr. Maidenhead, Buckinghamshire, SL6 0JA
	Booking Tel No.01628 605069. Booking Fax No. 01628 669461
Email:	cliveden@nationaltrust.org.uk
Website:	www.nationatrust.org.uk
Location:	M4 Junction 7 to A4 or M40 Junction 4 to A404 and follow brown signs.
	Coach entrance on Bourne End Road

Please quote this guide when making a booking

Waddesdon Manor and Gardens were bequeathed to the National Trust by the Rothschilds in 1957. The garden today is essentially the one laid out by Baron Ferdinand de Rothschild and his French, landscape designer, Elie Lainé.

It is considered one of the finest Victorian gardens in Britain with a parterre, seasonal displays, colourful shrubs, carpet bedding, statuary, fountains and parkland. At its heart lies the rococo-style Aviary housing exotic birds and known for breeding endangered species. The Aviary glade is the location of a new acquisition called Perceval by Sarah Lucas, a life-sized, bronze horse and cart. Sarah is of the same generation of artists as Damien Hirst and the late Angus Fairhust, whose gorilla sculpture can be seen in an area called the Tulip Patch.

The garden can be enjoyed at any season. Guided walks take place from April to September.

Fact File

Opening times: Gardens, Aviary, Woodland Playground, Shops and Restaurant - 10.00-5.00

Admission Rates: Winter Season, 3 Jan-29 Mar (weekends only), Adult: £5.50, Child: £2.75, Family: £13.75
Peak & Christmas Season, 01 Apr-23 Dec (Wed-Fri), Adult: £5.50, Child: £2.75, Family: £13.75
01 Apr-23 Dec (weekends & BHs), Adult: £7.00, Child: £3.50, Family: £17.50,
27 Dec-31 Dec (Wed-Fri) Adult: £5.50, Child: £2.75, Family: £13.75, 27 Dec-31 Dec (weekends) Adult: £7.00, Child: £3.50, Family £17.50, (Including Monday & Tuesday 28 & 29 Dec)
NT members free. RHS members free, gardens only, September and October only

Group Rates: Minimum Group Size: 15.
Group rates available see www.waddesdon.org.uk or phone the booking contact (see below).

Facilities: Shops, Plant Centre, Restaurant, Woodland Playground

Disabled Access: Yes. Wheelchair loan available.

Toilets on site: Yes

Car Parking on site: Yes

Coach Parking: Yes

Guided Walks: Yes

Length of Visit: 1 – 4 hours

Special Events: Yes

Booking Contact: Deborah Read, Waddesdon Manor, Waddesdon, Nr. Aylesbury, Buckinghamshire HP18 0JH
Booking Tel No.01296 653226. Booking Fax No. 01296 653212

Email: deborah.read@nationaltrust.org.uk

Website: www.waddesdon.org.uk

Location: 20 minutes from Junction 7 (northbound) and 9 (southbound) off the M40, off the A41 between Aylesbury and Bicester.

Anglesey Abbey, Gardens & Lode Mill   Cambridgeshire

A visit to the gardens at Anglesey Abbey offers a surprise around every corner. Throughout the year, the changing colours and scents provide a unique experience.

Rare varieties of snowdrops create a popular display in January and February. Thousands of hyacinths are a highlight in the spring, while summer is celebrated by the colourful herbaceous borders and dahlia gardens. Magnificent autumn foliage is followed by glorious winter colours and fragrances, making Anglesey a garden for all seasons.

The gardens are the vision of one man, Huttleston Broughton, 1st Lord Fairhaven. He created them between 1930 and his death in 1966. His attention to style and planting has given Anglesey the reputation as one of the great gardens of the twentieth century. His enthusiasm for collecting statuary can also be seen within the gardens.

Lord Fairhaven gave the gardens and the house to the National Trust on his death.

Fact File

Opening times: Gardens Open 1 January – 31 December, Wednesday to Sunday.
Closed Mondays (except Bank Holiday Mondays) & Tuesdays and 24 – 29 December.
Gardens open at 10.30 and close at 17.30 in summer, 16.30 in winter.
House open 8 April - 1 November, 11.00 – 17.00

Admission Rates: Gardens only (1 January – 15 March) Adult: £4.75*, Child: £2.40*
Gardens only (from 18 Mar) Adult: £5.80*, Child: £2.90*, Family: £14.50*, Family (1 adult): £8.70*
Includes a voluntary 10% gift aid donation which will be put towards the restoration and upkeep of the property.
NT Members Free. RHS Members Free – garden only

Group Rates: Minimum Group Size: 15 Gardens only (1 January – 15 March) Adult: £4.00, Child: £2.00
Gardens only (from 18 March) Adult: £4.95, Child: £2.45

Facilities: Visitor Centre, restaurant, shop, plant sales, second-hand bookshop

Disabled Access: Yes. Disabled toilets and parking avaialble. Wheelchairs and PMVs available to borrow, booking essential. Mill: access to lower floor only, ramp available.

Toilets on site: Yes

Parking: Car Parking on site. Coach Parking booking essential.

Length of Visit: Minimum 2 hours

Guided Tours: Yes, booking essential.

Special Events: Special events programme, for details please visit
www.nationaltrust.org.uk/angleseyabbey or telephone 01223 810080

Booking Contact: Administrator, Anglesey Abbey, Gardens & Lode Mill, Quy Rd, Lode, Cambridge CB25 9EJ
Booking Tel No.01223 810080. Booking Fax No. 01223 810088

Email: angleseyabbey@nationaltrust.org.uk

Website: www.nationaltrust.org.uk/angleseyabbey

Location: 6 miles north-east of Cambridge on B1102. Signed from A14, junc 35.

Please quote this guide when making a booking

Elgood's Brewery Gardens   Cambridgeshire

A beautiful 4-acre garden, situated behind Elgood's Brewery, on the banks of the River Nene in Wisbech, in the heart of the Fens.

The garden is famous for its maze and its trees, some over 200 years old, including Ginkgo Biloba, Tulip Tree, and Tree of Heaven. There is a lake with golden and ghost carp, a pond, which is home to Great Crested Newts, and a hot-house with many exotic plants.

The Visitor Centre houses a museum with brewery artefacts and pub memorabilia. A variety of freshly prepared snacks are available in the licensed cafe-bar and there is a well-stocked shop selling quality beers, gifts and plants.

Close by are The Octavia Hill Museum, The Wisbech & Fenland Museum, and the National Trust's Peckover House. These attractions, together with several excellent pubs along the riverbanks, add up to an enjoyable and interesting visit.

Fact File

Opening Times:	28th April - 24th September 2009 11.30am - 4.30pm.
Admission Rates:	Garden & Brewery - Adults £6.50, Senior Citizens £6.50, Child (6-16) £4.00
	We regret that children under 6 are not permitted on Brewery Tours
	Garden only - Adults £3.00, Senior Citizen £2.50, Child £2.50
Groups Rates:	Minimum group size 10
	Garden & Brewery - £5.50, Garden Only - £2.50
Facilities:	Visitor Centre, Gift Shop, Plant Sales, Teas, Licensed bar, Free Parking.
	No dogs except guide dogs.
Disabled Access:	Yes. Toilets and parking for disabled on site. Wheelchairs on loan. Booking Advisable.
Tours/Events:	Brewery Tours Tues, Wed, and Thurs 2pm (not suitable for disabled) Garden show and Craft Fair 10th May & 6th September 10am - 4pm
Coach Parking:	Yes
Length of Visit:	1 - 2+ Hours
Booking Contact:	Kate Pateman
	North Brink, Wisbech, Cambridge, PE13 1LN
	Telephone: 01945 583160 Fax: 01945 587711
Email:	info@elgoods-brewery.co.uk
Website:	www.elgoods-brewery.co.uk
Location:	Wisbech

Elton Hall Gardens — Cambridgeshire

Elton Hall Gardens have been stunningly restored during the last twenty years. The modern design is loosely based on an Edwardian interpretation of the medieval and Victorian gardens. Immaculately kept hedges of hornbeam and yew encompass four different areas.

The main lawn has a mass of topiary and an enchanting sunken lily pond which is surrounded with beds containing a number of specimen plants.

The former rose garden has recently been redesigned and is now a magical flower garden with a modern fountain and wisteria clad arches.

The Millennium was celebrated by the building of an orangery and this is set in a colourful Mediterranean garden with lemon and orange trees.

A small shrubbery area, with such gems as Paulownia Tomentosa, leads the visitor back into the Box Walk to enjoy another view of the house set in these magnificent gardens.

Fact File

Opening Times: 2.00 p.m. – 5.00 p.m.: May Bank Holiday Sunday 24th May and Monday 25th May; Wednesdays in June; Wednesday, Thursday and Sundays in July and August; August Bank Holiday, Monday 31st August.

Admission Rates: Adults: £5.00, Senior Citizens: £4.50, Children: Accompanied children under 16 admitted free

Group Rates: Minimum Group Size: 20. Adults: £5.00

Facilities: Shop, plant sales, restaurant, teas, toilets.

Disabled Access: Yes – to garden

Car Parking on site: Yes

Coach Parking: Yes

Tours/Events: Free flow or guided tours available. Booking required.

Length of Visit: 1 hour

Booking Contact: The Administrator
Elton Hall Gardens, Elton Hall
Nr. Peterborough, Cambridgeshire PE8 6SH
Booking Telephone No. 01832 280468
Booking Fax No. 01832 280584

Email: office@eltonhall.com

Website: www.eltonhall.com

Location: Elton is located just off the A605 between Peterborough and Oundle.

Please quote this guide when making a booking

Peckover House & Garden   Cambridgeshire

Peckover House is an elegant Georgian merchant's house within the heart of Wisbech, built in 1722. For one hundred and fifty years it was lived in by the Peckover family, a Quaker banking dynasty. The outstanding two-acre garden is a rare gem of surprising size, hidden behind the backs of neighbouring properties. It is regarded as one of the finest walled town gardens in the country, and its "gardenesque" character offers a rambling perambulation through distinct areas, with vistas through gaps and internal walls. The garden contains notable trees, such as Ginko Biloba (Maidenhair tree), Liriodendron tulipiferum (Tulip Tree), and possibly the largest specimen of Cornus mas in the country. The garden also contains three summerhouses, two pool gardens, over 70 species of rose and a croquet lawn. The Victorian glasshouses include an Orangery with 300-year-old orange trees which still fruit prolifically.

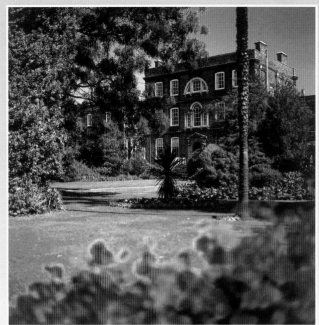

Fact File

Opening times: 14th March – 1st November 2009. Saturday, Sunday, Monday, Tuesday, Wednesday 12 – 5pm
Also open Good Friday and 2nd and 3rd July for Wisbech Rose Fair

Admission Rates: Adults: £5.80, Children: £2.90, Family: £14.70
National Trust members: Free

Group Rates: Minimum Group Size: 15. Adults: £4.90 Booking necessary

Facilities: Shop, Plant Sales, Restaurant, Secondhand bookshop

Disabled Access: Yes, level access. Wheelchair loan available + PMV loan (book in advance)
Toilet on site. No parking on site – drop-off point available.

Tours/Events: House and garden tours, day and evening tours available.

Coach Parking: No, available nearby

Length of Visit: 2+ hours.

Booking Contact: Property Secretary
Peckover House and Garden, North Brink, Wisbech, Cambridgeshire PE13 1JR
Tel: 01945 583463

Email: peckover@nationaltrust.org.uk

Website: www.nationaltrust.org.uk/peckover

Location: Centre of Wisbech, on north bank of River Nene.

Please quote this guide when making a booking

Arley Hall & Gardens   Cheshire

The award winning gardens, recently voted in the top 50 in Europe and in Britain's top 10, have been lovingly created over 250 years with each generation of the family making its own contribution. The result is a garden of great atmosphere, interest and vitality, which blends strong elements of design from earlier centuries with modern ideas in both planting and design. Arley is, therefore, a wonderful example of the idea that the best gardens are living, changing works of art. Outstanding features are the renowned double herbaceous border (c1846) the Quercus Ilex and pleached Lime Avenues, Victorian rootree, walled gardens, yew hedges and shrub rose collection. The family tradition continues today with the current Viscount Ashbrook, who over the last 30 years has created the less formal Grove and Woodland Walk, where 300 varieties of rhododendron grow amongst a collection of rare trees and shrubs in a delightful tranquil setting.

Fact File

Opening Times: Garden, Chapel & Grove: 11am – 5pm Tuesday - Sunday, 22 March – 27 September, Weekends in October. Gardens open in October 2009 weekend only.
The Hall: 12 noon – 5pm, Tuesdays and Sundays plus Bank Holidays*, April through September Sundays only in October. *If your primary reason to visit is to see The Hall, please call The Estate Office on 01565 777353 to confirm opening times.

Admission Rates: Gardens: Adults £5.50; Seniors £5, Children 5-16 £2, Family £13, UNDER 5's free.
Hall: Adults £2.50, Seniors £2, Children 5-16 £1.

Group Rates: Gardens £5; Seniors £4.50; Hall & Gardens £6.50; Seniors £5.75.
Season tickets: Individual £28, Joint £46, Family £64.

Facilities: Shop, Plant Nursery, Licensed Restaurant, Teas, Picnic & Play Area, Chapel, Estate Walks.

Disabled Access: Yes. Toilet and parking on site. Wheelchair available booking (recommended for special events).

Tours/Events: Please check website for details.

Coach Parking: Yes.

Length of Visit: 2 hours

Booking Contact: Caroline Fearon, Arley Hall & Gardens, Northwich, Cheshire CW9 6NA
Telephone: 01565 777353 Fax: 01565 777465

Email: caroline.fearon@arleyhallandgardens.com

Website: www.arleyhallandgardens.com

Location: M6 – Junction 19 or 20, M56 Junction 9 or 10. Brown tourist signs from Northwich and Knutsford, both 6 miles approximately.

Please quote this guide when making a booking

Ness Botanic Gardens Cheshire

Ness Botanic Gardens – Winner of The Mersey Partnership Large Visitor Attraction of the Year '08 and the Visit Chester and Cheshire – Large Attraction of the Year 2008.

The superb gardens at Ness on the Wirral Peninsular, overlooking the Dee Estuary were founded in 1898 by Arthur Kilpin Bulley, a Liverpool cotton merchant with a passion for gardens and for plant collecting.

Our Visitor Centre provides a warm welcome to the Gardens incorporating the Four Seasons café, gift shop and plant sales area.

An extensive events programme runs throughout the year including; guided walks, Sunday lectures, courses, children's half term activities, see our website for details www.nessgardens.org.uk   Winner of a coveted Gold Medal display garden at the RHS Flower Show at Tatton Park – a must see garden feature.

Much of the garden is accessible for those of limited mobility and both courtesy wheelchairs and motorised buggies are available for advance booking.

Fact File

Opening Times:	1st February – 31st October: 10 a.m. - 5 p.m.
	1st November - 31st January: 10 a.m. - 4.30 p.m.
Admission Charges:	Adults: £5.75, Senior Citizens: £5.25, Children: £2.75, Under 5 years: FREE
Group Rates:	Minimum Group Size: 20, Adults: £5.25.
On-Site Facilities:	Visitor Centre, Shop, Plant Sales, Licensed Restaurant, Teas, Lecture Theatre
Disabled Access:	Yes, partial. Wheelchair and mobility scooter loan available, booking required.
Toilets on site:	Yes
Car Parking on site:	Yes
Coach Parking:	Yes
Guided Tours:	Yes, booking required
Length of Visit:	Approx. 2½ hours
Special Events:	See www.nessgardens.org.uk
Booking Contact:	Val Hall, visitor Services Manager, Ness Botanic Gardens, Ness, Neston, South Wirral, Cheshire CH64 4AY
	Booking Tel No.0151 353 0123 Booking Fax No. 0151 353 1004
Email:	nessgdns@liv.ac.uk
Website:	www.nessgardens.org.uk
Location:	Road: off A540 Chester-Hoylake Road.

Please quote this guide when making a booking

Rode Hall Gardens were created by three notable landscape designers; Humphry Repton drew up the plans for the landscape and Rode Pool in his 'Red Book' of 1790. Between 1800 and 1810 John Webb, a Cheshire landscapist, constructed the Pool, an artificial lake of approximately 40 acres and at the same time he created the terraced rock garden and grotto. This area is covered in snowdrops in February followed by daffodils and bluebells and colour continues with the flowering of many specie and hybrid rhododendrons and azaleas in May.
In 1860 William Nesfield designed the rose garden and terrace where the flowerbeds are now filled with roses and a variety of herbaceous plants.
The two-acre walled kitchen garden dates from 1750 and grows a wide variety of flowers, vegetables and fruit. An Italian garden is being developed in the ruins of the old `Tenants Hall.
There is a fine icehouse and the Hall is open to the public on Wednesdays.

Fact File

Opening times: Snowdrop walks: From 24th January to 1st March – daily except Mondays and Tuesdays 12–4pm. 1 April to 30 September: Tuesdays, Wednesdays, Thursdays and Bank Holidays (not Good Friday): 2 – 5pm.

Admission Rates: Adults: £3.00, Senior Citizens £2.50, Children (over 12): £2.50

Group Rates: Minimum Groups Size: 15

Facilities: Shop, plant sales, teas, light lunches for snowdrop walkers in February only.

Disabled Access: Limited. Toilet and car parking on site

Tours/Events: Guided tours available.

Coach Parking: Yes

Length of Visit: 1 hour.

Booking Contact: Valerie Stretton. Rode Hall Gardens, Rode Hall, Scholar Green, Cheshire ST7 3QN
Telephone: 01270 882961 Fax: 01270 882962

Email: richard.wilbra@btconnect.com

Website: www.rodehall.co.uk

Location: 5 miles south of Congleton, between A34 and A50.

Please quote this guide when making a booking

Stapeley Water Gardens

Cheshire

Stapeley Water Gardens is the perfect destination all year round! The Palms Tropical Oasis is home to beautiful floral displays - from the Mediterranean splendour of the centre palms to the myriad of dazzling and exotic plants in the tropical house.

See aristolochia, beautiful orchids, variegated hibiscus, spectacular bougainvillea and the largest waterlily in the world, the Giant Amazonian Waterlily.

For a breath of fresh air, you can take a stroll outside to the beautiful and tranquil Italian Garden and unwind by the Japanese Koi Carp pool and Waterlily display. For some retail therapy you can take a trip to the enormous garden centre. Here you'll find everything you need for the graden and inspiration from the striking water gardens, with the National Collection of Waterlilies in bloom from mid June to September.

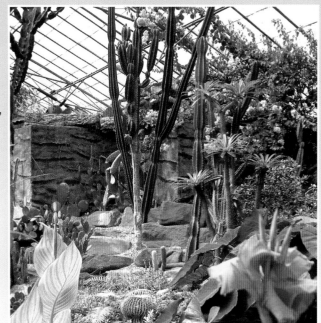

Fact File

Opening Times:	Garden Centre: 9am–6pm. (summer), 9am – 5pm. (winter), Sundays: 10am– 4pm.
	Palms, Tropical Oasis: 10am–6pm. (summer), 10am– 5pm. (winter), Sundays: 10am– 5pm.
Admission Rates:	(Admission to Palms Tropical Oasis only)
	Adults: £4.95, Senior Citizens: £4.45, Children: £2.95, Family tickets (2A, 2C) £12.60.
Group Rates:	Minimum Groups Size: 15 Adults: £3.95, Senior Citizens: £3.55, Children: £2.35
Facilities:	Shop, plant sales, restaurant, teas. Feeding schedule at the Palms Tropical Oasis every Sunday, plus a choice of three group entertainment packages (please request a leaflet).
Disabled Access:	Yes. Toilet and car parking on site. Wheelchair Loan booking available.
Tours/Events:	Different events throughout the year.
Coach Parking:	Yes
Length of Visit:	Approximately 3 hours.
Booking Contact:	Palms Reception. Stapeley Water Gardens, London Road, Nantwich, Cheshire. CW5 7LH Telephone: 01270 628628 Fax: 01270 624188
Email:	palms@stapeleywg.com
Website:	www.stapeleywg.com
Location:	Signposted from J16, M6. 1 mile south of Nantwich on A51

Please quote this guide when making a booking

Bosvigo is a 'must see' Cornish Colourist's garden created by owner Wendy Perry; an essential contrast to the grandeur and scale of the great Cornish Spring gardens. Wrapping around the lovely old house are a series of enclosed gardens with dazzling colour displays.

This is a garden both to love and to learn from. A spectacular Spring display of hellebores in the Woodland Garden is followed by breathtaking Summer herbaceous borders and on to the high drama of an Autumn finale of bold hot 'Firework' colours.

Visiting groups are treated to a private tour of the house and to tea in the historic kitchens which have been restored to their original Georgian glory. Bosvigo is a well-loved and lived-in family home, complete with a resident ghost reputed to linger in the Blue bedroom!

Fact File

Opening times: 1 March – 29 September: Wednesday, Thursday & Friday 11 a.m. – 6 p.m.

Admission Rates: Adults: £4.50, Senior Citizens: £4.50, Children: Under 5 free, Children 5 – 15 years £2.00

Group Rates: Minimum Group Size: 15. Adults: £4.50, Senior Citizens: £4.50, Children: Under 5 free, Children from 5 – 15 years £2.00

Facilities: Plant Sales, Help-yourself Teas

Disabled Access: Yes, but limited

Toilets on site: Yes

Car Parking on site: Yes

Coach Parking: Yes – Lane at side of house, by appointment only.

Guided Tours: Yes (of the house only), booking required.

Length of Visit: 1 – 2 hours, depending on level of plant interest

Special Events: Fantastic Hellebore day, second week in February (look on website for date, or ring) Woodland walk open in aid of local charity, teas/lunches in old kitchens.

Booking Contact: Mrs. Wendy Perry Bosvigo, Bosvigo House, Bosvigo Lane, Truro, Cornwall TR1 3NH Booking Tel No.01872 275774. Booking Fax No. 01872 275774

Email: bosvigoplants@talktalk.net

Website: www.bosvigo.com

Location: OS SW8145 in the western suburbs of Truro by A390. At Highertown, turn down Dobbs Lane by Aldi Store. Bosvigo is 500 yards on the left after the nasty bend!

Please quote this guide when making a booking

This 30-acre woodland gardens and nursery boasts award-winning displays and flowering features to captivate garden-enthusiasts and horticultural amateurs alike.

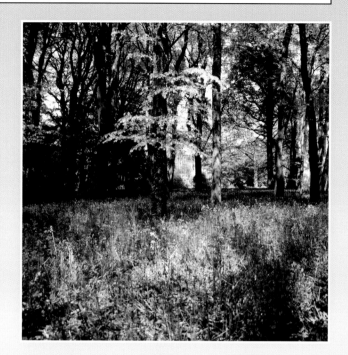

Perched on a hilltop, is home to one of the most diverse ranges of plants in the region. Its sprawling woodland gardens and old flower garden are rich with the likes of camellias, azaleas and rhododendrons, as well as over 20 species of bamboo.

Its vast acreage is packed with prolific blooms all year round and you can take self-guided wanders to appreciate the beauty of the successive seasons.

On a Spring ramble witness the drifts of snowdrops, primroses and wild violets, and later the daffodils and blankets of nodding bluebells. On a Summer wander it is the hydrangeas that spread their purple-blues and swamp the fading blooms of Spring. Take an Autumn amble, when more subtle colours and hardy specimens still leave much to be discovered

Fact File

Opening Times:	Monday – Saturday: 8.30 – 5 p.m. Sunday 11 a.m. – 5 p.m.
Admission Charges:	(to gardens only, nursery free): Adults: £2.00. Conducted tour £2.50 each
On-Site Facilities:	Shop, Plant Sales, Teas
Disabled Access:	Yes
Toilets on site:	Yes
Car Parking on site:	Yes
Coach Parking:	Yes
Length of Visit:	$1\frac{1}{2}$ - 2 hours
Booking Contact:	Stephen Dance, Burncoose Nurseries, Gwennap, Redruth, Cornwall TR16 6BJ Telephone No. 01209 860316 Fax No. 01209 860011
Email:	info@burncoose.co.uk
Website:	www.burncoose.co.uk
Location:	On A393 betweenRedruth and Falmouth approximately half-way between villages of Lanner and Ponsanooth.

This informal woodland garden created in the late 19th and early 20th century by J C Williams, is today the home of many fine examples of plants brought back by the intrepid plant hunters of the early 20th century and also a wide range of rhododendrons, camellias and magnolias, both bred and raised here, which the Williams family and Caerhays Gardens have become famous for worldwide.

Caerhays Castle is of the very few Nash built castles still standing and is situated within the 60 acre garden. Caerhays Garden is home to the famous williamsii camellias and also home to a National Magnolia Collection and was found, by a representative of the Tree Register, recently to contain no less than 78 Champion Trees (thought to be the most in a private garden in England).

Fact File

Opening Times: Garden:16th February to 31st May 2009   Seven days a week 10.00 am to 5.00 pm
last admission 4.00 pm
House: 16th March to 29th May 2009   Week days only (inc Bank Hols) 12.00 to 4pm

Admission Rates: Garden or House, £5.50 (adults), £5.00 (OAP) £2.50 (Under 16)
Combined Ticket, £9.50 (adults), £4.50 (Under 16)

Group Rates: Special group rates (Min 15 pers) or Private guided tours of the garden only by appointment

Facilities: Shop, plant sales area, licensed tea rooms serving lunches and snacks

Disabled Access: Partial, steep paths to top of garden but drive and lower routes fully accessible.
Disabled toilet in courtyard. Disabled parking by entry.

Tours\Events: Contact Estate Office for more details

Coach Parking: Yes. Coaches may drive up to entrance and unload before parking at beach.
Limited parking for small coaches by entrance.

Length of Visit: At least 2 hours for garden and 1 hour for house

Booking Contact: Cheryl Kufel, Estate Office, Caerhays, St Austell, Cornwall PL26 6LY
Tel: 01872 501310   Fax: 01872 501870

e-mail: estateoffice@caerhays.co.uk

Website: www.caerhays.co.uk

Location: South Cornwall coast between Mevagissey and Portloe, 9 m SW of St Austell

Please quote this guide when making a booking

Carwinion

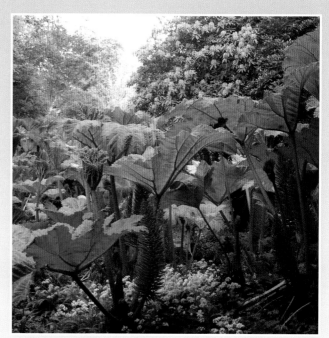

Lush, lovingly restored and utterly magical, Carwinion Garden lies in a sheltered Cornish valley on the Helford River. Ponds, waterfalls and sheltered pathways are dotted amongst the towering trees, bamboos and well-established plants in this twelve acre family run garden.

The garden contains a plethora of specimen plants, immense tree ferns over a hundred years old, gunnera with leaves spanning over two metres and ferns and Hellebores which flourish in the dappled sunlit woodland. Carwinion has one of the largest collections of bamboos in England; over two hundred different varieties (some exceedingly rare in cultivation) can be found growing throughout the garden and are at their best during the summer months.

The garden is at its pinnacle in Spring-time when the impact of colour, the bluebell carpeted woodland, the fragrance of the Azaleas and the continued blooming of the Camellias provides a sensual experience not to be missed.

Fact File

Opening Times:	All Year, every day 10am - 5.30pm
Admission Rates:	Adults £4.00, Senior Citizens £3.50, Child Free (under 16).
Group Rates:	Minimum group size: 10
	Adults £3.50, Senior Citizens £3.50.
Facilities:	Plant Sales, Teas (2 - 5.30pm from May - Sept), Small Gift Shop.
Disabled Access:	Partial. Toilet and parking for disabled on site.
Tours/Events:	Occasional Art Exhibits & Theatre displayed in Gardens and House.
Coach Parking:	yes, by arrangement
Length of Visit:	1 - 2 hours
Booking Contact:	Jane Rogers
	Carwinion, Carwinion Road, Mawnan Smith, Nr Falmouth, Cornwall, TR11 5JA
	Telephone: 01326 250258 Fax: 01326 250903
Email:	jane@carwinion.freeserve.co.uk
Website:	www.carwinion.com
Location:	Five miles South-West of Falmouth, in the village of Mawnan Smith, North side of the Helford River.

Please quote this guide when making a booking

Eden Project   Cornwall

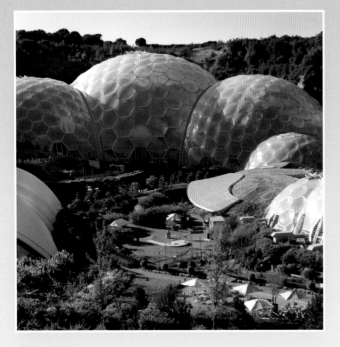

An unforgettable experience in a breathtaking epic location. Eden is a gateway into the fascinating world of plants and people and a vibrant reminder of how we need each other for our mutual survival.

Its home is a dramatic global garden the size of thirty football pitches, nestling like a lost world in a crater overlooking St. Austell Bay. One of its giant conservatories is a majestic rainforest cathedral, the other is host to the fruits of the Mediterranean and the flowers of South Africa and California. Outside in the landscaped grounds you will find tea and lavender, sunflowers and hemp.
It is a place to tell a hundred plant stories from cocoa and coffee to bananas and rubber. From plants and medicine to plants in construction. From paper and wine and from perfume to brewing.

For details of seasonal events such as Bulb Mania and our winter festival 'A Time of Gifts; please visit our website.

Fact File

Admission Rates:	Adults: £15.00, Senior Citizens: £10.00, Children: £5.00 (under 5s free), Family £36.00
Group Rates:	Minimum Group Size 10
	Adults: £11.00, Senior Citizens: £8.00, Children@ £4.00
Facilities:	Visitor Centre, Shop, Plant Sales, Restaurant
Disabled Access:	Yes, toilet and car parking on site.
Tours/Events:	See website www.edenproject.com for special events
Coach Parking:	Yes.
Length of Visit:	4 hours
Booking Contact:	Carol Barrett,
	Eden Project, Bodelva, St. Austell, Cornwall PL24 2SG
	Tel: 01726 811903, Fax: 01726 811912
Email:	Information@edenproject.com
Website:	www.edenproject.com
Location:	Brown tourism signs on A30, A39 and A390.

Enys is considered to be the oldest garden in Cornwall. Robert de Enys lived there during the reign of Edward 1. The 1709 edition of Camden's Magna Britannia mentioned that Enys was noted for its fine gardens.

One of the main features is the Ladies Garden, later called the Flower Garden. This garden leads in to the Colonel's Garden, named after Colonel Enys (1757 -1818) and is currently being replanted as a scented garden.

J D Enys, an inveterate traveller, greatly enriched Enys with seeds and plants he regularly sent home from New Zealand and Patagonia.

In spring the bluebells in the parkland, known as Parc Lye, are a sight to behold. This area is believed to be undisturbed since ancient times.

Probably the most valuable asset to the garden is its microclimate together with its peaceful and tranquil setting.

Fact File

Opening Times: Tuesdays, Thursdays, and the first Sunday of the month from 2 p.m., 1st April to 30th Sept.
Admission Rates: Adults: £3.00, Senior Citizens: 2.50, Children and students: £1.00.
Facilities: Teas.
Disabled Access: Yes, wheelchair loan available.
Toilets on site: Yes.
Tours/Events: Guided tours available, booking required.
Coach Parking: Yes.
Car Parking on site: Yes.
Length of Visit: 1-2 hours.
Booking Contact: W. H. Ward
Enys Gardens, St Gluvias, Penryn, Cornwall
Telephone: 01872 274536 or 07770 662849
Fax: 01872 223421
Email: whwone@supanet.com
Website: www.enystrust.org.uk
Location: Off Truro to Falmouth road, A39.
From Truro: 2nd left after Norway Inn. Follow signs.
From Falmouth: to Penryn (B3292). At Cross Keys pub, right fork into Truro Hill and follow signs.

.

The Lost Gardens of Heligan   Cornwall

Heligan, seat of the Tremayne family for more than 400 years, is one of the most mysterious estates in England. At the end of the nineteenth century its thousand acres were at their zenith; but only a few years after the Great War of 1914, bramble and ivy were already drawing a green veil over this sleeping beauty.

After decades of neglect, the devastating hurricane of 1990 should have consigned the Lost Gardens of Heligan to a footnote in history. Instead, fired by a magnificent obsession to bring these once glorious gardens back to life, a small band of enthusiasts has grown into a large working team with its own vision for Heligan's future.

Today "The Nation's Favourite Garden" offers 200 acres for exploration including restored productive gardens, working buildings and historic glasshouses, atmospheric pleasure grounds and a subtropical "Jungle" valley, surrounded by a sustainably managed estate incorporating a pioneering wildlife project.

Fact File

Opening Times: From 10am daily, all year round. (Except Christmas Eve and Christmas Day).

Admission Rates: Adults £8.50, Senior Citizens £7.50, Child £5.00, Family (2 adults and 3 children) £23.50

Groups Rates: Minimum group size 20, prior booking is essential.
Adults £7.50, Senior Citizens £6.50, Child £5.00. Pre-booked guided tour additional £1pp.

Facilities: Licensed Tea Rooms, Lunchtime Servery, Heligan Shop and Plant Sales, Lobbs Farm Shop. No Dogs March - October incl.

Disabled Access: Yes. All facilities and throughout most of the garden restoration and wildlife hide. Wheelchairs are available on a first come first served basis. Contact us for information in various formats.

Tours/Events: Please telephone for seasonal details or see our website.

Coach Parking: Yes, by prior arrangement.

Length of Visit: At least 4 hours

Booking Contact: Group Bookings Department.
The Lost Gardens of Heligan, Pentewan, St Austell, Cornwall, PL26 6EN.
Telephone: 01726 845120   Fax: 01726 845101

Email: info@heligan.com

Website: www.heligan.com

Location: From St Austell, take the Mevagissey Road (B3273) and follow the brown tourist signs to "The Lost Gardens of Heligan".

Please quote this guide when making a booking

One of only three Grade 1 listed Cornish Gardens set within the 865 acres of the Country Park overlooking Plymouth Sound. Sir Richard Edgcumbe of Cotehele built a new home in his deer park at Mount Edgcumbe in 1547. Miraculously the walls of this red stone Tudor House survived a direct hit by bombs in 1941 and it was restored by the 6th Earl in 1958. It is now beautifully furnished with family possessions.

The two acre Earl's Garden was created beside the House in the 18th century. Ancient and rare trees are set amidst classical garden houses and an exotic Shell Seat. Colourful flowers and heather grace the re-created Victorian East Lawn terrace. Also formal 18th Century Gardens in Italian, French & English style, modern American & New Zealand sections. There are over 1000 varieties in the National Camellia Collection which received the international award of 'Camellia Garden of Excellence'.

Mount Edgcumbe, RHS Britain in Bloom Public Park Awards 2007.

Fact File

Opening Times:	House & Earls Garden open 1st April - 30th September, Sunday to Thursday 11am - 4.30pm; Country Park open all year.
Admission Rates:	House & Earls Garden - Adults £5.00, Senior Citizen £4.00, Child £2.50, Country Park Free.
Groups Rates:	Minimum group size: 10 (April - September) Adults £4.00, Senior Citizen £4.00, Child £2.20
Facilities:	Shop & Tea Room in House. Orangery Restaurant (limited opening in winter), Civil Weddings, Conference Facilities.
Disabled Access:	Yes. Toilet and parking for disabled on site. Wheelchairs on loan, booking necessary.
Tours/Events:	Guided tours of the gardens available all year. Historic buildings, Camellia Collection in season. Exhibition and events programme. Introductory talk given to booked groups.
Coach Parking:	Yes
Length of Visit:	2 hours
Booking Contact:	Secretary. Mount Edgcumbe House, Cremyll, Torpoint, Cornwall, PL10 1HZ Telephone : 01752 822236 Fax: 01752 822199
Email:	mt.edgcumbe@plymouth.gov.uk
Website:	www.mountedgcumbe.gov.uk
Location:	From Plymouth Cremyll Foot Ferry, Torpoint Ferry or Saltash Bridge. From Cornwall via Liskeard - to A374, B3247, follow brown signs.

Please quote this guide when making a booking

Pencarrow, the much-loved home of the Molesworth-St Aubyn family for nearly 500 years, is set in 50 acres of Grade II* woodland and garden where dogs and children are most welcome.

Superb specimen conifers from around the world tower over a profusion of azaleas, magnolias and camellias galore, with 700 varieties of rhododendron adding to the blaze of spring colour; blue hydrangeas line the mile-long carriage drive throughout the summer.

Start exploring and you'll find a surprise around every corner – ancient Celtic cross, a 2, 000 year old Iron Age hill fort, Victorian lake and ice house, grotto, restful Italian gardens with fountain and an enormous rockery that was once the largest in the country.

The Georgian house boasts an impressive library with secret door (think of Harry Potter meets Narnia), elegant but "lived in" reception rooms, period bedrooms and collections of family prams, dolls, oriental porcelain, fascinating antique furniture and portraits.

Fact File

Opening times:	Gardens: daily 9.30 – 5.30 from March 1st – October 31st. House, café and shop: Sunday – Thursday inclusive: 11 a.m. – 5 p.m. from 5 April – 24 September (last tour of house at 3 p.m.)
Admission Rates:	Adults: House: £8.50, Gardens: £4.00, Senior Citizens: £8.50, Gardens: £4.00, Children: House: £4.00 Gardens: £1.00. Under 5s: free Historic Houses Association Members Free
Group Rates:	Minimum Group Size: 20. Adults: from £6.00, Senior Citizens: £6.00 Children: Please contact administrator
Facilities:	Shop, Plant Sales, Teas
Disabled Access:	Yes (partly). Wheelchair loan available – booking required
Toilets on site:	Yes
Car Parking on site:	Yes
Coach Parking:	Yes
Guided Tours:	Yes, booking required on arrival at house.
Length of Visit:	House: 1 hour; gardens 2+ hours
Special Events:	Please see website for craft fairs, outdoor theatre etc.
Booking Contact:	Sally Harvey, Pencarrow, Washaway, Bodmin, Cornwall PL30 3AG Booking Tel No.01208 841369, Booking Fax No. 01208 841722
Email:	info@pencarrow.co.uk
Website:	www.pencarrow.co.uk
Location:	4 miles north of Bodmin on A389

Please quote this guide when making a booking

St Michael's Mount Cornwall

A unique and extraordinary maritime garden created in terraces just above the sea, at the foot of a magical castle St. Michael's Mount.

Visitors to St. Michael's Mount are often surprised to find there are gardens here at all, clinging to a granite rock face that is almost vertical, falling some 200 feet from the castle to the sea far below.

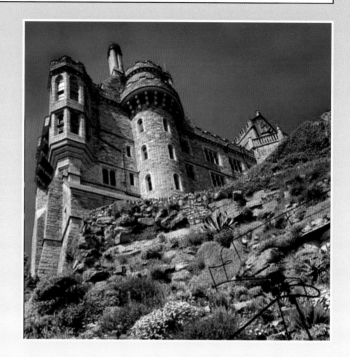

The gardens are buffeted by the winter gales and drenched in salt spray, then they become a tranquil oasis during the summer months. The warm Gulf Stream coupled with the heat retentive granite cliffs and walls enable a wide range of tender and exotic plants to be grown in the south facing gardens.

Access to the island is by motorboat or causeway.

Fact File

Opening times:	Garden: 1st May – 30th June, Monday to Friday. 1st July – 30th October, Thursdays and Fridays only. Castle: 29th March - 1st November - Sunday to Friday. Combined Castle & Garden ticket also available. All visits subject to favourable weather conditions
Admission Rates:	Adults: £3.00, Children: £1.00, NT members Free. Garden evenings available - a guided tour of the garden followed by a gourmet buffet at the award-winning Sail Loft Restaurant. Please telephone or check the website for details.
Group Rates:	Minimum Group Size: 15 Guided tour of Gardens with one of Mount Gardeners £5.00 per person.
Facilities:	National Trust Sail Loft Restaurant and Island Café, shops and plant sales
Disabled Access:	Bookable Sand wheelchair available for loan.
Tours/Events:	Guided tours available. Free trail available for younger children. Garden Evenings available - a guided tour of the garden followed by a gourmet buffet at the award-winning Sail Loft restaurant. Please telephone or check the website for details.
Coach Parking:	On mainland.
Length of Visit:	2 – 3 hours
Booking Contact:	Clare Sandry, Manor Office, Marazion, Cornwall TR17 0EF Tel: 01736 710507 Fax: 01736 719930
Email:	clare@manor-office.co.uk
Website:	www.stmichaelsmount.co.uk
Location:	½ mile South of A394 at Marazion

Please quote this guide when making a booking

Steeply wooded 25 acre sub-tropical valley garden falls 200 feet from 18th century house to private beach on Helford River.

A stream cascades over waterfalls through ponds full of Koi Carp and exotic water plants, winds through 2 acres of blue and white hydrangeas and spills out over the beach. Huge Australian tree ferns and palms mingle with shrubs of ever changing colours and scent beneath over-arching canopy of 100 year old rhododendrons and magnolias. A giant plantation of gunnera and clumps of huge bamboos give the garden a unique and exotic wildness matched by no other garden in the British Isles.

The newly built Hibbert Centre houses a distinctive restaurant, garden and gift shop. Children love Trebah, as do dogs (welcome on leads).

Fact File

Opening Times:	Open every day of the year normallly 10.30am to 5pm, or dusk if earlier. Winter times may vary slightly.
Admission Rates:	Adults £7.50, Senior Citizen £6.50, Child £2.50. 1st Nov 2009 - 28th Feb 2010, Adults £3.00, Senior Citizen £2.50, Child £1.00. RHS Members Free entry: Nov, Dec, Jan, Feb & March. NT Members Free entry: Nov, Dec, Jan & Feb.
Group Rates:	Minimum group size: 12 Adults £6.00, Senior Citizen £6.00, Child £2.50.
Facilities:	Visitor Centre, Shop, Plant Sales, Teas, Restaurant.
Disabled Access:	Yes, Toilet and parking for disabled on site. Wheelchairs on loan, booking advised.
Tours/Events:	Free welcome talk on arrival, full guided tour of one and a half hours at an extra £2.00 per head - must be booked in advance.
Coach Parking:	Yes.
Length of Visit:	2 1/2 - 3 hours
Booking Contact:	V Woodcroft Trebah Garden, Mawnan Smith, Falmouth, Cornwall, TR11 5JZ. Telephone: 01326 252200 Fax: 01326 250781
Email:	mail@trebah-garden.co.uk
Website:	www.trebah-garden.co.uk
Location:	From north - A39 from Truro to Treliever Cross Roundabout, follow brown and white tourism signs to Trebah.

Please quote this guide when making a booking

Trevarno Estate & National Museum of Gardening   Cornwall

A unique and unforgettable garden experience comprising of 70 acres of gardens and grounds, with abundant wildlife and one of Cornwall's largest and most diverse plant collections. Follow the progress of major restoration projects and walk the 2km Estate walk passing the spectacular National Daffodil Collection and visit Santa's reindeer while they holiday in Cornwall.

More formal areas include the Serpentine Yew Tunnel, Italian Garden and Great Lawn. Relax in the Fountain Garden Conservatory and enjoy homemade refreshments. Visit the remarkable National Museum of Gardening, fascinating Soap Museum or nostalgic Vintage Toy Museum, plant sales or shop, which sells our own Organic Skincare products. For the youngsters there is the Woodland Play area to let off steam.

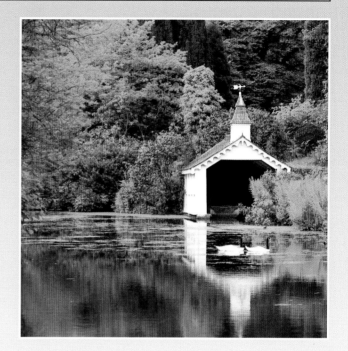

Fact File

Opening Times:	10.30am - 5pm all year except Christmas Day & Boxing Day.
Admission Rates:	Adults £6.50, Senior Citizens £5.75, Child £2.25, Disabled £3.25.
Group Rates:	Minimum group size: 12
	Adults £4.45, Senior Citizen £3.95, Child £1.25.
Facilities:	The National Museum of Gardening, Shop, Plant Sales, Tea Room, Vintage Soap Collection, Craft Workshops, *Vintage Toy Collection (*small additional charge).
Disabled Access:	Partial. Toilet and parking for disabled on site. Wheelchairs on loan, booking essential.
Tours/Events:	Numerous events throughout the year. Please call for details or visit www.trevarno.co.uk.
Coach Parking:	Yes, for up to 6 coaches.
Length of Visit:	4 hours
Booking Contact:	Garden Co-ordinator
	Trevarno Estate, Trevarno Manor, Crowntown, Nr Helston, Cornwall, TR13 ORU
	Telephone: 01326 574274 Fax: 01326 574282
Email:	enquiry@trevarno.co.uk
Website:	www.trevarno.co.uk
Location:	Trevarno is located immediately east of Crowntown village - leave Helston on Penzance Road and follow the brown signs.

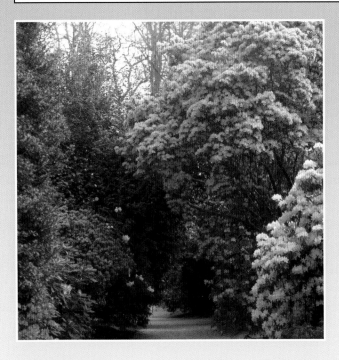

Trewithen means 'house of the trees' and the name truly describes this fine early Georgian house in its splendid setting of wood and parkland.

Country Life described the house as 'one of the outstanding West Country houses of the 18th century' and Penelope Hobhouse has described the garden as 'perhaps the most beautiful woodland garden in England'.

2004 was the 100th year in which George Johnstone inherited Trewithen and started developing the gardens as we know them today. The great glade on the south side is a masterpiece of landscape gardening and is a monument to the genius of George Johnstone. These gardens covering some thirty acres are renowned for their magnificent collection of camellias, rhododendrons, magnolias and many rare trees and shrubs which are seldom found elsewhere in Britain. The extensive woodland gardens are surrounded by traditional landscaped parkland.

Fact File

Opening Times:	Open 1st March to 30th September, 10am to 4.30pm Monday to Saturday. Sundays (March to May only).
Admission Rates:	Adults £5.00 (2008)
Groups Rate:	Minimum group size: 20
	Group £4.50 (2008)
Facilities:	Trewithen Tea Shop, Plant Sales, Camera Obscura, Viewing Platforms.
Disabled Access:	Yes. Toilet and Parking for disabled on site. Wheelchairs on loan.
Tours/Events:	Guided tours available, prior booking is essential. Occasional special events please telephone for details.
Coach Parking:	Yes
Length of Visit:	2 - 2½ hours
Booking Contact:	Glenys Cates
	Trewithen Gardens, Grampound Road, Nr Truro, Cornwall, TR2 4DD
	Telephone: 01726 883647 Fax: 01726 882301
Email:	gardens@trewithen-estate.demon.co.uk
Website:	www.trewithengardens.co.uk
Location:	On the A390 between Truro and St Austell.

Please quote this guide when making a booking

Brantwood

Brantwood's gardens and estate are like no other. Mature Victorian landscape gardens lead to Ruskin's own experimental landscapes, to ancient woodlands, high Moorland and spectacular views. Completion of the Zig-Zaggy, a garden begun by John Ruskin 130 years ago, and the High Walk, a spectacular Victorian viewing platform, brings a total of eight gardens restored at Brantwood. Expect the unexpected and explore 250 acres of fascinating landscape.

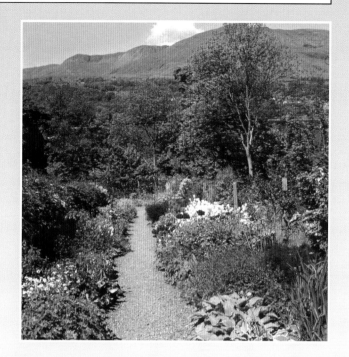

Whichever season you choose to visit you are assured year round interest. Spectacular azaleas in springtime; a collection of ferns, herbs and colourful herbaceous borders in summer; the vibrant colours of autumn; or a winter snowfall can transform the gardens into a winter wonderland.

Stroll the paths, sit and marvel at the magnificent views. Whatever you choose to do, you will take home with you the discovery of John Ruskin's legacy and inspiration.

Fact File

Opening Times:	Mid - March to mid - November daily 11am - 5.30pm.
	Mid - November to mid - March Wednesday - Sunday 11am - 4.30pm.
Admission Rates:	Adults £5.95 / £4.00 garden only, Child £1.20
Groups Rates:	Minimum group size: 10
	Adults £4.95 / £3.50 garden only, Child £1.20
Facilities:	Shop, Plant Sales, Restaurant, Craft Gallery.
Disabled Access:	Partial. Toilet and parking for disabled on site. Wheelchairs on loan, booking necessary.
Tours/Events:	A wide variety of events await, please check website for details.
Coach Parking:	Yes but limited.
Length of Visit:	4 - 6 hours
Booking Contact:	Heather Chislett
	Brantwood, Coniston, Cumbria, LA21 8AD
	Telephone: 01539 441396 Fax: 01539 441263
Email:	heather@brantwood.org.uk
Website:	www.brantwood.org.uk
Location:	2¼ miles east of Coniston. signposted from Coniston.

Please quote this guide when making a booking

Ideally situated between the South Lakeland hills and the expanse of Morecambe Bay, Holker Hall and Gardens combine the beauty of nature with the richness of local heritage. The Hall is Victorian, built on a grand scale in a style best described as neo-Elizabethan. The surrounding gardens cover 24 acres of woodland and formal garden areas. They are highly acclaimed and offer a richness and variety peculiar to the micro-climate of the South Lakes. Throughout the year the gardens are a riot of colour & texture.

The great Holker Lime is one of the highlights, its girth measuring over seven metres at its widest. This magnificent 17th Century tree is one of Britain's 50 greatest trees. Another treat during the summer is the blooming of the National Collection of Stryracaceae. The gardens contain some truly unique features, such as the stunning cascade, the mystical labyrinth and the slate sundial, fashioned to an ancient design. In April and May there is a spectacular display of Rhododendrons. Summer sees the blooming of the National Collection of Stryracaceae and the colours of the gardens in the Autumn never fail to thrill and excite.

Bespoke Garden Tours can be arranged upon request and can be tailored to suit the varied interest of each particular group.

Fact File

Opening Times: Hall 22nd March - 1st November, Sunday - Friday 11am - 4pm (closed Saturday)
Gardens 22nd March - 1st November, Sunday - Friday 10.30am - 5.30pm (closed Saturday)

Group Rates: Applicable only to groups of 10 or more - please call for details.
Hall & Gardens, Adults £6.70, Senior Citizen / Student £6.25, Children Free when accompanied by an adult.
Gardens, Adults £4.70, Senior Citizen / Student £4.25, Children Free when accompanied by an adult.

Facilities: The Holker Food Hall, Courtyard Cafe & Gift Shop - open daily from 1st February - 24th December - from 10.30am.

Disabled Access: Yes. Toilet and parking for disabled on site. Wheelchairs & Scooter to hire, booking advised.

Tours/Events: The Holker Garden Festival 29th - 31st May. Other seasonal events, please ring for details.

Coach Parking: Yes

Length of Visit: 2 - 4 hours

Booking Contact: Alex Wilson, House Opening Office, Holker Hall and Gardens, Cark-in-Cartmel, Nr Grange-over-Sands,Cumbria, LA11 7PL
Telephone: 015395 58328 Fax: 015395 58378

Email: groups@holker.co.uk

Website: www.holker.co.uk

Location: Cark-in-Cartmel. Leave M6 at junction 36, follow Brown & White Tourist Signs through Grange-over-Sands.

Please quote this guide when making a booking

Winderwath is a garden of five acres originally laid out at the beginning of the twentieth Century. The mature trees including Wellingtonia, Cut Leaf Beech and Cedar, date from this time. Extensive work has been carried out on the rockeries and herbaceous borders since the 1950s. More recently the pond area has been opened up

There is now a large collection of Alpine and Himalayan plants, including Arisaema and Moconopsis. There are many rare and unusual perennials including a good display of Salvias. We are well known for the display of Aconites and Daffodils in the Spring. There is a working vegetable garden in the Edwardian walled garden with apricots, nectarines and peaches in the greenhouses.

A selection of plants grown are for sale and we also sell second-hand garden tools. There are picnic tables round the pond area where you are welcome to enjoy a quiet lunch.

Fact File

Opening times:	10.00 a.m. – 4.00 p.m. Monday – Friday. Saturday: 9 a.m. – 12 noon
Admission Rates:	Adults: £3.50. Senior Citizens: £3,50
Group Rates:	Minimum Group Size: 12
Facilities:	Plant Sales, Second-hand garden tools for sale. Toilets.
Disabled Access:	Partial
Car Parking on site:	Yes
Tours/Events:	Guided tours available. Booking required.
Length of Visit:	1½ hours
Booking Contact:	Jane Pollock
	Winderwath Gardens
	Winderwath, Nr. Temple Sowerby
	Penrith, Cumbria CA10 2AG
	Booking Telephone No: 01768 88250
	Booking Fax No: 01786 88250
Location:	5 miles east of Penrith on A66, Take B6412 to Culgaith and Temple Sowerby, from Temple Sowerby bypass, turn left onto old A66, 200 yards on right.

Please quote this guide when making a booking

Renishaw Hall is the home of the Sitwell family, as it has been for 400 years. Its eight-acre Italianate gardens, designed by Sir George Sitwell, were laid out more than 100 years ago, and are among the most beautiful in the country. There are several garden rooms, hedged with sharply-cut yew, and there is always the sound of moving water in the background, often reflected in still pools.

On 22 February, we have our Fanfare for Spring, the only opportunity for visitors to see the structure of the garden at its best. There will also be specialist plant nurseries displaying and selling rare winter flowering plants.

From 23 April until 10 May Renishaw's bright bluebells are out in the ancient woods, with rhododendrons, camellias and magnolias in the newly-created woodland garden. 1000 roses bloom in June, which is the month the delphinums also reach their peak. The Laburnum Tunnel is bright yellow around the end of May, and later in the summer the herbaceous borders come into their own.

Sir George's classical structure remains, but for the past year Head Gardener David Kesteven has been working with internationally-famous designer Anthony Noel, known for his dramatic design and use of colour and shape. Children can work off their energy in the new Fairytale Garden designed especially for them to play in and explore.

Fact File

Opening Times:	Open March 20th to September 28th 10.30am - 4.30pm. Thurs to Sun & Bank Holidays.
Admission Rates:	Adults: £6.00, Senior Citizens: £4.20, Children under 10 Free. Free Car Parking.
Group Rates:	Minimum group size for the Hall tour 25. £9.95 and £11.00
Facilities:	Café. Shop. The Sitwell Museum, the Performing Arts Gallery (2008 exhibition: Dame Edna Everage), the John Piper Museum. Free film: Renishaw Hall and the Sitwells. The Rex Whistler Conference Room. The Wedding Lawn for marquees for weddings – only 14 a year.
Disabled Access:	Yes. Toilet and car parking on site £1.00 per car.
Tours/Events:	The Hall is open to the public only for group tours which must be booked in advance. Guided tours of vineyard and garden. Fanfare for Spring: 22 February 23 April - 10 May: Bluebell Fortnight. Delphinium Day: 21 June Other events all year (information on these and all activities at Renishaw Hall can be found on the website)
Coach Parking:	Yes
Length of Visit:	Hall tour – 1½ hours
Booking Contact:	Administrator Renishaw Hall Gardens, Renishaw Hall, Renishaw Park, Renishaw, Nr. Sheffield, S21 3WB. Telephone: 01246 432310 Fax: 01246 430760
Email:	Info2@renishaw-hall.co.uk
Website:	www.renishaw-hall.co.uk
Location:	Junction 30 off the M1. A6135 to Sheffield/Eckington.

Please quote this guide when making a booking

Bicton Park Botanical Garden   Devon

Spanning nearly 300 years of horticultural history, Bicton
Park Botanical Gardens are set in the picturesque Otter
Valley, where the gentile climate ensures a magnificent
display of exotic plants throughout the year. From the
classical grandeur of the 18th Century Italian Garden, Bicton's
63 acres (25.5 ha) extend through less formal gardens to a
superbly landscaped parkland with lakes, streams, a nature
trail and Devon's largest collection of record-holding trees.
Twenty five conifers and broadleaf specimens have been
officially recognised as the tallest or the largest of their kind in
the British Isles. Bicton's 19th Century Palm House is one of
the World's most beautiful garden buildings. Many other
tropical plants and cacti are also displayed under cover, as
are the fascinating exhibits in the Countryside Museum and
Shell House. For a small extra charge, visitors may tour
Bicton Park on Britain's only 18-inch gauge
passenger-carrying railway.

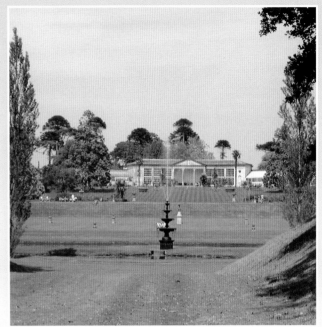

Fact File

Opening Times: Daily all year (except Christmas Day & Boxing Day) from 10am - 6pm in Spring/Summer and
10am - 5pm in Autumn/Winter.

Admission Rates: Adults: £6.95, Children: £5.95, Concessions: £5.95 (over 60yrs of age or disabled),
Family (2 Adults and up to 2 Children): £22.95, Dogs (on a lead at all times): £1.00,
Children under 3yrs: Free.

Group Rates: Adults: £3.95, Children: £2.95.

Facilities: Restaurant, Gift Shop, Garden Centre, Kiosk's, picnic area, Children's indoor and outdoor play
areas, mini-golf course.

Disabled Access: Yes. Toilet and parking for disabled on site. Wheelchairs on loan by prior arrangement.

Tours/Events: Walks for groups by prior arrangement. Tours may be tailored to your special interests,
including history, trees, wildlife.

Coach Parking: Yes.

Length of Visit: 3 hours minimum, all day maximum.

Booking Contact: Heather/valerie/Simon.
Bicton Park Botanical Gardens, East Budleigh, Budleigh, Salterton, Devon, EX9 7BJ
Telephone: 01395 568465 Fax: 01395 568374

Email: info\@bictongardens.co.uk

Website: www.bictongardens.co.uk

Location: Bicton is 10 miles SE of Exeter. From M5 leave at junction 30 and
follow the brown 'Bicton Park' signs. The gardens are midway
between Budleigh Salterton and Newton Poppleford on the B3178.

Broomhill lies in one of the most glorious valleys in North Devon, surrounded by hundreds of acres of woodland and bound by its own stream. The garden presents a wonderful balance between art and nature, with more than 300 sculptures by over 60 sculptors.

The Woodland Gardens provide all year round interest and are home to numerous birds and insects. The gardens are full of colour in the Summer, Autumn and are particularly beautiful in the spring, with a successions of Spring flowers including Snowdrops, Daffodils, Primroses, Bluebells and Azaleas.

The award-winning Broomhill Kitchen is based around the 'Slow food' ethos. Consisting of mainly Mediterranean cuisine using fresh, organic, fair-trade and fresh produce from neighbouring farms and the coast, the menu affords splendid choice and excellent value. Group lunches and cream teas are available (booking required).

Broomhill hosts a variety of exciting events throughout the year, such as art exhibitions, workshops, music concerts, lectures and food events.

We look forward to welcoming you.

Fact File

Opening times:	July – August: Monday – Sunday: 11:00 – 16:00. General: Wednesday – Sunday: 11:00 – 16:00. Closed 20 December – 15 January
Admission Rates:	Adults: £4.50, Senior Citizens: £3.50, Children: £1.50, 15 and under, Family ticket: £10.00 (2 adults + 2 under 5)
Facilities:	Visitor Centre, Shop, Restaurant, Teas
Group Rates:	Minimum Group Size: 10. Adults: £3.50, Senior Citizens: £2.50, Children: £1.50
Facilities:	Shop, Restaurant, Teas. Shop includes postcards + art + T-shirts, Art Gallery, Accommodation, Conference/meeting rooms.
Disabled Access:	Hotel and Art Gallery yes, gardens, partly
Toilets on site:	Yes
Car Parking on site:	Yes
Coach Parking:	Yes, for up to 2 coaches
Wheelchair Loan:	Yes
Guided Tours:	Yes, booking required
Special Events:	Jazz concert every month – see site for details. We host art exhibitions regularly.
Length of Visit:	2 – 3 hours
Booking Contact:	Broomhill Sculpture Gardens, Broomhill Art Hotel, Muddiford Rd, Barnstaple, Devon, EX31 4EX Booking Tel No.01271 850262
Email:	info@broomhillart.co.uk
Website:	www.broomhillart.co.uk
Location:	From Barnstaple, A39 towards Lynton, left onto the B3230 towards Ilfracombe. Broomhill is signposted 2 miles after the NDD Hospital

Please quote this guide when making a booking

This inspirational garden blends seamlessly into a timeless Devon landscape, and offers magnificent views in all directions. Today, the garden extends to 8 acres and is several gardens in one, using over 6,000 varieties of plants to great effect in both traditional and naturalistic planting styles.

In spring – admire magnificent collections of camellias, magnolias and rhododendrons. Enjoy the Bulb Meadow with its masses of woodland plants such as erythroniums, anemones, cyclamen and bluebells.

In summer – experience the delights of the famous Walled Garden built around medieval ruins, wisteria bridges, the exotic South African Garden as well as the romantic Cottage Garden and Wild Flower Meadow.

In autumn – over 50 Japanese maples provide a kaleidoscope of autumnal colour.

Plant Sales has an excellent range of plants, including many of the beautiful ones grown in the garden.

The Garden Tearooms are situated in the 18th century former vicarage and serve delicious homemade cakes, Devon cream teas and light lunches.

Fact File

Opening times:	10.30 a.m. – 5.00 p.m. daily 28 February – 1 November 2009. Weekends only February and November.
Admission Rates:	Adults: £5.90, Senior Citizens: £5.40, Children: £2.50 (5 – 16 years)
Group Rates:	Minimum Group Size: 15. Standard Rate: £5.00
Facilities:	Plant Sales, tearooms serving lunches and teas
Disabled Access:	Limited disabled access. Not all areas are flat.
Toilets on site:	Yes
Car Parking on site:	Yes
Coach Parking:	Yes
Guided Tours:	Yes, booking required.
Length of Visit:	2 hours
Special Events:	A full event programme throughout the year. Please telephone for details or see our website.
Booking Contact:	Rachel Young, Administrator, The Garden House, Buckland Monachorum, Yelverton, Devon, PL20 7LQ Booking Tel No.01822 854769.
Email:	office@thegardenhouse.org.uk
Website:	www.thegardenhouse.org.uk
Location:	10 miles north of Plymouth. Signed off A386 at Yelverton.

Please quote this guide when making a booking

Created by Dr. Jimmy Smart – a fine plantsman. Marwood Hill has 20 acres of beautiful gardens and three small lakes set in a sheltered valley setting. A haven for trees and shrubs from around the world as well as herbaceous and alpine plants giving all year round interest and colour.

The gardens are well known for the extensive collection of Camellias and National Collections of Astilbe, Japanese Iris and Tulbaghia. There are many areas where the visitor can rest, experience the tranquillity and enjoy the many inspiring aspects of the gardens.

The walled garden plant centre sells a wide range of plants, most of which have been grown and propagated in the gardens. Knowledgeable staff are usually available to help and advise.

The Garden Tearoom overlooking the garden offers a selection of light lunches, home baked cakes and Devon cream teas.

You could also visit Broomhall Art & Sculpture Garden nearby all in one day.

Fact File

Opening Times: Gardens: Daily except Christmas Day 9.30 – 5.30, Plant Centre: March – October, Garden Tea Room: March – October

Admission Rates: Adult: £4.50, Children: Under 12 free.

Group Rates: Minimum Groups Size: 10. By appointment only.
Adult: £4.00, including introductory talk by Head Gardener.

Facilities: Plant Centre and Garden Tea Room.

Disabled Access: Yes, but limited. Toilet and car parking on site.

Tours/Events: Guided tours available. Contact the booking office for details.

Coach Parking: Yes

Length of Visit: 2 hours – all day.

Booking Contact: Mrs. Patricia Stout
Marwood Hill Gardens, Marwood, Barnstaple, North Devon EX31 4EB
Telephone 01271 342528 Fax: 01271 342528

Email: info@marwoodhillgarden.co.uk

Website: www.marwoodhillgarden.co.uk

Location: 9 miles from Ilfracombe. 4 miles north of Barnstaple.

Please quote this guide when making a booking

Paignton Zoological & Botanical Gardens — Devon

The 80 acre gardens of Paignton Zoo consist of mature shrubberies and newer areas developed over the past 10 years. The plantings are designed to create the feeling of a natural habitat by using geographic and educationally themed displays. New garden areas include a Mediterranean climate garden, an economic plant garden and a medicinal garden.

There are three glasshouses, which contain tender and tropical plants from around the world. The newest is Crocodile Swamp which opened last year and displays wetland tropical plants.

The warm climate in the South West allows the Zoo to grow many tender plants outside as part of the exhibits as well as some of the rarest plants in the world. Palms, bananas and citrus are amongst the plants that contribute to the tropical feel. The Zoo is also home to the NCCPG National Collection of species Buddleja.

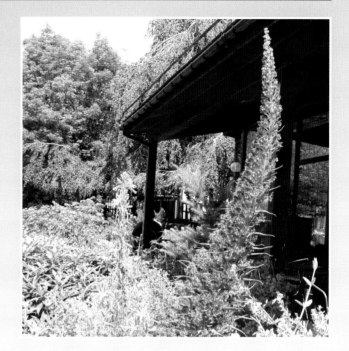

Fact File

Opening Times: Open daily from 10 a.m. Closing times vary according to the season.
Admission Rates: Adults: £11.90*, Senior Citizens: £9.80*, Children: £8.40*
*Includes a 10% voluntary donation (These are 2008 prices, 2009 will change).
Group Rates: Minimum Group Size: 15. Adults: £8.95, Senior Citizens: £7.30, Children: £6.00.
Facilities: Visitor Center Shop, Restaurant, Teas.
Disabled Access: Yes. Bookable wheelchair loan available.
Toilets on site: Yes.
Tours/Events: Guided tours available. Booking required. Extra charge.
Coach Parking: Yes - free.
Car Parking on site: Yes - free.
Length of Visit: 4-5 hours.
Booking Contact: John Rea
Paignton Zoological & Botanical Gardens, Totnes Road, Paignton, Devon TQ4 7EU
Telephone: 01803 697515
Fax: 01803 523457
Email: groupvisits@paigntonzoo.org.uk
Website: www.paigntonzoo.org.uk
Location: We are located on the A3022 Totnes Road, 1 mile from Paignton town centre.

Come and see this enchanting 65-acre garden set in the beautiful Torridge Valley. Whatever the season, Rosemoor is a unique place that people return to time and again for ideas, inspiration or simply to enjoy a relaxing day out.

From Lady Anne's original garden to rose gardens (with over 200 varieties), formal and informal gardens, the fruit and vegetable garden, the arboretum, stunning lake and cottage garden, as well as woodland walks, there is something for everyone to enjoy.

Over 80 exciting events are also held at Rosemoor throughout the year, such as art exhibitions and workshops, horticultural lectures and walks, family events, craft fairs, and musical events. For information, please ring 01805 624067 for a FREE brochure.

Licensed Restaurant, Tea Room, Plant Centre and Shop also on site and free parking.

Fact File

Opening times: April - September 10am - 6pm, October - March 10am - 5pm, open every day except Christmas Day. Visitor Centre Closed noon Christmas eve and re-opens 10am 27th Dec.

Admission Rates: Adults £6.00, Senior Citizen £6.00, Child (6-16yrs) £2.00, (under 6yrs Free), RHS Members + 1 Guest Free

Group Rates: Minimum group size: 10. £5.00 per person
RHS members + 1 guest, Free, Carers for diabled people Free.

Facilities: Visitor Centre, Shop, Restaurant, Wisteria Tea Room, Plant Centre.

Disabled Access: Yes. Toilet and Parking for disabled on site. Wheelchairs on loan, booking necessary.

Tours/Events: Full programme of events throughout the year.

Coach Parking: Yes

Length of Visit: Half to full day

Booking Contact: Admin Department
RHS Garden Rosemoor, Great Torrington, North Devon, EX38 8PH
Telephone 01805 624067 Fax: 01805 624717

Email: rosemooradmin@rhs.org.uk

Website: www.rhs.org.uk/rosemoor

Location: 1 mile south of Torrington on the A3124 (formerly B3220)

Please quote this guide when making a booking

Abbotsbury Subtropical Gardens　　　　　Dorset

Established in 1765 by the first Countess of Ilchester. Developed since then into a 20-acre grade 1 listed magnificent woodland valley garden. world famous for it's Camellia Groves, Magnolias, Rhododendron and Hydrangea collections. In summer it is awash with colour.

Since the restoration after the great storm of 1990 many new and exotic plants have been introduced. The garden is now a mixture of formal and informal, with a charming walled garden and spectacular woodland valley views.

Facilities include a Colonial Tea-house for lunches, snacks and drinks, a Plant Centre and quality Gift Shop. Events and concerts are presented during the year.
The Floodlighting of the Garden at the end of October (Oct 14th - Nov 1st 2009) should not be missed.

Fact File
Opening Times: Summer: 10am - 6pm last entry at 5pm.
Winter (November - February) - 10.00am - 4pm or dusk, last entry 1 hour before.
Admission Rates: Adults £9.00, Senior Citizen £8.50, Child £6.00
Groups Rates: Minimum group size 10
Adults £7.00, Senior Citizen £6.50, Child £4.50
Facilities: Colonial Tea-house, Gift Shop, Plant Centre.
Disabled Access: Yes. 50% of garden accessible. Toilet and parking for disabled on site. Wheelchairs F.O.C.
Tours/Events: £1 per person (minimum charge £20) on top of the group rate (minimum 10 people). Special events see web site.
Coach Parking: Yes
Length of Visit: 2 hours
Booking Contact: Jess Owen/Jessica Lambert. Abbotsbury Sub Tropical Garden, Bullers Way, Abbotsbury, (Nr Weymouth), Dorset, DT3 4LA. Telephone: 01305 871130   Fax: 01305 871092
Email: info@abbotsbury-tourism.co.uk
Website: www.abbotsbury-tourism.co.uk & www.abbotsburyplantsales.co.uk
Location: On the B3157 between Weymouth and Bridport in Dorset. come off the A35 near Dorchester at Winterborne Abbas.

Please quote this guide when making a booking

The 8 acres of gardens here hold National & International Plant Collections of Water Lilies, flowering from late spring to autumn, creating one of the most outstanding displays of water lilies in Britain with a Monet style Japanese Bridge as a centrepiece.

Many of the original lilies planted here by the Bennett family in 1959 came from the same nursery in France that supplied Claude Monet's garden in Giverny. These same varieties that Monet painted are among the collections on display.

Grass pathways lead you through the series of lakes surrounded by wetland plants, native trees, palms, wild plants and flowers. The gardens are a 'Site of Nature Conservation Interest' and home to abundant wildlife.

The Museum contains local history including Chesil Beach & Fleet lagoon, plus the fascinating story of this site from Brickworks & Clay Pits in 1859 through to the gardens today.

Fact File

Opening times:	Mid-March to Mid-October: 10 a.m. – 5 p.m. daily except Saturdays
Admission Rates:	Adults: £6.95, Senior Citizens: £6.25, Children: £3.95 (5 – 16 years)
Group Rates:	Minimum Group Size: 15. Adults: £4.75, Senior Citizens: £4.75, Children: £3.25
Facilities:	Visitor Centre, Shop, Plant Sales, Restaurant, Teas
Disabled Access:	Yes
Toilets on site:	Yes
Coach Parking:	Yes
Car Parking on site:	Yes
Guided Tours:	Yes, booking required
Special Events:	Please see website
Length of Visit:	2 hours+
Booking Contact:	Angie or James Bennett, Bennetts Water Gardens, Putton Lane, Chickerell, Weymouth, Dorset DT3 4AF Booking Telephone No. 01305 785150. Booking Fax No. 01305 781619
Email:	info@waterlily.co.uk
Website:	www.waterlily.co.uk
Location:	2 miles west of Weymouth on the B3157 – follow brown signs for Water Gardens from the A354 at Weymouth

Please quote this guide when making a booking

Forde Abbey & Gardens

Forde Abbey is a treasure in an area already known for its outstanding beauty. More than 900 years of history are encapsulated in this elegant former Cistercian monastery and its 30 acres of award winning gardens. In the peaceful solitude of its secluded position it is possible to imagine just how it looked to many of its previous owners: monks going about their daily round of work and prayer, prosperous parliamentary gentlemen discussing the cavalier threat, gifted philosophers debating the imponderable, elegant Victorian ladies fanning themselves by the fireside and country gentlemen going about their work on the estate.

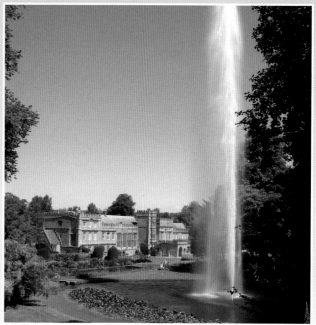

The architectural beauty of the house, with its striking interior, and the varied garden, including a mature arboretum, rockery, bog garden and working walled kitchen garden makes Forde Abbey a delightful destination. The cascade of lakes provides a wonderful setting for the Centenary Fountain, the highest powered fountain in England.

However, Forde Abbey is first and foremost a family home giving it an atmosphere of warmth and ease not often found in stately homes. The fruits of the garden and farm can be sampled in the Undercroft restaurant with a wide selection of delicious homemade lunches and cakes. A gift shop, plant centre and pottery exhibition add to the day.

Enjoy England Awards for Excellence, Silver winner 2008

Fact File

Opening times:	Gardens open daily throughout the year from 10am (last admission 4.30pm). House open, 1st April to end of October, 12noon-4pm on Tue -Fri, Sundays & Bank Holiday Mondays.
Admission Rates:	Tel: 01460 221290
Groups Rates:	Minimum group size 20, Tel: 01460 220231.
Facilities:	Shop, Plant Sales, Teas, Restaurant and Pottery Exhibition.
Disabled Access:	Yes. (house not suitable for wheelchairs) Toilet and parking for disabled on site. Wheelchair and Battery Car on loan, booking necessary. To book 01460 221699.
Tours:	Tours for pre-arranged groups only.
Coach Parking:	Yes
Length of Visit:	3 hours
Booking Contact:	Mrs Carolyn Clay Forde Abbey, Chard, TA20 4LU Telephone: 01460 220231 Fax: 01460 220296
Email:	info@fordeabbey.co.uk
Website:	www.fordeabbey.co.uk
Location:	Signposted from A30 Chard to Crewkerne & from A358 Chard to Axminster. 4 miles south east of Chard.

Please quote this guide when making a booking

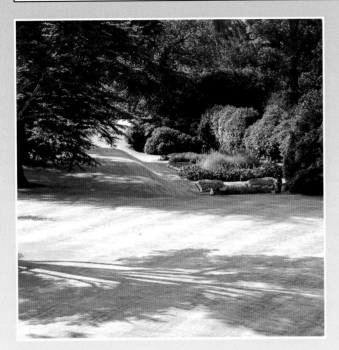

Laid out by successive members of the Bankes family over the last three centuries, the grounds of this extensive estate are presented by the National Trust in their Edwardian splendour. Most recent of the restoration projects is the Japanese Gardens of Henrietta Bankes, the formal Tea Gardens of which were opened in 2005, set in seven acres of the southern shelter-belt and include an Acer Glade, a Quarry Garden, an Evergreen Garden and a Cherry Garden. Closer to the magnificent Mansion are the Sunk Garden and the Parterre, both of which remain true to their early twentieth century planting patterns throughout the year. The Fernery, with over thirty-five varieties, is also the home of the National Collection of Anemone nemorosa, while the surrounding three hundred-acre Parkland reflects the Bankes' passion for specimen trees whether as single examples or as groups and avenues.

Fact File

Opening Times: 14th March – 1st November: Daily 10.30 a.m. – 6 p.m.
6th November – 20th December: Friday, Saturday and Sunday: 10.30 a.m. – 4 p.m.

Admission Rates: Gardens Only: Adults: £5.00, Children: £2.50. Includes a voluntary donation but visitors can choose to pay the standard prices displayed at the property and on the website.

Group Rates: Minimum Groups Size: 15
Group rates for House and Gardens only: Adults: £8.00, Children: £4.00.

Facilities: Woodland Walks, Children's play areas.

Disabled Access: Yes – gardens only. Lavatory and car parking on site. Wheelchair Loan booking available.

Tours/Events: Guided tours available. Events leaflet available.

Coach Parking: Yes – booking essential.

Length of Visit: 2 hours +

Booking Contact: Carol Dougherty, Property Administrator, Kingston Lacy, Wimborne Minster, Dorset BH21 4EA
Telephone: 01202 883402 Fax: 01202 882402

Email: kingstonlacy@nationaltrust.org.uk

Website: www.nationaltrust.org.uk

Location: 1½ miles west of Wimborne Minster, on B3082.

Please quote this guide when making a booking

Kingston Maurward Gardens & Animal Park Dorset

Set in idyllic surroundings Kingston Maurward Gardens are one of Dorset's best kept secrets. A tranquil, and peaceful spot, the gardens are situated in undulating Dorset countryside, with a large ornamental lake, broad sweeping and formal gardens.

The gardens were laid out in the "Jardin Anglais" style popularised by Capability Brown in the 18th Century. The formal gardens consist of a matrix of small gardens each with its own theme. The Rainbow beds and beautiful herbaceous borders compliment the Croquet lawn and an extensive display of tender perennials. The charming Japanese style garden lies adjacent to the north shore of the lake, with stately Chusan Palms, Bamboos and Japanese Maples. There are also tree trails, lakeside walks and a delightful walled garden.

The Animal Park has an interesting collection of animals, including Rabbits, Guinea Pigs, Sheep, Goats, Shetland ponies, Alpacas and lots more. There is plenty of space for picnics and the Visitor Centre has a wide variety of plants and gifts for sale.

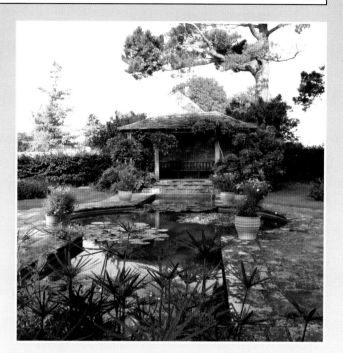

Fact File

Opening times:	5th January 2009 to 21st December 10am - 5.30pm.
Admission Rates:	Adults £5.00, Senior Citizen £4.50, Child £3.00, Family £15.50.
Group Rates:	Minimum group size: 10
	Adults £4.50, Senior Citizen £4.50, Child £3.00.
Facilities:	Visitor Centre, Shop, Tea Room, Plant Sales, Picnic Area
	Children's Play Area, Animal Park.
Disabled Access:	Yes. Toilet & parking for disabled on site. Wheelchairs on loan, booking necessary.
Tours/Events:	Guided walks are available if booked in advance.
	Special events take place throughout the year, telephone for details.
Coach Parking:	Yes
Length of Visit:	Minimum 2 hours
Booking Contact:	Ginny Rolls
	Kingston Maurward, Dorchester, Dorset, DT2 8PY
	Telephone 01305 215003 Fax: 01305 215001
Email:	events@kmc.ac.uk
Website:	www.kmc.ac.uk/gardens
Location:	Signposted from the roundabout at the eastern end of the Dorchester by-pass A35.

Please quote this guide when making a booking

Home of the Churchill and Digby families for 350 years, Minterne, described by Simon Jenkins as 'a corner of paradise', was landscaped after the manner of Capability Brown in the 18th century with small lakes and cascades. The first Arboreum Rhododendrons were planted in the 1850's, many more from Himalayan expeditions by George Forrest, Wilson and Rock around 1905, and from Kingdon Ward's expedition in 1924.

Wander peacefully through 20 wild woodland acres of hidden gardens laid out in a horseshoe over a mile round; March sees the Magnolias, and early Rhododendrons. April and May, Japanese cherries and a profusion of rhododendrons and azaleas. Late May and June many fine specimens of Davidia Involucrata (the Pocket Handkerchief Tree) are a particular feature. Eucryphias, Hydrangeas, water plants and water lilies provide a new vista at each turn. The autumn colouring is quite sensational.

Fact File

Opening times:	10 a.m. – 6 p.m. daily, 1st March – 9th November.
Admission Rates:	Adults: £4.00, Senior Citizens: £4.00, Children under 16: FOC if accompanied.
Disabled Access:	Not suitable for wheelchairs.
Toilets on site:	Yes.
Tours/Events:	See website events page.
Coach Parking:	Yes.
Car Parking on site:	Yes. Free car park with picnic facilities.
Length of Visit:	1-2 hours.
Booking Contact:	Minterne Gardens
	Minterne Magna, Dorchester, Dorset DT2 7AU
	Telephone: 01300 341370
	Fax: 01300 341747
Email:	enquiries@minterne.co.uk
Website:	www.minterne.co.uk
Location:	Situated in the village of Minterne Magna on the A352 Dorchester/Sherborne road, 2 miles north of Cerne Abbas.

Please quote this guide when making a booking

Marks Hall Gardens & Arboretum Essex

There is much to see in over 100 acres of gardens and arboretum throughout the year.

In the Walled Garden the five individual gardens and the longest double herbaceous border in East Anglia are a unique blend of traditional and contemporary, combining unusual landscaping and creative and colourful planting. The garden is at its best from early summer through to autumn but on the opposite lake bank there is the Millennium Walk, designed to be at its best on the shortest days of the year. Here stems of dogwood, rubus and birch reflect in the lake and the scent of Hamamelis lingers.

Each year new plantings mature, surprise and delight.

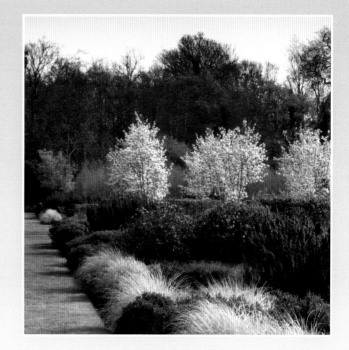

Fact File

Opening Times: 1st April-31st October Tuesday to Sunday & Bank Holidays 10.30am - 5pm.
1 November-31st March Fridays, Saturdays & Sundays 10.30am to dusk.
Admission Rates: £3.80 Adult, Child £1.00 (5 to 16, under 5's Free), £3.30 Concessions.
Groups Rates: Minimum group size 12
£2.50 per person
Facilities: Visitor Centre, Shop, Plant Sales, Tea Room.
Disabled Access: Yes. Toilet and parking for disabled on site. Wheelchairs and buggy on loan.
Tours/Events: Please telephone for details.
Coach Parking: Yes
Length of Visit: 2-3 hours
Booking Contact: Visitor Centre Manager
Marks Hall, Coggeshall, Essex, CO6 1TG
Tel: 01376 563796 Fax: 01376 563132
Email: enquiries@markshall.org.uk
Website: www.markshall.org.uk
Location: Signed from A120 Coggeshall by-pass.

Batsford Arboretum & Wild Garden - The Cotswolds Secret Garden and former home of the Mitford family.

One of the largest private collection of trees in Great Britain. See spring flowers as they cascade down the hillside. Many wild orchids and fritillaries adorn the arboretum. In autumn the many rare and unusual trees explode into their magnificent reds, golds and purples.

Follow the stream through pools and waterfalls to its source, make a wish with the giant Buddha. find the Foo Dog hidden amongst the trees, then negotiate the waterfall without getting too wet. See if you can find Algernon and Clemantine on the lake, then rest awhile and view the deer in the Deer Park. Fifty acres of peace, traquillity - pure Cotswold magic!

Fact File

Opening Times: Open every day 9am - 5pm. (May close Wednesdays in December and January - Check before travelling long distances).
Also open Boxing day & New Years Day.

Admission Rates: Adults £6.00, Senior Citizen £5.00, Child £2.00.

Groups Rates: Minimum group size 20. Admission Rates less 10%

Facilities: Visitor Centre, Shop, Plant Sales, Teas, Restaurant, Garden Centre and Falconry Centre.

Disabled Access: Partial. Toilet and parking for disabled on site, wheelchairs on loan, booking necessary.

Tours/Events: Tours by arrangement. Events to be arranged.

Coach Parking: Yes new area.

Length of Visit: 2 Hours

Booking Contact: Mr Chris Pilling
Batford Arboretum, Batsford Park, Moreton in Marsh, Glos GL56 9AB.
Telephone: 01386 701441 Fax: 01386 701829

Email: arboretum@batsfordfoundation.co.uk

Website: www.batsarb.co.uk

Location: 1 mile west of Moreton in Marsh on A44 road.

Please quote this guide when making a booking

Berkeley Castle is England's oldest inhabited castle and most historic home. Over 24 generations of Berkeley's have transformed a savage Norman fortress into a stately home full of treasures.

Successive generations softened the stern aspect of the Castle walls with flowers, until finally the present planting of the terraces was carried out with the help of Gertrude Jekyll at the turn of the last century. The gardens specialise in scent and the roses are a delight in June. Rare plants, shrubs and trees are to be enjoyed and a butterfly house.

From the Lily Pond, first built as a swimming pool during the time of the last Earl, sweeping curved steps lead down to the Great Lawn on which the remaining Culloden pine stands, said to have been brought back as a pine cone from the Battle of Culloden by the 4th Earl of Berkeley.

Fact File

Opening Times:	11 - 5pm. Every Sunday Easter to end October. All Bank Holiday Weekends. Open Sun - Thurs, June, July, & August. Open for groups all year round by appointment.
Admission Rates:	Adults: £7.50, Senior Citizens: £6.00, Children: £4.50
Group Rates:	Minimum Group Size 25 Adults: £7.00, Senior Citizens: £5.50, Children: £3.50
Facilities:	Visitor Centre, Shop, Teas
Disabled Access:	Partial access only.
Tours/Events:	Yes, see website for details
Coach Parking:	Yes.
Length of Visit:	1.5 hours gardens. 1.5 hours castle
Booking Contact:	David Exworth Berkeley Castle, Berkeley, Gloucestershire GL13 9BQ Tel: 01453 810332 Fax: 01453 512995
Email:	info@berkeley-castle.com
Website:	www.berkeley-castle.com
Location:	Just off the A38, midway between Bristol and Gloucester. 10 minutes from Junctions 13 or 14, M5

Bourton House Garden Gloucestershire

Intensively planted, this three-acre garden features excitingly planted herbaceous borders full of stunning plant and colour combinations.

Neatly clipped box and yew is found in knots, parterres and spiralling topiary. Water wends it way through small fountains, pools and ponds. Wide use of sub-tropical plants, a shadehouse, raised alpines troughs; all provide further variety in this continually evolving garden. And add to the whole, a myriad of magically planted pots and containers. There is excellent late season interest to be enjoyed.

Planted just over 10 years ago with a wide variety of trees, the seven-acre field opposite already boasts some sizeable specimens.

The imposing 16th century Tithe barn creates a striking gateway to this delightful garden.

The garden is no longer open to the general public and looks forward to welcoming pre-booked groups.

Fact File

Opening Times:	From mid-May until the end of July, then September and October, Closed in August.
Groups Rates:	Minimum group size 20, £5.50.
Facilities:	Teas and delicious home made cakes or light meals may be ordered when booking
Disabled Access:	There is limited access for wheelchairs: 70%
Coach Parking:	Yes
Length of Visit:	1½ hours
Booking Contact:	Monique Paice
	Bourton House, Bourton-On-The-Hill, Moreton-in-Marsh, Glos, GL56 9AE
	Tel: 01386 700121 Fax: 01386 701081
Email:	cd@bourtonhouse.com
Website:	www.bourtonhouse.com
Location:	2 miles west of Moreton-in Marsh on the A44.

Please quote this guide when making a booking

Cerney House Gardens are a romantic, secret step back into the past. Set amongst parkland, this family-run estate bulges with old-fashioned splendour. The central walled garden boasts a working kitchen garden complemented with generous herbaceous borders and roses of every description. A quieter knot garden plays host to the annual 'Floral Fireworks' tulip festival. There is a well-labelled herb garden that leads to the woodland, which is carpeted in the spring with snowdrops followed by bluebells. The avenue beds lead to genera borders that map out plant connections and end in turn amongst the ever-growing arboretum.

There are plant collections throughout, including the national collection of Tradescantia. The air is full of scents and nature's sounds. But this is still essentially a family garden where your guide will often be one of the many resident pets.

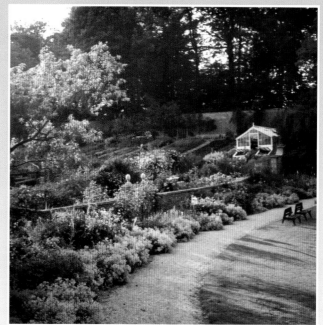

Fact File

Opening Times:	Open from Mid January for Snowdrops until the end of July or by appointment. Open: Tuesday, Wednesday, Friday, Sunday.
Admission Rates:	Adults: £4.00, Children: £1.00.
Group Rates:	Adults: £4.00, organiser entrance free, Children: £1.00
Facilities:	Shop, Plant Sales, Teas, Pottery.
Disabled Access:	Yes. Toilet and car parking on site. Wheelchair loan available please book.
Tours/Events:	Guided tours available. Annual Tulip Festival.
Coach Parking:	By arrangement.
Length of Visit:	1 1/2 hours
Booking Contact:	Barbara McPherson Cerney House Gardens, North Cerney, Cirencester, Gloucestershire GL7 7BX Telephone 01285 831300/831205 Fax: 01285 831421
Email:	barbara@cerneygardens.com
Website:	www.cerneygardens.com
Location:	On the A435 at North Cerney. Turn up behind village church, 400 metres from main road.

Please quote this guide when making a booking

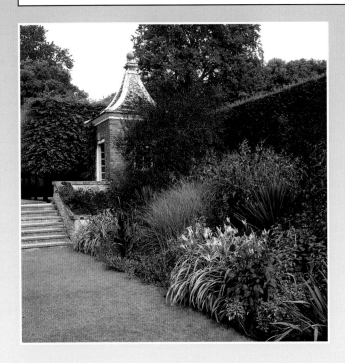

Hidcote Manor Garden is one of England's great Arts and Craft gardens. Created by the American horticulturist Major Lawrence Johnston in 1907, Hidcote is famous for its rare trees and shrubs, outstanding herbaceous borders and unusual plants from all over the world.

The garden is divided by tall hedges and walls to create a series of outdoor 'rooms' each with its own special and unique character. From the formal splendour of the White Garden and Bathing Pool to the informality and beauty of the Old Garden, visitors are assured of a surprise around every corner.

The numerous outdoor rooms reach their height at different times of the year, making a visit to Hidcote Manor Garden enjoyable whatever the season.

Fact File

Opening Times:	14 March - 1 November: Monday, Tuesday, Wednesday, Saturday & Sunday 10am - 6pm (last admission 5pm). From October last admission 4pm. Also open Thursdays & Fridays in July & August. Please call the property for further seasonal openings.
Admission Rates:	Adults £9.00, Senior Citizen £9.00, Child £4.50. (National Trust members free)
Groups Rates:	Minimum group size: 15
	Adults £7.80, Senior Citizen £7.80, Child £3.90 (National Trust members free)
Facilities:	Shop, Plant Centre, Teas & Restaurant.
Disabled Access:	Partlal. Toilet and parking for disabled on site. Wheelchairs on loan.
Tours/Events:	Please contact the property for a list of special events.
Coach Parking:	Yes. Groups must book in advanced.
Length of Visit:	2 hours
Booking Contact:	Lisa Edinborough,
	Hidcote Manor Garden, Hidcote Bartrim, Chipping Campden, Gloucestershire, GL55 6LR
	Telephone: 01386 438333 Fax: 01386 438817
Email:	hidcote@nationaltrust.org.uk
Website:	www.nationaltrust.org.uk
Location:	4 miles north east of Chipping Campden; 8 miles south of Stratford Upon Avon & signposted from B4632 Stratford/Broadway road, close to the village of Mickleton.

Please quote this guide when making a booking

William Morris chose Kelmscott Manor, a Grade 1 listed Tudor farmhouse adjacent to the river Thames, as his summer home in 1871. Morris loved the house, a "dear, sweet old place," which he described as having "grown up out of the soil."

The garden and surrounding countryside were inspirational to Morris' work. His letters refer to crocuses, aconites, "snowdrops everywhere," violets, primroses and tulips. Morris' daughter, May, writes of the garden "gay with thousands of tulips", the "white foam" of cherry and the "first purple-red rose."

The restoration of the Manor's garden reflects the rich botanical content of Morris's designs – wild tulips and snakeshead fritillaries under the mulberry tree, herbaceous beds filled with hollyhocks, cottage annuals, poppies, China asters and Sweet Sultans; the Yew hedge in the front garden with the topiary dragon clipped by Morris into "Fafnir", the mythical dragon of his Icelandic poems.

Fact File

Opening Times:	April to Sept 2009.
	General public open days House & Garden: (visits not bookable in advance)
	Every Wednesday 11am to 5pm. First and third Saturdays 11am to 5pm April 4th & 18th, May 2nd & 16th, June 6th & 20th, July 4th & 18th, August 1st & 15th & September 5th & 19th
	Ticket office opens 10.30am. Last admission to Manor 4.30pm.
	The Manor has limited capacity. Admission to the house is by timed ticket
	Garden only: Thursdays, May and June, 2pm to 5pm (as well as Wednesdays and open Saturdays)
Admission Rates:	House & Garden: Adults £8.50; Children (aged 8-16) £4.25; Students in full-time education with a valid student's card £4.25. One carer accompanying a disabled person FREE. Garden only: £2.
Group Rates:	please contact for details. Must be booked in advance.
Facilities:	Shop, Restaurant
Disabled Access:	Access to groundfloor; wheelchair available; toilet on site; disabled persons parking.
Tours/Events:	Guided tours available.
Coach Parking:	Yes – 2 coaches.
Length of Visit:	1¹/₂ - 2 hours
Booking Contact:	Kelmscott Manor, Kelmscott, Lechlade, Gloucestershire GL7 3HJ
	Tel: 01367 252486 Fax: 01367 253754
Email:	admin@kelmscottmanor.co.uk
Website:	www.kelmscottmanor.org.uk
Location:	Kelmscott Manor is situated approximately 3 miles from Lechlade and is signposted from the A417 and the A4095. On entering the village, please follow the signs to the Manor

Please quote this guide when making a booking

Kiftsgate is a glorious garden to visit throughout the seasons with spectacular views to the Malvern Hills and beyond. Three generations of women gardeners have designed, planted and sustained this garden.

The upper gardens around the house are planted to give harmonious colour schemes, whilst the sheltered lower gardens recreate the atmosphere of warmer countries. The latest addition is a modern water garden which provides an oasis of tranquillity and contrast to the exuberance of the flower gardens.

On open days plants grown from the garden are for sale. A wide and interesting selection are always available. The tearoom in the house offers delicous home made cream teas and light lunches in June and July.

"Winner of the HHA/Christies Garden of the Year award 2003"

Fact File

Opening times:	May, June & July - Saturday to Wednesday 12noon - 6pm. August - Saturday to Wednesday 2pm - 6pm. April & September - Sunday, Monday & Wednesday, 2pm - 6pm.
Admission Rates:	£6.50 Adults, £2.00 Children.
Groups Rates:	Coaches by appointment, 20 adults or more £5.50 per person
Facilities:	Plants for Sale, Tea Room, Gift Shop.
Disabled Access:	Limited
Tours/Events:	None
Coach Parking:	Yes.
Length of Visit:	1 ½ hours
Booking Contact:	Mrs Anne Chambers Kiftsgate Court Garden, Chipping Campden, Gloucestershire, GL55 6LN Telephone: 01386 438777 Fax: 01386 438777
Email:	anne@kiftsgate.co.uk
Website:	www.Kiftsgate.co.uk
Location:	3 miles north east of Chipping Campden. Follow signs towards Mickleton, then follow brown tourist signs to Kiftsgate Court Gardens.

Please quote this guide when making a booking

A place of tranquil beauty amidst fine formal gardens, Lydney Park is home to Viscount Bledisloe, and is steeped in history from Iron Age to the present day. In early season, the visitor to Lydney Park drives between a resplendent display of daffodils and narcissi, and beyond the car park are the Spring Gardens, a secret wooded valley with lakes, providing a profusion of Rhododendrons, Azaleas and other flowering shrubs. Discover an important Roman Temple Site and the site of a Normal Castle. Picnic in the Deer Park amongst some magnificent trees, and visit our museums, which includes a New Zealand Museum. Home made teas in Dining Room of House. Dogs welcome on leads.

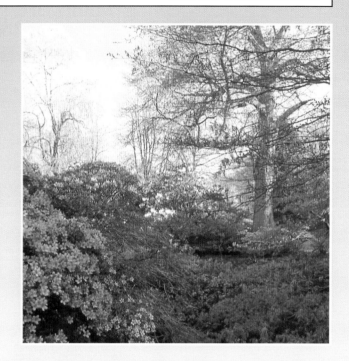

Fact File

Opening times:	10am - 5pm Sundays, Wednesdays and Bank Holidays Monday from 29th March until 3rd May Then daily from 3rd May until 7th June (except Fridays and Saturdays).
Admission Rates:	Adults £4.00, Children 50p.
Groups Rate:	Minimum group size: 25 - Phone for group rates.
Facilities:	Tea Rooms, Roman Temple Site, Museums, Gift Shop, Plant Sales.
Disabled Access:	Not Suitable.
Tours/Events:	Tour of Garden can be made available.
Coach Parking:	Yes
Length of Visit:	1 - 2 hours
Booking Contact:	Sally James Lydney Park Gardens, Lydney Park, Estate Office, Old Park, Lydney, Gloucestershire, GL15 6BU. Telephone: 01594 842844 or 01594 842922 Fax: 01594 842027
Email:	mrjames@phonecoop.coop or tracey_lydneype@btconnect.com
Website:	None
Location:	Situated off A48 between Chepstow and Gloucester.

Please quote this guide when making a booking

Surrounding a very old watermill, and hugging the sides of a tiny valley, Mill Dene Garden really is hidden in the Cotswolds and is a place of beauty, tranquillity and rest.

The stream behind the house has an air of mystery with a misty grotto and shade plants. The herb potager has the village church as a backdrop and there are views over the hills to the Salt Way. The gentle sounds of water in rills and basins abound, as does scent, particularly along the Rose Walk.

The feel of the garden is light-hearted with the use of mirrors, trompe l'oeil, concealment and surprise apparently altering the boundaries and size of the garden. The owner, Wendy Dare, with help from Rupert Golby, has designed a highly individual garden. She started from nothing and, responding to the strong sense of place, has made a garden in the 'English Country Garden' style – the result is delightful.

enjoyEngland.com

QUALITY ASSURED VISITOR ATTRACTION

Fact File

Opening Times: Open April 1st to September 30th. Weds to Fri. 10.30 to 5pm, last entry 4pm. Also open Saturdays 9.30 to 12.30.

Admission Rates: Adults: £5.00, Senior Citizens: £4.75, Children: 5 - 15: £1.00 includes free garden trail. A short 10/15 min. talk can be given by the owner for individuals. Book ahead. £10 a head.

Group Rates: Minimum Group Size: 20. £4.50 a head, must be booked ahead. Short talk: £25. Guided tour £65. Bank Holidays 2 - 5pm. Closed one week July 12th to 17th . Free access for RHS - April and September

Facilities: Plant sales, gift shop, light lunches and cream teas available.

Disabled Access: 50% no toilets for disabled. Please ring ahead for reserved parking space and for ramps to be put out.

Toilets on site: Yes

Car Parking: Yes - limited. Coach Parking nearby.

Length of Visit: 2.5 hours

Special Events: Open Easter Monday, April 13th 2-5 for NGS. April 27th RHS lunch and tour. May 10th-15th & 16th-18th September Art Course. May 11th, 22nd June, 27th July, 24th August, 14th. September Photographic course. 27th September Pebble mosaic course Open Dec 5th for LINC: 6.30 to 9, for Garden lighting.

Booking Contact: Wendy Dare, School Lane, Blockley, Moreton in Marsh, Glos. GL56 9HU Booking Tel No.01386 700457. Booking Fax No. 01386 700526

Email: info@milldene.co.uk **Website:** www.milldenegarden.co.uk

Location: Take the Blockley turn off the A44 at Bourton on the Hill only. Coaches follow brown signs, stop at 1st left turn behind village gates by School Lane, and unload, then park where directed.

Please quote this guide when making a booking

This lovely, timeless garden, with spectacular views over both deer park and rolling Cotswold hills beyond, was created in the 17th Century and still retains a wonderful sense of peace and quietness. There are extensive yew hedges, including a notable yew walk, a Lutyens loggia hung with wisteria and a wide York stone terrace overlooked by a fine specimen of Magnolia soulangeana. Beneath the terrace splendid grass steps, fringed with campanula, lead to the South Lawn and an ancient mulberry tree, believed planted in 1620. West of the house, a rill with fountain and a stone summerhouse are recent garden additions to commemorate the Millennium. Beyond the rill a large walled garden boasts extensive double borders which have undergone a total re-plant over the last two years and now contain a wide range of roses, clematis, shrubs and herbaceous, all arranged in individual colour sections and planted to provide flower and interest from spring to autumn.

Fact File

Opening Times:	10am - 5pm, Tuesday, Wednesday & Thursday, 1st April - 30th September.
Admission Rates:	Adults £4.00, Senior Citizen £4.00, Child Free
Group Rates:	Minimum group size: 20
	Adults £3.60, Senior Citizen £3.60, Child Free
Facilities:	Nurseries Adjacent.
Disabled Access:	Yes. Parking for disabled on site.
Tours/Events:	None.
Coach Parking:	Yes
Length of Visit:	1 1/2 hours
Booking Contact:	Estate Office
	Misarden Park, Miserden, Stroud, Glos, GL6 7JA
	Telephone 01285 821303 Fax: 01285 821530
Email:	estate.office@miserdenestate.co.uk
Website:	None
Location:	Follow signs to Misarden from A417 or from B4070.

Please quote this guide when making a booking

"Owlpen, in Gloucestershire - ah, what a dream is there!" - Vita Sackville-west, 1941

This garden, set within a beautiful Cotswold valley, is a rare survival of an early formal garden on a manorial scale... 'possibly the earliest domestic garden in England to survive in something approaching completeness' -Sir Geoffrey jellicoe. It was re-ordered with terraces and strong symmetry in 1723 by Thomas Daunt IV.

The garden became an icon to the designers of the early twentieth century, as a 'Sleeping Beauty'. Gertrude Jekyll visited the garden several times and featured it in her influential book, Gardens for Small Country Houses (1914). After being uninhabited for over 100 years, iit was restored sympathetically in 'Old English' style by Norman Jewson in 1926. Vita Sackville-West described the garden between the wars as a 'dream', one of 'the places one has seen and loved', whose yew rooms were precursors to those in her great garden at Sissinghurst.

The garden has been reordered since 1975 by Sir Nicholas and Lady Mander with magnificent yew topiary, old roses, hornbeams and box parterres on seven hanging terraces.

Fact File

Opening Times:	Beginning of May - End of September 2009 on Tues, Thurs & Sun, Gardens & Restaurant from 12.00 noon and House open from 2pm until 5pm (last admission at 4.30pm).
Admission Rates:	Garden Only - Adults £3.75, Senior Citizen £3.75, Child £1.75
	House & Garden - Adults £5.75, Senior Citizen £5.75, Child £2.75
Groups Rates:	Minimum group size: 25
	Adults £5.00, Senior Citizen £5.00, Child £2.50
Facilities:	Restaurant, Lunches and Teas.
Disabled Access:	No. Parking for disabled on site.
Tours/Events:	None.
Coach Parking:	Yes.
Length of Visit:	1½ - 2 hours
Booking Contact:	Jayne Simmons, Owlpen Estate Office, Owlpen Manor, Uley, Dursley, Gloucestershire, GL11 5BZ Telephone: 01453 860261 Fax: 01453 860819
Email:	sales@owlpen.com
Website:	www.owlpen.com
Location:	Approach from Uley village, 1/2 mile east off B4066 at village green in Uley (near the Old Crown pub) between Dursley and Stroud.

Please quote this guide when making a booking

Painswick Rococo Garden Gloucestershire

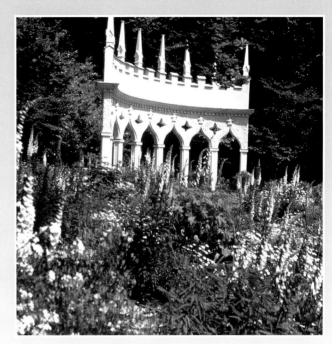

Painswick Rococo Garden is a fascinating insight into 18th century English garden design. The only complete Rococo garden in England, it dates from a brief period (1720-1760) when English gardens where changing from the formal to the informal. These Rococo gardens combined formal vists with winding woodland walks and more natural planting. However Rococo gardens were so much more, their creators showed off their wealth and included features that were both flamboyant and frivolous. The gardens featured buldings of unusual architectural styles, to be used as both eye catchers and view points. These gardens became regency playrooms, an extension of the house to be enjoyed by the owner and his guests.

We are restoring the Garden back to how it was shown in a painting dated 1748. We have contemporary buidings, woodland walks, herbaceous borders, and a large kitchen garden all hidden away in a charming Cotswold valley with splendid views of the surrounding countryside. Visit our Anniversary Maze, or come in early spring to see our stunning snowdrop display.

Fact File

Opening times:	10th January - 31st October. Daily 11am - 5pm.
Admission Rates:	Adults £5.50, Senior Citizen £4.50, Child £2.75
Groups Rates:	Minimum group size: 20 (includes free introductory talk) Adults £4.50.
Facilities:	Visitor Centre, Shop, Plant Sales, Teas, Restaurant.
Disabled Access:	No. Toilet for disabled on site.
Tours/Events:	None yet booked - see website for details.
Coach Parking:	Yes.
Length of Visit:	2 hours
Booking Contact:	Paul Moir Painswick Rococo Garden, Gloucestershire, GL6 6TH Telephone: 01452 813204 Fax: 01452 814888
Email:	prm@rococogarden.org.uk
Website:	www.rococogarden.org.uk
Location:	½ mile outside Painswick on B4073

Please quote this guide when making a booking

Rodmarton Manor is the supreme example of the Cotswold Arts and Crafts Movement. The garden was laid out as the house was being built (1909-1929) as a series of outdoor rooms covering about 8 acres. Each garden room has a different character and is bounded by either walls or hedges. One "garden room" has 26 separate beds with a wide variety of planting dominated by yellow shrubs and roses. There is a collection of stone troughs with alpines as well a rockery with bigger alpines. Topiary is a feature of the garden with extensive yew, box beech and holly hedges and clipped features including some new topiary. The herbaceous borders are magnificent from May but peaking late June but with plenty flowering into September. Many different types of roses flourish in the garden including old fashioned well-scented ones. There is a walled Kitchen Garden which has other plants besides vegetables including trained apples and pears. There is a big snowdrop collection. Most people who visit Rodmarton see the house which has specially made furniture as well as seeing the garden.

Fact File

Opening times:	1st, 8th, 12th, 15th February from 1.30pm, (Garden only for snowdrops). House and Garden Easter Monday 2pm - 5pm. Wednesdays, Saturdays, Bank Holidays May - September 2pm - 5pm. Private coach bookings also at other times.
Admission Rates:	House and Garden £7.00 (5-15yrs £3.50). Garden only £4.00 (5 - 15yrs £1.00) (no dogs)
Facilities:	Teas
Disabled Access:	Yes. Most of garden and ground floor of house.
Tours/Events:	Guided tours of house and garden available.
Coach Parking:	Yes
Length of Visit:	2 hours for house and garden
Booking Contact:	Simon Biddulph, Rodmarton Manor, Cirencester, GL7 6PF. Telephone 01285 841253 Fax: 01285 841298
Email:	simon.biddulph1@btinternet.com
Website:	www.rodmarton-manor.co.uk
Location:	Off A433 between Cirencester and Tetbury.

Please quote this guide when making a booking

This 2½-acre garden has been created over the last 15 years. It is made up of a series of rooms that flow around the house each holding their own special magic.

Many woodland plants give interest and colour in the early months. The borders are full to overflowing with bulbs from March to late May, along with countless herbaceous treasures, and in summer over 65 different varieties of roses scent the garden. Autumn brings exotic colour tones from many different species of shrubs and trees.

A tiny Potager with raised beds shows how to make growing vegetables easy on terrible ground. The Stream has been graded into a gently flowing water garden awash with musk-scented Primula Floridae.

This is a Garden for all Seasons.

4 Rare Plant Sales are held here each year when some of the finest Specialist Nurseries sell their treasures.

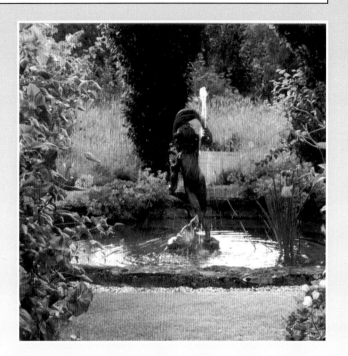

Fact File

Opening Times:	1st March until the end of October.
Admission Rates:	Adults: £5.00, Children: Free
Facilities:	Teas, morning coffee or light lunches by arrangement.
Disabled Access:	Yes. Good wheelchair access. Toilet and car parking on site.
Tours/Events:	Guided tours available.
	Rare Plant Sales: Hellebore Sale 6th March, 10am – 1pm. Primula Auricula & Woodland Plants 17th April, 10am - 1pm. Summer Plant Sale 25th May, 10am - 2pm. Autumn Plant Sale 15th September 10am – 3pm.
	Open for NGS on Sunday 19th April 2pm - 6pm. Plants and tea available.
Coach Parking:	Yes.
Length of Visit:	1 hour.
Booking Contact:	Katie Lukas
	Stone House, Wyck Rissington, Cheltenham, Glos. GL54 2PN
	Tel: 01451 810337 Fax: 01451 810340
Email:	katielukas@globalnet.co.uk
Website:	www.stonehousegarden.co.uk
Location:	Last house on right in village coming from the A429.

Please quote this guide when making a booking

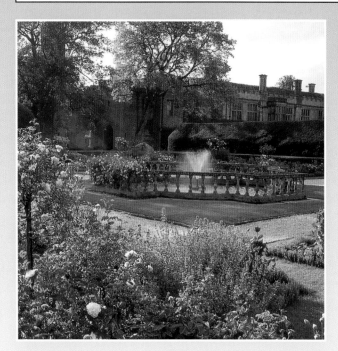

14 acres of glorious, organically managed gardens. Bold areas of planting such as those surrounding the 15th century Tithe Barn ruins contrast with intricate detail as seen in the Tudor Knot Garden. Topiary features strongly throughout and the famous Queens Garden, full of English roses, is furnished on two sides by magnificent double yew hedges planted in 1860. A Victorian Kitchen Garden links with the HDRA to help preserve rare and endangered vegetables. More recent additions include the East Garden, its arbour and beds planted with white wisterias, oriental clematis and tree peonies, and a landscaped Pheasantry area.

Fact File

Opening Times:	Open 30th March to 1st November 2009. Daily; 10.30am - 5.00pm. Please ensure you telephone or visit our website for updated information before visiting.
Admission Rates:	Adults £7.20, Concessions £6.20, Children £4.20. Family (2 adults and 2 children) £20.80.
Group Rates:	Group rates available.
Facilities:	Visitor Centre, Plant Sales, Coffee Shop, Picnic Area and Children's Play Area.
Disabled Access:	Limited - garden only. Toilet and Parking for disabled on site.
Tours/Events:	Group guided tours available - must be pre-booked. Special events programme, please call for details. (Information may be subject to change, please call or check website).
Coach Parking:	Yes
Length of Visit:	3 hours
Booking Contact:	Group Bookings Sudeley Castle, Winchcombe, Cheltenham, Gloucestershire, GL54 5JD Telephone: 01242 602308 Fax: 01242 602959
Email:	enquiries@sudeley.org.uk
Website:	www.sudeleycastle.co.uk
Location:	On B4632, 8 miles north east of Cheltenham.

Please quote this guide when making a booking

Tortworth Court Four Pillars Hotel	Gloucestershire

Tortworth Court is a Grade Two listed property built by Lord Ducie in the Victorian Gothic style and set in 32 acres of recently restored grounds. The grounds are split in two main areas. There is a formal garden with a parterre, which has now been replanted with over six hundred roses and then the arboretum which has around one thousand trees many of which are rare and some of the first of their kind in the country.

In its day Tortworth Court rivalled Westonbirt the famous arboretum nearby. Today the arboretum is still extremely important and is recognised as one of the finest of its type in the British Isles. One of our most famous trees is the original Corkscrew Hazel made famous by Sir Harry Lauder as his twisted walking stick.

Fact File

Opening Times: N/A
Admission Charges: Adults: N/A, Senior Citizens: N/A, Children: N/A
On-Site Facilities: Restaurant, Teas, Bar
Disabled Access: Yes. Toilet and parking on site. Wheelchair loan available – booking advisable.
Toilets on site: Yes
Car Parking on site: Yes
Coach Parking: Yes – 200 yards away
Guided Tours: Yes (must be booked in advance)
Length of Visit: 2 hours
Booking Contact: Clive Smith, Tortworth Court Four Pillars Hotel, Wotton Under Edge, South Glos. GL12 8HH
Booking Tel No. 01454 263000 Booking Fax No. 01454 263001
Email: tortworth@four-pillars.co.uk
Website: www.tortworth-court-hotel.co.uk
Location: From the north: leave the M5 at junction 14. Follow the B4509 towards Wotton.
On the hill and take the first right into Tortworth Road. After half a mile,
the hotel is on the right up a long drive.
From the south: leave M5 at junction 14, signposted to Dursley.
At the T Juncton turn right on the B4509 and follow directions above.

Please quote this
guide when
making a booking

Westonbirt The National Arboretum   Gloucestershire

Westonbirt, The National Arboretum, situated in the glorious Cotswolds, is one of the outstanding tree collections in the world covering an area of 600 acres. Westonbirt is noted for its vast range of stunning mature specimen trees.

A short walk from the original arboretum is Silkwood, with collections of native Asian and American species that in spring are carpeted with primroses, wood anemones and bluebells. There are in excess of 17,000 numbered trees, including an exceptional National Collection of Japanese maples, extended in 2006 by the newly planted Rotary Glade. Colour is best in May (rhododendrons, magnolias, etc.) and October (Japanese maples, Persian ironwoods, Katsuras etc.). The plant centre offers some rare, interesting shrubs and trees, especially Japanese maples, conifers and specimen trees. Westonbirt arboretum is an inspiring place to relax, get back to nature and indulge your senses. You will want to return to explore time and time again ...

Fact File

Opening times: 9 a.m. – 8 p.m. or dusk

Admission Rates: Adults: £5.00 - £8.00 (subject to seasonal variation), Senior Citizens: Concessions available
Children: £2 - £3 for children aged 5-18, Under 5 – Free
RHS members free at certain times

Group Rates: Minimum Group Size: 16, Adults: £5.50, Senior Citizens: £4.50, Children: £1.00

Facilities: Visitor Centre, Shop, Plant Sales, Restaurant, Teas, play areas for under 5s, play zones for up to age 10

Disabled Access: Yes. Wheelchair loan available – booking required.

Toilets on site: Yes   **Car Parking on site:** Yes   **Coach Parking:** Yes

Guided Tours: Yes, weekend tours, just turn up. Booking required for groups

Length of Visit: 3 hours plus

Special Events: Main Events: Festival of the Tree August, Enchanted Christmas: December. Dog Days, February, Summer concerts, June/July, Many more smaller events all through the year.

Booking Contact: Helen Daniels, Westonbirt The National Arboretum, Westonbirt, Tetbury, Gloucestershire GL7 2RW
Booking Tel No.01666 881200 Booking Fax No. 01666 880559

Email: helen.daniels@forestry.gsi.gov.uk   **Website:** www.forestry.gov.uk/westonbirt

Location: From the southwest, Wales and London – we are 15 minutes north of Junction 18 of the M4 (Bath junction) on A433
From Cheltenham, the North and Oxfordshire – go to Tetbury via Cirencester and follow the brown signs south on the A433.

Please quote this guide when making a booking

Natural beauty is in abundance at Exbury Gardens, a 200 acre woodland garden on the east bank of the Beaulieu River in the New Forest National Park. Created by Lionel de Rothschild in the 1920's the Gardens are a stunning vision of his inspiration. The spring displays of rhododendrons, azaleas, camellias and magnolias are world famous. The daffodil meadow, rock, exotic, iris and herbaceous and grasses gardens ensure year round interest. Summer is a favoured time for cool and shady walks, whilst the River Walk offers magnificent views over the Solent to the Isle of Wight. The autumn sees spectacular colours from acers, sweet gums and dogwoods and magnificent displays from *Nyssa* and *Oxydendrums*, two of Exbury's National Plant Collections.

Visitors can enjoy over 20 miles of pathways, or "let the train take the strain" with a 20 min journey around part of the Yard Wood, with magnificent vistas over the Rock Garden and features which include a bridge, viaduct and tunnel. Chauffeur driven buggy tours ensure access for all.

Copyright Murray Sanders

Fact File

Opening Times: 7 March – 8 November daily, 10am – 5.00pm last admission. Gates close 6pm. Please call for winter opening dates / Exbury Santa Steam Specials in Dec.

Admission Rates: Adult £8.00; Senior Citizen £7.50; Child (3-15) £1.50 under 3's free. Family £18.50 (2 Adults & 3 Children 3-15). Railway + £3.50. (includes tour of engine shed) Rover ticket (unlimited daily travel) + £4.50. Buggy Tours (30/45 mins) + £3.50 / + £4.00. "Exbury Experience Ticket" £13.00 – inclusive of entry, railway journey, buggy tour and Tree Trail leaflet, and discounts based on a minimum spend in restaurant and gift shop. Available from early June onwards.

Groups Rates: Minimum group size: 15 – Adults / Sen Cits £7.00. Group organiser free entrance. Coach Driver incentives.

Facilities: Gift Shop; Plant Sales; Teas; restaurant; Buggy Tours.

Disabled Access: Yes. Toilet and parking for disabled on site. Wheelchairs available on free loan. Accessible carriages on train. Carers admitted free of charge on 1:1 basis to gardens.

Tours/Events: Guided tours of Gardens (including specialist interest)and "Meet & Greets" are available.

Coach Parking: Yes, free. We endeavour to meet groups on arrival in main season, April / May.

Length of Visit: 2½ - 3½ hours min, but between 4-6 hours in main flowering season, April / May.

Booking Contact: Reception, Exbury Gardens, Estate Office, Exbury, Southampton, Hants SO45 1AZ. Telephone: 023 80 891203 Fax: 023 80 899940

Email: nigel.philpott@aol.com

Website: www.exbury.co.uk

Location: Junction 2 west of M27, just follow A326 to Fawley, off B3054, 3 miles Beaulieu, in New Forest National Park. B&W signposted.

Please quote this guide when making a booking

The gardens at Houghton Lodge are listed Grade II* and surround an enchanting and unique example of an 18th Century "Cottage Orne", with sweeping lawns and fine trees that overlook the tranquil beauty of the River Test. Chalk Cob walls enclose a traditional Kitchen Garden with espaliers, herbs and heated greenhouses, a hydroponicum and an orchid collection. The Gardens are both formal and informal with a woodland walk, stunning herbaceous border and topiary peacock garden. Do not miss the topiary puffing dragon! Houghton Lodge is a popular TV/film location including the film 'Wilde' and BBC TV productions of 'Murder at the Vicarage', 'The Buccaneers' and 'David Copperfield'. A further 14 acres adjoining the garden provide an experience of the natural world with meadow walks through the peaceful and unspoiled surroundings of the River Test where you will meet Tom, Dick and Harry, our new Alpacas.

Licensed for Civil Weddings.

Fact File

Opening times: 1st March – 31st October: 10 a.m. – 5 p.m. every day but not Wednesdays. Wednesdays and House by appointment only

Admission Rates: Adults: £5.00, Children: Under 14 – Free
14-acre meadow walks with Alpacas, an additional £2.50. Dogs welcome on short leads.

Group Rates: Coach tours and groups welcomed on any day by appointment only – special rates if booked in advance.

Facilities: Visitor Centre, Teas

Disabled Access: Yes. Wheelchair loan available.

Toilets on site: Yes

Car Parking on site: Yes

Coach Parking: Yes

Guided Tours: Yes, booking required.

Length of Visit: 2 hours

Booking Contact: Anthea Busk, Houghton Lodge Gardens, Stockbridge, Hants. SO20 6LQ
Booking Tel No. 01264 810502. Booking Fax No. 01264 810063

Email: info@houghtonlodge.co.uk

Website: www.houghtonlodge.co.uk

Location: Houghton Lodge Gardens are 1½ miles south of Stockbridge, signed to Houghton.

Please quote this guide when making a booking

Sir Harold Hillier Gardens

Sir Harold Hillier Gardens is one of the most important modern plant collections in the world. Established in 1953 by the distinguished plantsman Sir Harold Hillier, the magnificent collection of over 42,000 plants from temperate regions around the world grows in a variety of superb themed landscapes set over 180-acres of rolling Hampshire countryside.

Open throughout the year, the Gardens offer four seasons of beauty, inspiration and discovery and includes 11 National Plant Collections, over 250 Champion Trees and the largest winter Garden in Europe.

A £3.5 million Visitor & Education Pavilion offers fine views of the collection and surrounding countryside and features; a stylish licensed restaurant for home-cooked meals; light refreshments and afternoon teas; open-air terrace; gift shop; and interpretation area explaining the role and history of the Gardens. Entry to the Pavilion is free of charge with Group bookings welcome by prior arrangement.

Fact File

Opening Times:	Daily: 10am - 6pm or dusk if earlier. Open all year except Christmas Day and Boxing Day.
Admission Rates:	Adults £8.25, Concession £7.15, (seniors, jobseekers, full-time students and people with disabilities) Under 16 years - free of charge.
Group Rates:	Minimum group size 10, £6.60 per person.
Facilities:	£3.5 million Visitor & Education Pavilion, Open-air terrace and restaurant, Gift Shop, Plant Centre.
Disabled Access:	Yes. Toilet and parking for disabled on site. Wheelchairs on loan, booking advised. Mobility Scooters for hire.
Tours/Events:	Pre-booked guided tour with Curator, Botanist, Head Gardener and Horticultural staff available by arrangement. Please telephone for details about Special Events.
Coach Parking:	Yes (Free)
Length of Visit:	2 - 4 hours
Booking Contact:	Group Bookings. Sir Harold Hillier Gardens, Jermyns Lane, Romsey, Hampshire, SO51 0QA Telephone: 01794 369317/318 Fax: 01794 368027
Email:	info@hilliergardens.org.uk
Website:	www.hilliergardens.org.uk
Location:	The Gardens are situated, 2 miles north-east of Romsey. M3/M27 (West) to Romsey town centre. At Romsey follow brown heritage signs to the Hillier Gardens off the A3090. Alternatively, the Gardens can be approached from the A3057 Andover direction.

Please quote this guide when making a booking

Nestling in a woodland corner of Hampshire is this ravishingly attractive 1720's manor house, where busts of gods, emperors and dukes look down from the walls onto two major gardens. The inner gardens, enclosed by eighteenth century walls, are all devoted to parterres. One is filled with water lilles, another of classical design with box topiary and a third enacts the whimsy of Alice in Wonderland with the story's characters in ivy and box topiary surrounded by roses of red and white. The main walled garden is planted in subtle hues of mauve, plum and blue, contained in beds that have been faithfully restored to their original outlines. A decorative potager is centred around berry-filled fruit cages where herbs, flowers and unusual vegetables are designed into colourful patterns. All this is surrounded by a second garden, a remarkable new-classical park studded with follies, birdcages and monuments. A Paradise water garden. A Red Paeony Dragon Garden now join two new gardens in 2008. West Green House was the first garden to have a whole `Gardeners World' programme dedicated to itself.

Fact File

Opening Times:	Sunday 12th AprilSunday 26th April Sunday 3rd May Sunday 27th September.
Admission Rates:	Adults £5.50, Children £3.00.
Group Rates:	Groups by arangement please telephone for details. 1st May to 30th September 2009.
Facilities:	Tea Rooms, Nursery, Garden Shop.
Disabled Access:	Yes. Toilet and parking for disabled on site.
Tours/Events:	Opera. August 1st & 2nd, 8th & 9th. June Midsummer Concert date TBA, check website. July Summer Day Concert date TBA, check website.
Coach Parking:	Yes
Length of Visit:	2 hours approximately.
Booking Contact:	West Green House, Thackhams Lane, West Green, Hartley Wintney, Hants RG27 8JB Telephone: 01252 845582 Fax: 01252 844611
Email:	pip@westgreenhouse.co.uk
Website:	westgreenhousegardens.co.uk
Location:	10 miles north east of Basingstoke, 1 mile west of Hartley Wintney, 1 mile north of A30.

Please quote this guide when making a booking

Hampton Court Gardens are magnificent new gardens set in the grounds of a late medieval castle and surrounded by a thousand acres of parkland. Rescued from neglect in 1994, the gardens have been revived and transformed. Estate masons and carpenters have meticulously restored many original structures, and inspirational new features have been added. Today, water canals, island pavilions, avenues and borders complement the established planting of the earlier eras. The Gardens are a peaceful haven but also a place of exploration with a maze, Gothic Tower and secret tunnel to a waterfall. The Ornamental Kitchen Garden is both beautiful and productive and visitors can sample its delicious organic produce in the Orangery Restaurant, or enjoy a picnic on the lawn.

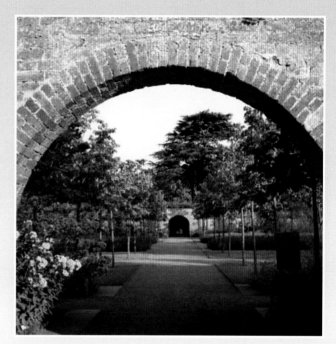

Fact File

Opening Times: 11 am – 5 pm, 10 April - 31 October inclusive. Open Tuesday to Sunday and Bank Holiday Mondays. Open every day in August. Open until 7 pm every Friday and Saturday throughout the summer. Last entry one hour before closing time.

Admission Charges: Adults £6.00 (includes free admission on a second midweek visit) OAP £5.50 (includes free admission on a second midweek visit) Children 5 –16 yrs £3.50. Under 5's FREE. Family ticket (2+3) £15. Prices may vary on special event days.

Group Rates: Minimum Group Size: 20. Adult £ 5.00 Children £2.50

On-Site Facilities: Shop, Plant Sales, Restaurant, Teas

Disabled Access: Yes, wheelchair loan available. Booking required.

Toilets on site: Yes

Car Parking on site: Yes

Coach Parking: Yes

Length of Visit: 1/2 day

Booking Contact: Ticket Office, Hampton Court Gardens, Hampton Court, Hope-under-Dinmore, Leominster, Herefordshire HR6 0PN
Booking Tel No.01568 797777 Booking Fax No. 01568 797472

Email: office@hamptoncourt.org.uk

Website: www.hamptoncourt.org.uk

Location: Situated on the A417 near to its junction with the A49 between Hereford and Leominster.

Hergest Croft Gardens   Herefordshire

From spring bulbs to autumn colour this is a garden for all seasons. Four distinct gardens with over 5,000 rare shrubs and trees and over sixty Champion trees are sure to delight everyone. Thirty foot high rhododendrons are fantastic in Park Wood. Azaleas in the Azalea Garden are spectacular in spring. The large Kitchen Garden contains the long colourful herbaceous borders, the Rose Garden, Spring Borders and unusual vegetables. Autumn colour throughout the gardens is superb. The Gardens hold the National Collections of maples, birches and zelkovas.

Teas and light lunches, by award-winning Ridgeway Catering, specialise in local homemade food, and are available in the old Dining Room of Hergest Croft. The Plant Sales area contains rare and unusual specimens from all over the world. A wide range of gifts are presented in the Hall.

There are special entry rates for pre-booked groups of 20 or more people.

Fact File

Opening times:	28 March – 1 November 2009: March: weekends 12 – 5.30 p.m. Daily: 12 – 5.30 p.m.
Admission Rates:	Adults: £6.00, Senior Citizens: N/A, Children: Free under 16 years
	RHS Members Free Between 1st and 30th April 2009, 1st July – 30th September 2009
Group Rates:	Minimum Group Size: 20 + pre-booked.
	Adults: £5.00, pre-booked, Senior Citizens: N/A, Children: Free under 16 years
	Guided tour 20+, pre-booked £7.00
Facilities:	Visitor Centre, Shop, Plant Sales, Tearoom
Disabled Access:	Yes – limited. One wheelchair available for loan. Booking required.
Toilets on site:	Yes + disabled
Car Parking on site:	Yes
Coach Parking:	Yes – 200 yards away
Guided Tours:	Yes, booking required.
Length of Visit:	2 hours
Special Events:	Flower Fair, Monday 4 May 2009 10.30 – 5.30 p.m.
	Plant Fair Sunday 18 October 2009 11.00 a.m. – 4.30 p.m. - Others as per website
Booking Contact:	Melanie Lloyd, Hergest Croft Gardens, Kington, Hereford HR5 3EG
	Booking Tel No.01544 230160. Booking Fax No. 01544 232031
Email:	gardens@hergest.co.uk
Website:	www.hergest.co.uk
Location:	A44 (Rhayader) signposted from Kington

Please quote this guide when making a booking

Moors Meadow Garden & Nursery   Herefordshire

Enjoy the mystery of leaving the beaten track to visit this hidden jewel of Herefordshire.

An enchanting and unique 7-acre organic garden overlooking the beautiful Kyre Valley and brimming with trees, shrubs, flowers and bulbs from around the world, it would tax even the most avid plantaholic trying to identify some of the many rarely seen species. It has been created by the same family over 50 years and includes an outstanding grass garden, fernery, herbaceous beds and borders, cottage-style gardens, herb garden and kitchen garden. It comprises of a little 'formal', through a lot of 'ordered chaos', to 'bring your own machete'; with secretive shrubberies and meandering paths there is something to surprise and fascinate at all times of year.

It is a garden full of inspiration and ideas with many intriguing features, seats and sculptures throughout the garden, and pools and ponds help to encourage myriad wildlife.

Fact File

Opening times: Friday, Saturday, Sunday and Bank Holidays: 11.00 a.m. – 5.00 p.m.
25th March – 7th September. If you would like to visit any other time, please ring.

Admission Rates: Adults: £4.00, Senior Citizens: £4.00, Children: £1.00

Group Rates: Minimum Group Size: 10. Adults: £4.00, Senior Citizens: £4.00, Children: £1.00
(Includes free introductory talk)

Facilities: Plant Sales. All the plants in the nursery are propagated from the garden.
Artist blacksmith on some days.

Disabled Access: Yes – very limited wheelchair access

Toilets on site: Yes

Car Parking on site: Yes

Coach Parking: Yes, by prior arrangement

Guided Tours: Yes, booking required. Guided tours conducted by the Head Gardener, subject to availability.

Length of Visit: 2 hours +

Booking Contact: Ros Bissell, Moors Meadow Garden & Nursery, Collington, Bromyard, Herefordshire, HR7 4LZ
Booking Tel No.01885 410318

Email: moorsmeadow@hotmail.co.uk

Website: www.moorsmeadow.co.uk

Location: 4 miles North Bromyard, 6 miles South Tenbury Wells on B4214,
half mile up lane – follow yellow arrows

Please quote this guide when making a booking

Broadview Gardens is a wonderful place in which to spend a couple of hours. Set in the peaceful picturesque Kent countryside it comprises 10 acres of beautifully manicured gardens each one of which is divided into smaller themed areas. You will be able to experience the wonders of a traditional Italian garden, wander around the Oriental garden as well as explore the sensory and water gardens. It is guaranteed to provide inspiration for both the amateur and professional.

Holding the National Collection of Hellebores and Japanese anemones we host a wide range of events throughout the year and, because each area is seasonally planted, there is always something interesting to see. Our spectacular dogwoods create a living flame effect during the winter which, combined with the peeling bark of birches and vibrant eranthis, iris reticula and other early flowering bulbs, means that there is a variety of colour on offer.

Fact File

Opening times:	Monday – Saturday: 9 a.m. – 5 p.m. Sunday: 10 a.m. – 4 p.m.
Admission Rates:	Free admission
Group Rates:	Minimum Group Size 20
Facilities:	Shop, Plant Sales, Restaurant, Teas, Garden Centre, Fresh Produce Shop
Disabled Access:	Yes
Toilets on site:	Yes
Car Parking on site:	Yes
Coach Parking:	Yes
Wheelchair Loan:	Yes, booking required
Guided Tours:	Yes, booking required
Length of Visit:	1 – 2 hours
Special Events:	Hellebore weekends – your chance to visit the National Collection of Hellebores, Feb 2009
Booking Contact:	Louise Yearwood, Broadview Gardens, Hadlow College, Tonbridge Road, Hadlow, Kent, TN11 0AL Booking Tel No.01732 853227. Booking Fax No. 01732 853207
Email:	enquiries@hadlow.co.uk
Website:	www.@hadlow.ac.uk
Location:	4 miles north of Tonbridge on the A26, just outside the village of Hadlow

Doddington Place Gardens Kent

Doddington Place is surrounded by wooded countryside in an area of outstanding natural beauty high up on the North Downs. The lovely landscaped gardens are set in the grounds of an imposing Victorian mansion and cover 10 acres. There is a notable woodland garden - spectacular in May and June - which includes many different varieties of rhododendron and azalea; also a large Edwardian rock garden with pools which has recently been renovated and re-planted; a formal sunk garden with borders; a new dahlia garden and a recently completed brick and flint folly. Extensive lawns and avenues are framed by impressive clipped yew hedges and many fine trees.

Fact File

Opening Times:	Sundays and Bank Holiday Mondays, 2 - 5pm from Easter Sunday until end of September.
Admission Rates:	Adults: £4.50, Children: £1.00.
Group Rates:	Minimum group size 12. Adults: £3.50, Children: £0.75p
Facilities:	Homemade cakes and cream teas, toilets.
Disabled Access:	Yes except to Rock Garden. One wheelchair available to loan.
Tours/Events:	Open air opera 10th and 11th July.
Coach Parking:	Yes
Length of Visit:	1 hour for garden and tea 1 1/2 hours.
Booking Contact:	Joan Webster
	Doddington Place Gardens, Doddington, Nr Sittingbourne, Kent, ME9 0BB
	Telephone: 01795 886101 Fax: 01795 886363
Email:	enquiries@doddingtonplacegardens.co.uk
Website:	www.doddingtonplacegardens.co.uk
Location:	From A20 at Lenham follow signs to Doddington. In Doddington turn left at Chequers Inn. After half mile turn right signed Doddington Church.
	From A2 at Ospringe Faversham follow sign to Doddington. Go into Doddington turn right at Chequers Inn. After half a mile turn right signed Doddington Church.

WINNER - Best Tourism Experience of the Year 2005 - Tourism Excellence Awards.

There's magic and mystery, history and romance at this enchanting award-winning venue - which provides such an unusual combination of a traditional heritage garden with the contemporary landscaping of the ancient woodland.

First laid out in 1674 on a gentle, south-facing slope, the formal walled gardens are set against the romantic backdrop of a medieval moat house (not open to the public). They include herbaceous borders, an exquisite white rose garden with over 20 varieties of roses, a secret garden, knot garden, nut walk, paradise walk and oriental garden plus the drunken garden with its crazy topiary, and there's wonderful seasonal colour throught spring, summer and autumn.

In complete contrast, in the ancient woodland of the 'Enchanted Forest" there are quirky and mysterious gardens developed by innovative designer, Ivan Hicks.

Fact File

Opening times: Open daily 28th March to 7th November 2009, 10am to 5.30pm (or dusk if earlier)

Admission Rates: Adults £8.95, Senior Citizen £7.45, Child (3-12yrs) £7.45, Family Ticket (2+2) £29.95.

Group Rates: Minimum group size: 12
Adults £7.25, Senior Citizens £5.50 (off peak) and £6.25 (July and August - Peak)
Students £6.25, and Children (3-12yrs) £5.50.

Facilities: Gift Shop, Licensed Restaurant, Plant Sales.

Disabled Access: Yes. Toilet & limited parking for disabled on site. Wheelchairs on loan.

Tours/Events: Guided tours for groups - pre booked only, £30 per guide. Packed programme of Special Events throughout the season.

Coach Parking: Yes

Length of Visit: 3 - 4 hours

Booking Contact: Carrie Goodhew
Groombridge Place, Groombridge, Tunbridge, Wells, Kent TN3 9QG
Telephone 01892 861444 Fax: 01892 863996

Email: office@groombridge.co.uk

Website: www.groombridge.co.uk

Location: 4 miles south west of Tunbridge Wells on B2110, just off the A264 between Tunbridge Wells and East Grinstead.

Please quote this guide when making a booking

Managed by Bexley Heritage Trust, Hall Place is a fine Grade I listed country house built in 1537 for Sir John Champneys, a wealthy merchant and former Lord Mayor of London. Surrounding the house are award-winning formal gardens with magnificent topiary, enclosed gardens and inspirational herbaceous borders. In the walled gardens there is a nursery selling plants grown in the Hall Place gardens, and a sub-tropical glasshouse where you can see ripening bananas in mid-winter.

The house, which boasts a panelled Great Hall with Minstrel's Gallery, ornate 17th century plaster ceilings and various other furnished historic rooms, has recently undergone extensive restoration. Following its reopening late in 2008, there are new displays including an introduction to the house's history and exhibits from Bexley's extensive museum collection. The new visitor centre in the grounds offers a riverside tearoom and a gift shop, as well as tourist information.

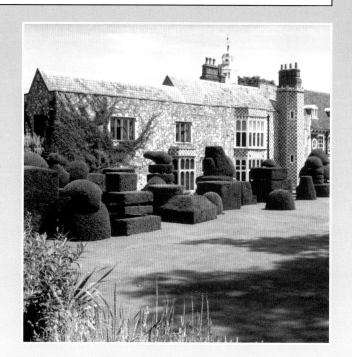

Fact File

Opening times:	Gardens open 9 a.m. – sunset throughout the year. Please telephone 01322 526574 for seasonal house, visitor centre and tearoom opening hours.
Admission Rates:	Free (except on special event days)
Group Rates:	Charges apply for guided tours and special events.
Facilities:	Free parking, Gift Shop, Plant Sales, Tearoom, Visitor Centre
Disabled Access:	Partial. Designated disabled toilet and parking on site.
Toilets on site:	Yes
Car Parking on site:	Yes
Coach Parking:	Yes
Guided Tours:	Pre-booked guided tours of the house and/or gardens available.
Special Events:	Extensive programme of events – please telephone 01322 526574 to request a leaflet.
Length of Visit:	3 – 4 hours
Booking Contact:	Sue Pothecary, Bourne Road, Bexley Kent, DA5 1PQ. Booking Tel No.020 8298 6951. Booking Fax No. 020 8303 6641
Email:	info@hallplace.org.uk
Website:	www.hallplace.org.uk
Location:	Black Prince Interchange of the A2, 3 miles from junciton 2 of the M25, towards London. Nearest rail connection: Bexley. Buses 229. 492, B15, 132 to the foot of Gravel Hill

Please quote this guide when making a booking

Discover 700 years of history at this romantic double-moated 13th century castle, once the childhood home of Anne Boleyn and set in award-winning gardens.

The spectacular gardens are the masterpiece of William Waldorf Astor who between 1904 and 1908 created a garden paradise. Visitors can view the stunning topiary, wander through pergolas of roses, climbing shrubs and perennial planting in the magnificent Italian gardens. Absorb the breathtaking scent of over 3000 roses in the walled rose garden and tapestries of colour in the 110-metre herbaceous border or take a peaceful stroll through Sunday Walk in this quintessential garden.

Enjoy the yew and water mazes, grottoes, cascades and fountains, 38-acre boating lake or walk around the newly-opened Hever Lake Walk with splendid mature trees, splashes, waterfalls.

A garden for all seasons and perfect for weddings, conferences and special occasions.

Fact File

Opening Times:	MAIN SEASON, 1 – 31st March: Wednesday – Sunday. 1 April – 31 October: Daily WINTER, 1 – 30 November: Thursday – Sunday. 3 – 20 December: Thursday – Sunday 10.30 opening; Castle 12 noon. Last admission 5 p.m., final exit 6 p.m. Winter: last admission 3 p.m., final exit 4 p.m.
Admission Charges:	Adults: £12.00, Senior Citizens: £10.00, Child: £6.50, Family: £30.50 Gardens Only: Adult: £9.50, Senior Citizens: £8.00, Child: £5.80, Family: £25.50
On-Site Facilities:	Restaurants, Picnic Areas, Shops, Plant Sales, Audio Tours
Disabled Access:	Partial. Toilet and parking for disabled and a limited number of wheelchairs
Toilets on site:	Yes
Car Parking on site:	Yes
Coach Parking:	Yes
Guided Tours:	Pre-booked guided tours available of castle and gardens. Full calendar of special events.
Length of Visit:	4 hours
Booking Contact:	Nicky Rees, Hever Castle, Hever TN8 7NG Telephone No. 01732 861701 Information Tel. No. 01732 865224
Email:	mail@hevercastle.co.uk
Website:	www.hevercastle.co.uk
Location:	30 miles from Central London. 3 miles SE of Edenbridge. Exit M25 junctions 5 or 6.

Please quote this guide when making a booking

Hole Park Gardens   Kent

Situated in the High Weald on the Kent and Sussex borders, Hole Park Garden is one of the Garden of England's best-kept secrets.

Spread over 15 acres is a garden for all seasons, set in the heart of the English countryside. Hole Park is located on the edge of the picturesque Weald village of Rolvenden. Hole Park has been owned by the Barham family for the past four generations. This outstandingly beautiful country house garden reflects the care and long-term planning that is unique to family-owned estates.

Formal, walled, meadow and woodland gardens are a feature and Hole Park is perhaps best noted for the extensive topiary, fine lawns and specimen trees and an amazing display of spring colour from the bluebells and rhododendrons.

Many visitors combine their visit to Hole Park Gardens with a trip to the historic Cinque Port of Tenterden, Sissinghurst Gardens or Great Dixter, only 6 miles distant.

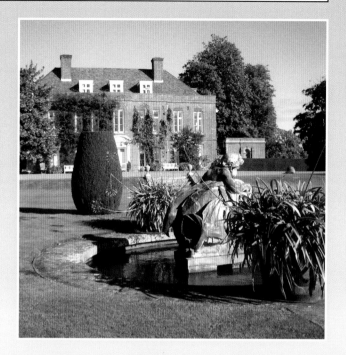

Fact File

Opening Times:	2pm – 6pm, Wednesdays and Thursdays from beginning of April to end of October. Sundays April to end of June. Bank Holiday Mondays 13th April, 4th & 25th May. Autumn Sundays, 4th, 11th, 18th and 25th October. Or by arrangement.
Admission Rates:	Adults: £5.00, Children: £0.50
Group Rates:	Group rates, including conducted tours available, please telephone for details.
Facilities:	Toilets, Plant Stall, Tea Room
Disabled Access:	Yes.
Tours/Events:	Tours, including all catering, to your requirements. Bluebell & Spring Spectacular, from 12th April to 10th May inclusive. Meet the Gardener 11th, 18th & 25th October (2.30 prompt)
Coach Parking:	Yes.
Length of Visit:	1½ - 2 hours.
Booking Contact:	Edward Barham, Hole Park Estate, Rolvenden, Cranbrook, Kent TN17 4JA Tel: 01580 241344 Fax: 01580 241386
Email:	info@holepark.com
Website:	www.holepark.com
Location:	4 miles south west of Tenterden, mid-way between villages of Rolvenden and Benenden on B2086

Please quote this guide when making a booking

Ightham Mote's 14-acre garden nestles in a sunken valley and surrounds the beautiful medieval moated manor house.

The North Lake and Woodland Garden with ornamental pond and cascade was created in the early 19th century with interesting trees to walk and sit amongst with pleasurable views to the house showing off its romantic setting. The Orchard, Enclosed Garden, Memorial Garden and Vegetable and Cutting Garden all contribute to the garden's sense of tranquillity for which it is famed.

The garden has "sat quietly" as a backdrop during the 15-year conservation project on the house. Now emerging out of the shadows for its moment of real glory, it is an exciting time to visit as a Conservation Plan is underway for the garden to become an attraction in its own right. These changes will be interpreted for our visitors as they occur.

Fact File

Opening Times: 14th March - 1st November 2009.
10.30am – 5.00pm (last entry at 4.30pm) every day except Tuesday and Wednesday.
For Winter opening times please visit ourwebsite.

Admission Rates: Adults: £10.40, Senior Citizens: N/A, Children: £5.20

Group Rates: Minimum Group Size: 15
Adults: £8.85, Senior Citizens: N/A, Children: £4.45

Facilities: Visitor Centre, Shop, Plant Sales, Restaurant, Teas

Disabled Access: Yes, wheelchair loan available. Toilet and parking on site.

Tours: Pre-booked only.

Coach Parking: Yes.

Length of Visit: 2 hours approximately

Booking Contact: Pamela Westaway
Ightham Mote, Mote Road, Ivy Hatch, Sevenoaks, Kent TN15 0NT
Tel: 01732-810378 Ext 100, Fax: 01732-811029

Email: linda.dillon@nationaltrust.org.uk

Website: www.nationaltrust.org.uk/ighthammote

Location: Between Sevenoaks and Borough Green, 1½ miles south of A25

Please quote this guide when making a booking

Lullingstone Castle & World Garden

Winner of the UK's Best New Tourism Project Awardin 2005. Set within 120 acres of beautiful Kent countryside, Lullingstone Castle is one of England's oldest family estates. The manor house and gatehouse – which overlook a stunning 15 acre lake – were built in 1497 and have been home to the same family ever since. In 2005, Tom Hart Dyke – 20th generation of Hart Dykes to live at Lullingstone – created within the Castle grounds a unique and inspiring 'World Garden' and filled it with thousands of rare, unusual and beautiful plants collected from all over the world (Tom came up with the idea for the garden whilst being held hostage at gunpoint in the Colombian jungle in 2000!) By the 2006 season these plants will have established and begun to fill the borders – which are designed in the shape of the continents.

Tom would now like to offer your group a chance to join him on a unique and personal tour of the 'World Garden'. You will also have the opportunity to view inside his home – Lullingstone Castle.

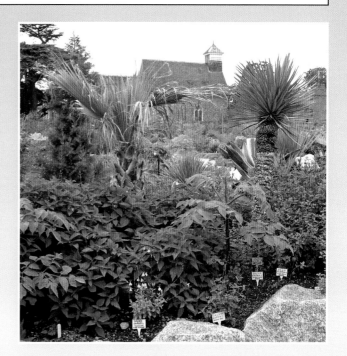

Fact File

Opening times:	April through September; Garden open Fridays and Saturdays 12-5pm (except Good Friday) Sundays and Bank Holidays 2-6pm. House open bank holidays! Special events at same times. Pre-booked groups on Wednesdays and Thursdays by arrangement.
Admission Rates:	Adults £6.00, Senior Citizen £5.50, Child £3.00, Family £15.00.
Group Rates:	Minimum group size: 20 Adults £8.00 per person plus £40.00 per group for Tom or a dedicated guide.
Facilities:	Toilets, book and plant sales on site. Refreshments available at nearby Visitor Centre (10 minutes walk), or why not bring a picnic?
Disabled Access:	Yes. Toilet and parking for disabled on site. Wheelchairs available upon request.
Tours/Events:	May 10th Lullingstone's Home Grown Plant Fair. July 26th Lullingstone's Eucalyptus Day. For more events See Website.
Coach Parking:	Yes.
Length of Visit:	Guided tour of House and Garden lasts approximately 2 - 2 1/2 hours.
Booking Contact:	Mr and Mrs G Hart Dyke Lullingstone Castle, Eynsford, Kent DA4 0JA. Tel: 01322 862114 Fax: 01322 862115
Email:	hartdyke@btinternet.com
Website:	www.lullingstonecastle.co.uk
Location:	Off the A225 near the village of Eynsford and just 10 minutes drive from Junction 3 of M25.

Please quote this guide when making a booking

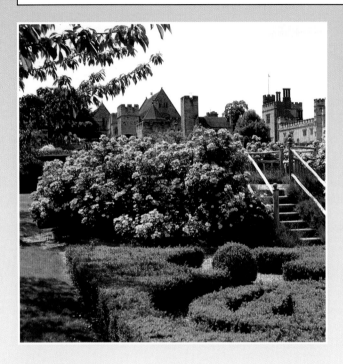

Ancestral home of the Sidney family since 1552, with a history going back six and half centuries, Penshurst Place has been described as "the grandest and most perfectly preserved example of a fortified manor house in all England".

See the awe-inspiring Baron's Hall with its 60ft high steeply angled roof and the State Rooms filled with fine tapestries, furniture, portraits and armour. The 11 acres of Gardens are as old as the original house - the walls and terraces were added in the Elizabethan era - and are divided into a series of self-contained garden rooms. Each garden room offers an abundance of variety in form, foliage and bloom and ensures a continuous display from Spring to Autumn. Victorian Herbaceous border restoration project taking place 2009-10

With Penshurst Place at its centre, there is the village of Penshurst to explore, ancient Parkland (walks leaflets available), Garden Tea Room serving hot lunches as well as lighter meals and refreshments, Gift Shop, Plant Centre and a Woodland Trail with a traditional Venture Playground for Children

Fact File

Opening Times: 28th February - 29th March open weekends and then daily from 30th March - Sunday 1st November 2009.

Admission Rates: 2008 prices held for 2009. To Gardens: Adults £7.00, Child (5-16) £5.00, Family Ticket (2+2) £20.00 Cyclists family £16.00 (or £1 off normal admission prices per person).

Groups Rates: 2008 prices held for 2009. Freeflow (non guided) House & Gardens Adults £7.00, School Children £4.00. Garden or House tours for groups (15+) available includes entrance to house & grounds. Adults £8.50, Children £4.50 .
Combined house & Garden tours: Adults £12.00, Children £7.50

Facilities: Gift Shop, Garden Tea Room & Garden History Exhibition in Garden Tower.

Disabled Access: Garden Yes, House DVD of state rooms in Baron's Hall
Toilet and parking for disabled on site, Wheelchairs on loan, booking necessary.

Tours/Events: Special joint entrance with other nearby attractions. Penshurst cream tea offer and high tea for groups if prebooked. Events programme.

Coach Parking: Yes.

Length of Visit: 2 - 3 hours

Booking Contact: Visitor Co ordinator
Penshurst Place, Penshurst, Nr Tonbridge, Kent TN11 8DG
Telephone: 01892 870307 Fax: 01892 870866

Email: groups@penshurstplace.com

Website: www.penshurstplace.com

Location: M25 junction 5, follow A21 to Hastings. Exit at Hildenborough then follow brown tourists signs.

Please quote this guide when making a booking

Normanby Hall Country Park

North Lincolnshire

Set in 300 acres of woodland and pleasure grounds, the Victorian walled garden is a unique experience. The garden has been carefully restored to its late Victorian heyday and grows fruit, flowers and vegetables dating from 1901 or earlier. Trained fruit, vegetable beds and cut flower borders are complemented by a range of glasshouses including a peach case, vinery, display house and fernery.

The huge herbaceous borders in the Secret Garden boast a colourful selection of unusual plants, whilst the Sunken Garden near the Hall is planted in pastel shades. There is also a parterre and rose beds, A 400ft long bog garden has been created in the base of the old ha-ha and a Victorian woodland garden is under development.

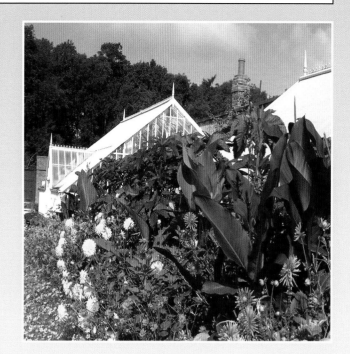

Fact File

Opening Times:	Park open all year, 9am - dusk.
	Walled Garden open 10.30am - 5pm in summer, 10.30am - 4pm in winter.
Admission Rates:	Adults £4.80, Senior Citizens (over 60's) £4.40, Child £2.40 (2008 prices).
	Season Ticket admits 2 Adults & Children all year for £18.00. (2008 prices).
Group Rates:	Minimum group size: 15. Freedom visit: Adults £4.20, Senior Citizens £4.00, Child £2.20.
	Visit with tour: Adults £6.70, Senior Citizens £6.10, Child £2.20 (includes admission to all areas).
Facilities:	Visitor Centre, Shop, Tea Room, Restaurant, Plant Sales.
Disabled Access:	Yes. Toilet & parking on site. Wheelchairs & motorised scooters on loan, booking necessary.
Tours/Events:	Guided tours of walled Garden & Hall available - approx 1 1/2 hours.
	Special gardening events throughout the year.
Coach Parking:	Yes
Length of Visit:	3 - 4 hours
Booking Contact:	Stuart Campbell
	Normanby Hall Country Park, Normanby, Scunthorpe, DN15 9HU
	Telephone: 01724 720588 Fax: 01724 721248
Email:	normanbyhall@northlincs.gov.uk
Website:	www.northlincs.gov.uk/normanby
Location:	4 miles north of Scunthorpe off the B1430.

Please quote this guide when making a booking

London's oldest botanic garden is a beautiful oasis of living history in the heart of the capital, home to a unique collection of medicinal and rare plants. Used as a place to teach people about plants and the environment for more than 300 years, today it exists as a self-supporting charity with two main goals: to help children understand more about the environment, and to conserve a 'living history' of medicinal herbs and plant introductions.

This four-acre walled garden is a haven for rare and tender plants, and also has several glasshouses, the largest fruiting olive tree grown outside in Britain and the oldest rock garden in Europe made from rubble from the tower of London. Particularly successful has been the Fortune Tank Pond, installed more than a hundred years ago by the famous collector of Chinese plants, Robert Fortune.

Fact File

Opening Times:	Wednesday - Friday: 12 - 5 p.m. & Sunday 12 - 6 p.m. Last entry 30 minutes prior to closing.
Admission Charges:	Adults: £8.00, Senior Citizens: £8.00, Children: £5.00
Group Rates:	£25 per guide + entrance fee Minimum Group Size: No minimum
	Adults: £8.00, Senior Citizens: £8.00, Children: £5.00
On-Site Facilities:	Shop, Plant Sales, Restaurant, Teas
Disabled Access:	Yes. Wheelchair loan available – booking required.
Toilets on site:	Yes
Car Parking on site:	No
Coach Parking:	No
Guided Tours:	Yes. Booking only required for large groups
Length of Visit:	45 minutes – 1 hour
Special Events:	Christmas Fair and snowdrop days – check our website for more details.
Booking Contact:	Neil Couzens, Chelsea Physic Garden, 66 Royal Hospital Road, London SW3 4HQ Telephone No. 0207 352 5646 Extension 21 Fax No. 0207 376 3910
Email:	enquiries@chelseaphysicgarden.co.uk
Website:	www.chelseaphysicgarden.co.uk
Location:	No. 170 bus from Victoria Flood Street stop or Clapham Junction. Circle/District line to Sloane Square

Please quote this guide when making a booking

Capel Manor Gardens Middlesex

Capel Manor gardens and estate surround a Georgian Manor House and Victorian Stables. The gardens are broadly divided into five zones:

Historic landscape – includes a walled garden, magnolia border, holly walk, Italianate maze and seventeenth century gardens.

Model gardens – a range of domestic gardens including Sunflower Street (relocated from The Chelsea Flower Show), a new garden designed by Kim Wilde and gardens dedicated to the late Queen Mother and Princess of Wales.

Trials garden – experimental and thought-provoking gardens, sponsored by Gardening Which?

Theme gardens

Wilderness and woodland gardens – best in Spring for daffodils, bluebells and azaleas.

All of this together with animal stock including Clydesdale horses, make the gardens an excellent family day out.

Visitors see behind the scenes of greater London's specialist college of Horticulture, Floristry, Garden Design, Animal Care, Arboriculture and Countryside Studies.

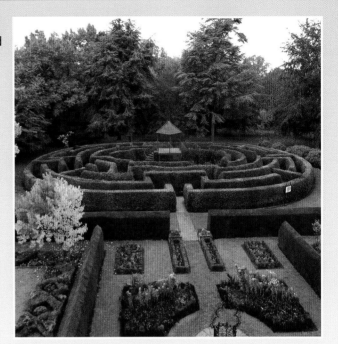

Fact File

Opening Times: Summer Opening: March to October, open daily 10am - 6pm (last ticket 4.30pm).
Winter Opening: November to February, open weekdays only 10am - 5pm (last ticket at 3.30pm) Closed Xmas eve to 2nd January.
Please telephone to check times.

Admission Rates: Adults £6.00, Senior Citizens £5.00, Child £3.00, Family Ticket £15.00 (from April 2008).

Group Rates: Minimum group size: 20. Adults £5.50, Concessions £4.50 (Senior Citizens, Disabled, Students, UB40 holders) Children £2.50 (5s and under go free).

Facilities: Visitor Centre, Shop, Restaurant, Dogs allowed entry on lead.

Disabled Access: Yes. Parking for disabled on site. Wheelchairs on loan, booking necessary.

Tours/Events: Please telephone for details of tours and events programme.

Coach Parking: Yes

Length of Visit: 2 - 3 hours

Booking Contact: Julie Ryan
Capel Manor Gardens, Bullsmoor Lane, Enfield, Middx, EN1 4RQ
Telephone: 08456 122 122 Fax: 01992 717544

Email: cservices@capel.ac.uk

Website: www.capelmanorgardens.co.uk

Location: Near junction 25 of M25

Please quote this guide when making a booking

Experience Myddelton House Gardens, one of Lee Valley Regional Park's unique and characterful sites. The house, which is not open to visitors, was the ancestral home of the Parker-Bowles family and is now the headquarters of the Lee Valley Regional Park Authority.

Born of one man's passionate interest in plants, Myddelton House Gardens were created by E.A. Bowles, a gifted botanist, author, artist, a philanthropist and a Fellow of the Royal Horticultural Society.

A modest man, E.A. Bowles was one of the giants of British horticulture. Within the gardens is the National Collection of award winning Iris, thousands of naturalised Crocus and Snowdrops and many original plantings.

Visit the "Lunatic Asylum" as Bowles lovingly called it because of it was home to unusual plants, Tom Tiddler's Ground (a collection of variegated plants) and the Tulip Terrace.

The Gardens feature many of Bowles original plantings, carpets of spring bulbs, box edged beds and scented shrubs. There are historical artefacts located in the grounds as well as a Victorian conservatory, summer house and a pergola garden. Seats beside the attractive carp lake offer some of the loveliest views in the Gardens for visitors who want to take a break. A visit to this hidden garden is a must at any time of the year.

Fact File

Opening Times: Open every day except for Christmas week. April – September 10.00 – 16.30
October - March 10.00 – 15.00. National Garden Scheme days 12.00 – 16.00

Admission Rates: Adults: £3.00 Concessions £2.50 (prices change 1 April 2009)

Facilities: Plant Sales, Teas

Disabled Access: Yes. Toilet and car parking on site (most, but not all, paths accessible).
Wheelchair Loan available (bookable)

Tours/Events: Guided tours available. National Garden Scheme days plus other events throughout the year e.g. Christmas Greenery sale.

Coach Parking: Yes.

Length of Visit: 2 hours

Booking Contact: Head Gardener,
Myddelton House, Bulls Cross, Enfield, Middlesex EN2 9HG
Tel: 08456 770600, Fax: 01992 719937

Email: info@leevalleypark.org.uk

Website: www.leevalleypark.org.uk

Location: The Gardens are located close to J25 of the M25 off the A10 near Enfield.
Turkey Street Station is within walking distance.

Please quote this guide when making a booking

Syon House Gardens & Park Middlesex

There have been gardens at Syon since the 15th century when a Brigettine abbey occupied the site of the present house. Recent archaeological excavations have revealed the remains of the 17th century formal gardens created around the house which were swept away by "Capability" Brown when he landscaped the park for the 1st Duke of Northumberland.

The centrepiece of the gardens is the spectacular Great Conservatory, built by the 3rd Duke in the 1820's by Charles Fowler.

The 40 acres of gardens open to visitors are renowned for their extensive collection of rare trees. Brown's lake is overlooked by a Doric column bearing Flora, Goddess of flowers. The vistas across the Thames-side water meadows, still grazed by cattle, give Syon a unique rural landscape so close to the heart of London.

Fact File

Opening Times:	Gardens: Mar – Oct daily (closed Dec 25th and 26th) – 10.30 – 17.00. Nov – Feb, weekends & New Year's Day only: 10.30 – 16.00. Last admission 1 hour before closing
	House open: 18th March - November 1st 2009 Weds, Thurs, Sundays, Bank Holiday Mondays
Admission Rates:	House & Gardens. Adults: £9.00, Concessions: £8.00, Child: £4.00, Family £20.00
	Gardens Only. Adults: £4.50, Concessions: £3.50, Child: £2.50, Family £10.00
Group Rates:	Available on request.
Facilities:	Garden centre, shops & Tropical Forest. Refectory open daily – drinks, snacks, light lunches.
Disabled Access:	Disabled access to the gardens. Limited access to the house. Toilet and car parking on site.
Tours/Events:	Guided tours + audio available for the house only.
Length of Visit:	1 hour house, 1 hour gardens.
Booking Contact:	Shirley Guest. Syon House Gardens & Park, Syon Park, Brentford, Middlesex, TW8 8JF. Tel: 020 8560 0882, Fax: 020 8568 0936
Email:	info:syonpark.co.uk
Website:	www.syonpark.co.uk
Location:	Location map on website. By rail from Waterloo to Kew Bridge then bus as below or North London line to Gunnersbury then bus 237 or 267 to Brentlea Bus stop. Pedestrian entrance 50 yards. Free car park. Vehicle entrance Park Road, Isleworth, TW8 8JF Sat Nav Ref: TW7 6AZ

The Birmingham Botanical Gardens & Glasshouses   W Midlands

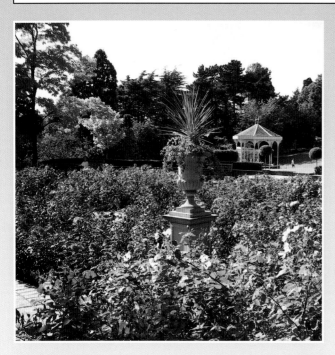

Opened in 1832, the Gardens are a 15 acre 'Oasis of Delight' with over 200 trees and the finest collection of plants in the Midlands. The Tropical House, full of rainforest vegetation, includes many economic plants and a 24ft lily pond. Palms, tree ferns and orchids are displayed in the Subtropical House. The Mediterranean House features citrus fruits and conservatory plants while the Arid House conveys a desert scene. There is colourful bedding on the Terrace plus Rhododendrons, Rose, Rock, Herb and Cottage Gardens, Trials Ground and Historic Gardens. The Gardens are notably home to the National Bonsai Collection.

Other attractions include a Children's Playground, Children's Discovery Garden, exotic birds in indoor and outdoor aviaries, an art gallery and Sculpture Trail. Bands play on summer Sunday afternoons and Bank Holidays.

Fact File

Opening times:
Open daily from 9am (10am Sundays)
Closing: April to September - 7pm, October to March - 5pm (or dusk).

Admission Rates:
Adults £7.50, Senior Citizen £4.75, Child £4.75

Groups Rates:
Minimum group size: 10
Adults £6.50, Senior Citizen £4.50, Child £4.50

Facilities:
Shop, Tea Room, Plant Sales, Children's Discovery Garden, Sculpture Trail, Aviaries, Organic Garden and many Themed Gardens.

Disabled Access:
Yes. Toilet and parking for disabled on site. Wheelchairs on loan, booking necessary.

Tours/Events:
Tours by appointment. Please telephone for details of Special Events programme.

Coach Parking:
Yes by appointment.

Length of Visit:
2 - 4 hours

Booking Contact:
Tony Cartwright
The Birmingham Botanical Gardens, Westborne Road, Edgbaston, Birmingham, B15 3TR
Telephone: 0121 454 1860   Fax: 0121 454 7835

Email:
admin@birminghambotanicalgardens.org.uk

Website:
www.birminghambotanicalgardens.org.uk

Location:
Access from M5 junction 3 and M6. follow the signs for Edgbaston then brown tourist signs to Botanical Gardens.

Please quote this guide when making a booking

David Austin Roses is home to the National Collection of English Roses. These combine all the charm and fragrance of the Old Roses with the wide colour range and free flowering nature of the modern roses. David Austin has built one of the best rose gardens in the world at his nursery in Albrighton. It is also one of the largest covering nearly two acres and containing nearly 700 different varieties of roses from the smallest to the largest and the oldest to the newest.

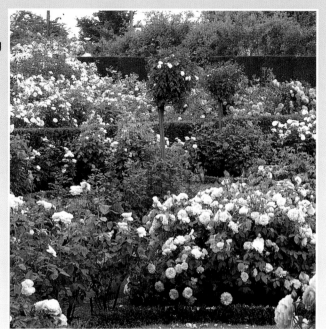

The garden is divided up into 5 separate gardens each with its own style. The Long Garden forms the core from which the other gardens lead off. The whole Garden is surrounded by and interlaced with pergolas, together with many Climbing and Rambling Roses.

The Victorian Garden is planted with English roses and other repeat flowering shrub roses.

The Renaissance Garden is perhaps the most beautiful of all. It is devoted entirely to English Roses.

The Lion Garden is under development this year. It is being replanted to show how delightful roses can be when combined with other plants.

The Species Garden contains the true wild roses and their near hybrids. At its most beautiful in early summer and again in autumn, when the hips are in full colour.

Fact File

Opening Times:	9am - 5pm (7 days a week) (Garden and Garden Shop)
	9.30am - 4.30pm Tea Room
Admission Rates:	Free entry
Groups Rates:	By prior appointment only, contact plant centre manager.
Facilities:	Shop, Plant Sales, Teas and Light Lunches
Disabled Access:	Yes. Parking for disabled on site.
Tours/Events:	Workshops with the RHS Design Days and Guided Tours. For full details of events please visit our website.
Coach Parking:	Yes
Length of Visit:	2 - 3 Hours
Booking Contact:	Cheryl Fellows-Bennett
	David Austin Roses, Bowling Green Lane, Albrighton, Wolverhampton WV7 3HB.
	Telephone: 01902 376342 Fax: 01902 372142
Email:	plantcentre@davidaustinroses.co.uk
Website:	www.davidaustinroses.com
Location:	Albrighton is situated between the A41 and A464 about 8 miles west of Wolverhampton and 2 miles south east of junction 3 on the M54.
	Look for the brown tourist information signs.

Please quote this guide when making a booking

An exceptional plant-lover's garden for all seasons. The house and garden walls are covered with unusual shrubs, climbers and fruit. The flower gardens are formally designed and richly planted within beautiful yew hedges: formal rose gardens, a paved garden, and herbaceous and shrub borders. The arboretum has a remarkable collection of trees – more than 800 different species, many of them rare or very rare. All are labelled. The walled kitchen gardens are traditionally managed, with vegetables, cut flowers, mixed borders, and two glasshouses. In spring, the parkland and arboretum are filled with daffodils – massed plantings of more that 90 carefully chosen and graded cultivars. A delight and an education.

Fact File

Opening times:	2.00 – 5.30 p.m. 2nd and 4th Sundays, June – September. Groups at other times by appointment
Admission Rates:	Adults: £4.00, Senior Citizens: £4.00, Children: FOC
Group Rates:	On application.
Facilities:	Plant Sales, teas, toilets.
Disabled Access:	Yes.
Car Parking on site:	Yes.
Tours/Events:	Guided tours available. Booking required.
Length of Visit:	2 – 3 hours
Booking Contact:	Chris Allhusen Bradenham Hall Gardens, Bradenham, Thetford Norfolk IP25 7QP Booking Telephone No. 01362 687279/243 Booking Fax No. 01362 687669 E-mail. info@bradenhamhall.co.uk
Location:	A47, 2 miles West of Dereham, Junction of Dale Road, then south to Bradenham, 2 miles on right.

Please quote this guide when making a booking

Those who haven't visited the Bressingham Gardens lately are certainly missing a treat, for there have been important additions and changes to make this a gardener's paradise.

The late Alan Bloom's Dell Garden created from 1953 with over 50 immaculate Island Beds of more than 4500 varieties of perennials, and Adrian Bloom's spectacular Foggy Bottom garden with views and vistas of year round colour are worth a visit on their own. But both now are linked with new gardens, in total covering 16 acres. Follow the Foggy Bottom Trail from the Summer Garden with its National Collection of Miscanthus, through the Dell Garden and the latest development of the Fragrant Garden, to Adrian's Wood, planted with a wide range of plants of North American origin to the final destination of the delightfully peaceful Foggy Bottom garden, famous too for its use of conifers.

New Winter Garden open from November to March 11-4. Groups Welcome.

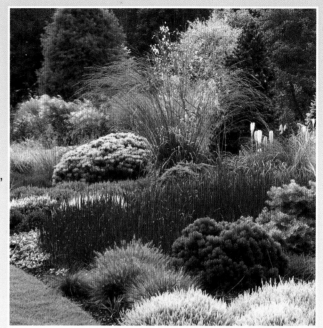

Fact File

Opening Times:	Normal opening daily 30th March - 1st November, Winter garden open November - March
Admission Rates:	Adults: £7.00, Senior Citizens: £6.00, Children: £4.00
	Winter garden, November – March only: £3.50
Group Rates:	Minimum Group Size: 12.
	Adults: £6.00, Children: £4.50
Facilities:	Visitor Centre, Shop, Plant Sales, Restaurant, Teas, Steam Museum
Disabled Access:	Yes, bookable wheelchair loan available. Toilet and car parking on site
Tours/Events:	Guided tours available. Special events: see website www.bressingham.co.uk
Coach Parking:	Yes.
Length of Visit:	2½ - 5 hours, (2 hours in Winter including Garden Centre).
Booking Contact:	Sue Warwick
	The Bressingham Gardens, Bressingham, Nr. Diss, Norfolk IP22 2AB
	Tel: 01379 686900 Fax: 01379 686907
Email:	info@bressingham.co.uk
Website:	www.bressingham.co.uk & for plant, garden details, www.bressinghamgardens.com
Location:	On A1066 Thetford – Diss road, 3 miles west of Diss, Norfolk.

Please quote this
guide when
making a booking

The Exotic Garden   Norfolk

Such is the extraordinary plethora of plant life at the Exotic Garden in Norwich, it is difficult to work out which part of the world you are in! This south-facing hillside garden, has a sub-tropical micro-climate which has allowed Will Giles to create a personal paradise of distinctly tropical-looking plants, many of which we commonly think of a 'house-plants', including an ever expanding collection of Bromeliads.

This garden powers up to a grand crescendo in August and September, but is exciting from spring right through until the first frosts. The emphasis is on big, over-the-top foliage with dazzling flowers including several species of banana which tower over the garden, under planted with Colocasias and a host of fabulous gingers, ornamental sweet potatoes and Cannas.

The garden also boasts the biggest tree house in East Anglia as well as several raised pools and a large waterfall dripping with plants. Recently, a new xerophytic garden (arid planting) has been created with large agaves, aloes and tall Trichocerus

Fact File

Opening Times:	1.00 – 5.00 p.m. Sundays only
Admission Charges:	Adults £4.50, Senior Citizens: £4.50, Child: Free
Group Rates:	(Groups can visit any day of the week by arrangement) Minimum Group Size: 10
	Adults: £5.50 pp, £6.00 with tea/coffee and biscuits Senior Citizens: £5.50, Child: Free
On-Site Facilities:	Plant Sales, Teas
Disabled Access:	No
Toilets on site:	Yes
Car Parking on site:	Yes
Coach Parking:	Yes
Length of Visit:	1 – 2 hours
Special Events:	Guided tours available, contact for further information
Booking Contact:	(Mail only) 6, Cotman Road, Thorpe, Norwich, Norfolk NR1 4AF
	Booking Telephone No. 01603 623167
Email:	info@exoticgarden.com
Website:	www.exoticgarden.com
Location:	Entrance to The Exotic Garden can be found at the left side of the Alan Boswell Insurance building – 126 Thorpe Road, Norwich NR1 1UL (postal code essential for those with satnav).

Please quote this guide when making a booking

Fairhaven Woodland & Water Garden Norfolk

Fairhaven Woodland and Water Garden is a haven of peace and tranquillity in the heart of the Norfolk Broads.

Three miles of scenic paths. Environmentally managed for the thriving and varied wildlife. Delightful in Spring; primroses, daffodils, skunk cabbage (Lysichiton americanus), bluebells, followed by a spectacular display of the largest naturalised collection of Candelabra primulas in England, and azaleas and rhododendrons. An oasis in Summer, with boat trips on our private broad, flowering shrubs and wild flowers which attract several species of butterflies. Glorious Autumn colours and quietly beautiful in Winter with wonderful reflections in the still water and new Winter Garden.

A full programme of special events is available including our Green/Environmental festival. Please ring for deails or visit our website.

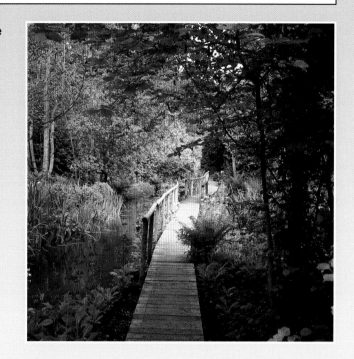

Fact File

Opening times: Open daily 10am - 5pm (10am - 4pm Dec, Jan & Feb) also open until 9pm on Wednesday and Thursday evenings from May to the end of August (Closed Christmas Day).

Admission Rates: Adult £5.00, Senior Citizen £4.50, Child £2.50 under 5 Free, Dogs 25p.
Annual Membership: Family £42.00, Single £18.50, Dogs £2.50.

Groups Rates: Minimum group size: 15
Adults £4.75, Senior Citizen £4.25, Child £2.25

Facilities: Visitor Centre, Gift Shop, Tea Room, Plant Sales, Boat trips April to end October, Sensory Garden.

Disabled Access: Yes. Toilet and parking for disabled on site. Wheelchairs on loan. Booking necessary.

Tours/Events: Guided walks or introductory talk for pre-booked groups. Programme of Special Events available, including guided walks, music in the Garden, Green/Environmental Festival and Halloweén event. Telephone or visit our website for details.

Coach Parking: Yes

Length of Visit: 2 - 3 hours or preferably all day.

Booking Contact: Louise Rout
Fairhaven Woodland & Water Garden, School Road, South Walsham, Norwich NR13 6DZ
Telephone/Fax: 01603 270449

Email: enquiries@fairhavengarden.co.uk

Website: www.fairhavengarden.co.uk

Location: 9 miles east of Norwich, off B1140.
Signposted on A47 at junction with B1140.

Most people long for tranquillity, a garden they are happy to be in ; such is Gooderstone Water Gardens.

Billy Knights, with no training but great enthusiasm began his garden in 1970, according to his own taste; his likes and dislikes were not dictated by fashion. When he died aged 93 in 1994 he left behind an entrancing 6-acre garden that sits comfortably in the Norfolk countryside. From the natural stream he created ponds and flowing waterways spanned by thirteen bridges. With its additional 8-acre Nature Trail and Kingfisher Hide it's truly a haven for people and wildlife.

Combining native and cultivated plants in informal beds, his daughter Coral is endeavouring to further enhance this atmospheric garden. From well-placed seats visitors can enjoy enchanting vistas and the changing moods of the sky reflected in the clear spring water. And the homemade cakes are delicious!

Fact File

Opening times:	10 a.m. – 5.30 p.m. (dusk in winter)
Admission Rates:	Adults: £4.75, Senior Citizens: £4.25, Children: £1.50
Group Rates:	Minimum Group Size: 15. Adults: £4.50, Senior Citizens: £4.00, Children: £1.25
Facilities:	Plant Sales, Teas
Disabled Access:	Yes
Toilets on site:	Yes
Car Parking on site:	Yes
Coach Parking:	Yes
Length of Visit:	2 – 3 hours
Special Events:	A wonderful show of astilbe first two weeks July.
Booking Contact:	Gooderstone Water Gardens, The Street, Gooderstone, King's Lynn, Norfolk, NR13 4HG Booking Tel No.01603 712913/07730 551945
Email:	
Website:	www.gooderstonewatergardens.co.uk
Location:	In west Norfolk, 6 miles SW of Swaffham between Cockley Cley and Oxburgh Hall (N.T.). Brown signed from Swaffham and Oxborough. Swaffham is on A47.

Set in the Norfolk Broads area, the gardens offer an exceptional range of plants, design features, landscape and inspiration throughout the season for garden and plant lovers. In early spring masses of narcissi, including many rare and unusual varieties collected during the 20th century, flower in drifts by the lakes and streams in the woodland areas. From late April to end of May the fragrance of the azaleas and rhododendrons is spectacular on the woodland walks; the lake and Water Garden area has beautiful displays of candelabra primulas and other moisture loving plants. During summer, hydrangeas from deep blue to pale pink and purple flank the sides of the main drive whilst the herbaceous borders and Clematis Walk are at their height of displays.

With lakes, streams and wetland areas meandering through the estate together with a large wood, the gardens are also home to extensive birdlife, both migratory and native species.

Fact File

Opening times: April - Easter Sunday 12th, BH Monday 13th and proceeding Wednesdays, Thursdays, Fridays and other Sundays (Please note the tea room will only be open on Sundays in April) May, June, July, August and to September 13th - all Wednesdays, Thursdays, Fridays, Sundays and BH Mondays. 10.30am to 5.00pm

Admission Rates: Adults: £5.00, Children: £2.50 (5-14 years), Wheelchair users & Carers: £3.00, Season Ticket Single: £15.00, Season Ticket Family: £25.00.

Group Rates: (25 or more) booking and paying in advance £4.50 per head on open days, Evening Visits £6.00 per head, Non Open Days 10.30am to 5.00pm £5.00 per head by arrangement.

Facilities: Plant Sales, Teas

Disabled Access: Partial.

Tours/Events: Yes

Coach Parking: Yes.

Length of Visit: 2 - 3 hours

Booking Contact: Barbara Buxton, Hoveton Hall Gardens, Norwich, Norfolk NR12 8RJ
     Telephone: 01603 782798 Fax: 01603 784564

Email: info@hovetonhallgardens.co.uk

Website: www.hovetonhallgardens.co.uk

Location: Follow brown and white signs off the A1151 just north of Wroxham

Please quote this guide when making a booking

The gardens around this medieval moated manor house feature a wide variety of plants, trees and shrubs in many different settings. Throughout the gardens are thousands of roses especially classic varieties. In the Heritage Rose and Twentieth Century Rose Gardens are roses in areas with designs reflecting their date of origin from the fifteenth century to the present day.

In the kiosk is a display about the garden's development. On the South Lawn is a classical temple and the Sensory Garden with plants selected for touch, sound and taste, as well as smell and colour.

New in 2008 was a link between the wood walk and the 20th Century Garden. The garden for the less able provides a shady area, near to the vegetable garden, which has been redesigned, and planted in 2007/8

Wildflowers are encouraged around the landscaped lakes and in the 'Chapel Garden' where follies surround the ruins.

Fact File

Opening times:	Sundays May – September: 12.00 – 5.00 p.m. Wednesday, Thursday & Friday June – August: 11.00 – 5.00 p.m.
Admission Rates:	Adults: £5.00, Senior Citizens: £4.00, Children: Under 16 – Free NGT members free. RHS members free.
Group Rates:	Minimum Group Size: 15. Adults/Senior Citizens: £3.50, Children: by arrangement
Facilities:	Visitor Centre, Shop, Plant Sales, Restaurant, Teas
Disabled Access:	Yes. Wheelchair loan available – booking required.
Toilets on site:	Yes
Car Parking on site:	Yes
Coach Parking:	Yes
Guided Tours:	Yes, booking required.
Length of Visit:	1½ hours plus
Special Events:	Drama, opera, music, etc.
Booking Contact:	Laurel Walpole, Mannington Gardens, Mannington, Norwich, Norfolk NR11 7BB Booking Tel No.01263 584175. Booking Fax No. 01263 761214
Email:	larelwalpole@manningtongardens.co.uk
Website:	www.manningtongardens.co.uk
Location:	Signposted from Norwich-Holt Road (B1149) at Saxthorpe/Corpusty

Please quote this guide when making a booking

Pensthorpe Norfolk

Set in the beautiful Wensum Valley in North Norfolk, Pensthorpe, the new home of BBC Springwatch is an award winning attraction for all those who love nature, wildlife and the outdoors.

Enjoy the inspirational Millennium Garden designed by Piet Oudolf, with swathes of perennials and grasses. Discover the striking lances of Astilbe chinensis var.taquetii 'Purpulanze' which are married perfectly with the spun gold Deschampsia cespitosa 'Goldtau'. The Garden builds dramatically to its peak in August, then settles into a stunning new aspect with thousands of seed heads in autumn.

The Wave Garden opened in 2006 and has year-round structure and interest, with Luzula dipping under the crests of yew and meandering through the resident trees in this lakeside garden. Thousands of bulbs and flowering fruit trees bring splashes of colour in winter and spring to this wooded lakeside garden. The Garden designed by Julie Toll works with nature using calm and naturalistic planting.

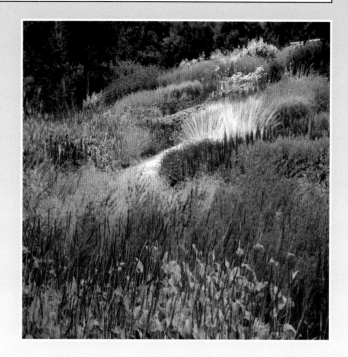

Fact File

Opening times:	10 a.m. – 4 p.m. (January – March)
	10 a.m. – 5 p.m. (April – December)
Admission Rates:	Adults: £8.50, Senior Citizens: £7.00, Children: £5.00.
Group Rates:	Minimum Group Size: 15.
	Adults: £7.50, Senior Citizens: £6.00, Children: £4.00. School parties £3.00.
Facilities:	Visitor Centre, Shop, Plant Sales, Restaurant, Teas.
Disabled Access:	Yes. Bookable wheelchair loan available.
Toilets on site:	Yes.
Tours/Events:	Guided tours available. Booking required.
Coach Parking:	Yes.
Car Parking on site:	Yes.
Length of Visit:	4-6 hours.
Booking Contact:	Kirsty Willingham
	Pensthorpe Nature Reserve, Norwich Road, Fakenham, Norfolk NR21 0LN
	Telephone: 01328 851465
	Fax: 01328 855905
Email:	info@pensthorpe.com
Website:	www.pensthorpe.com
Location:	1 mile from Fakenham on the A1067 to Norwich.

Please quote this guide when making a booking

Peter Beales Rose Gardens — Norfolk

Peter Beales Roses are world leaders in Classic Roses. In glorious full bloom, the inspirational rose gardens of Peter Beales are a must for any enthusiast, with over three acres of RHS Chelsea Flower Show gold medal winning varieties, the National Collection of Rosa species and many interesting and colourful companion plants and shrubs. The garden has many points of interest in its room-like layout including an attractive pond with koi carp, pergolas, arbours and archways. Visitors are free to wander and enjoy the beautiful flowers and sensuous perfumes. There is also an excellent licensed Bistro and Garden Centre on site where you can enjoy a meal and a glass of wine or stock up on gardening essentials, luxury gifts and, of course, lots of roses too. There are hundreds of container roses as well as other plants available during the summer or you can choose to order for winter delivery.

Fact File

Opening Times: Daily 9 a.m. – 5 p.m. Sundays and Bank Holidays: 10 a.m. – 4 p.m.
Admission Rates: Adults: Free, Senior Citizens: Free, Children: Free.
Group Rates: Minimum Group Size: 15. Please contact us for further information.
Facilities: Garden Centre, Gift Shop, Bistro, Gardens. Marquee available for hire.
Disabled Access: Yes. Bookable wheelchair loan available.
Toilets on site: Yes.
Tours/Events: Guided tours available. Booking required.
Pruning and Planting in the Peter Beales Rose Gardens. A full day of instruction with lunch included to help you get the most from your roses, please enquire.
Coach Parking: Yes.
Car Parking on site: Yes.
Length of Visit: 2 hours.
Booking Contact: Peter Beales Roses, London Road, Attleborough, Norfolk NR17 1AY
Telephone: 0845 481 0277 Fax: 01953 456845
Email: events@peterbealesroses.com
Website: www.peterbealesroses.com
Location: Approaching from the south – leave the A11 at the Breckland Lodge roundabout. The nursery is approximately 1/2 mile north on the old London Road. Approaching from Norwich, bypass Attleborough and turn left at the roundabout.

Please quote this guide when making a booking

A visit to Sandringham's sixty-acre gardens is a delight at any time of year. Woodland walks, lakes and streams are planted to provide year-round colour and interest; sheets of spring - flowering bulbs, avenues of rhododendrons and azaleas, beds of lavender and roses, dazzling autumn colour - there is always something to see. Other highlights include the formal North Garden, Queen Alexandra's summerhouse beside its own cascading stream, sixteen species of oak and many commemorative trees. Guided garden walks offered regularly.

Open Easter to mid-July and early August to end October, 10.30am to 5pm daily (4pm in October).

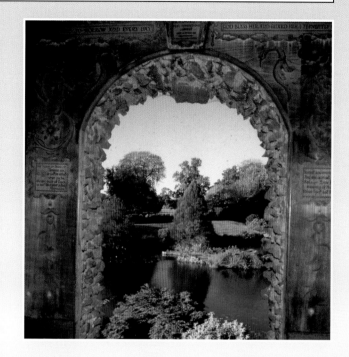

Fact File

Opening times:	Easter - mid July and early August - end October
Admission Rates:	Adults £6.50, Senior Citizen £5.50, Child £3.50.
Groups Rates:	Minimum group size: 20, Group discounts available.
Facilities:	Visitor Centre, Gift Shop, Plant Sales, Teas, Restaurant, Sandringham Museum (inc in ticket) Sandringham House (Extra Charge).
Disabled Access:	Yes. Toilet and parking for disabled on site, Wheelchairs on loan.
Tours/Events:	Guided garden walks offered regularly.
Coach Parking:	Yes
Length of Visit:	2 hours. (for Garden only, longer for House and Museum).
Booking Contact:	Mrs N Colman Sandringham, Norfolk. PE35 6EN. Tel: 01553 612908 Fax: 01485 541571
Email:	visits@sandringhamestate.co.uk
Website:	www.sandringhamestate.co.uk
Location:	8 miles northeast of Kings Lynn on A149.

Please quote this guide when making a booking

The Park is listed Grade One in the Register of Parks and Gardens of Special Historic Interest and originates from the 18th Century when Ralph, first Duke of Montagu created an ornamental and intricate landscape, inspired by the ones he had seen at Versailles whilst serving there as English Ambassador to Louis XIV. The River Ise was canalised and lakes, waterways, fountains, ornamental plantings and statuary were added by him and his son John, the Second Duke of Montagu. Avenues of trees created a network of rides stretching out for over seventy miles.

The benign neglect into which the House fell for the remainder of the 18th and 19th centuries was equally beneficial for the landscape. The bones survived, albeit hidden and now the landscape is being restored, inspired by the original plans of 1746. Waterways are being cleared and realigned to the original scheme, whilst many features and avenues are being re-created. Over the next ten years the landscape of Boughton will continue to be transformed to reflect its former glory.

Fact File

Opening Times: (2009) Grounds opening May 1st - July 31st, every day except Saturday, August 1st - September 1st every day, noon - 5pm.

Admission Rates: (2009) Adults £3.00, Children (5-16 years old) £1.50, Family Ticket £8.00 (2+2).

Group Rates: Please enquire.

Facilities: Shop, Plant Sales, Toilets.

Disabled Access: Yes. Wheelchair loan available for Gardens.

Coach Parking: Yes.

Booking Contact: Charles Lister, House Manager
The Living Landscape Trust
Boughton House
Kettering
Northamptonshire
NN14 1BJ
Booking Tel Number. 01563 515731 Booking Fax Number. 01536 417255

Email: llt@boughtonhouse.org.uk

Website: www.boughtonhouse.org.uk

Location: Boughton House is situated off the A43, 3 miles north of Kettering and the A14, through the village of Geddingdon.

Castle Ashby Gardens Northamptonshire

Castle Ashby House is the ancestral home of the 7th Marquess of Northampton. The house is set amidst a 10,000 acre working estate with an extensive 25 acres of gardens which are open to the public 365 days a year.

Castle Ashby Gardens are a mixture of many different styles including a beautiful butterfly garden, picturesque rainbow border, colourful fuschia house, large arboretum including a nature trail and the formal Italian gardens.

A children's farmyard with a wide selection of rare breed animals can also be found within the gardens and new attractions now also include a tea room and gift shop.

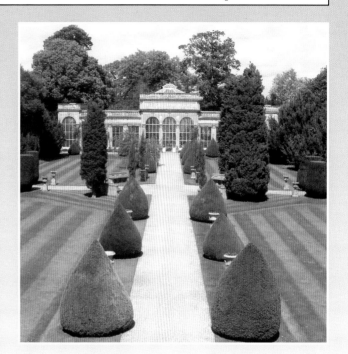

Fact File

Opening Times: 10am – 5;30 pm 1st April to 30th September
                        10am - 4;30 pm 1st October to 31st March
Admission Rates: Adults: £5.00, OAP/ children over 10 £4.50, Children under 10 free.
Group Rates: Minimum Group Size: 15
Facilities: Shop, plant sales, restaurant/teas, toilets.
Disabled Access: Yes.
Car Parking on site: Yes
Coach Parking: Yes
Tours/Events: Guided tours available. Booking required.
Length of Visit: 2 – 3 hours.
Special Events: TBC
Booking Contact: Mark Brooks - Head Gardener, Peter Cox - Assistant Head Gardener
                        Castle Ashby Gardens, Castle Ashby
                        Northampton NN7 1LQ
                        Booking Telephone No. 01604 695200 Booking Fax No. 01604 696516
Email: sales@castleashbygardens.co.uk
Website: www.castleashbygardens.co.uk
Location: Castle Ashby is situated off the A428 between Northampton and Bedford,
                        and is also accessible from the A45.

Please quote this guide when making a booking

Coton Manor lies in peaceful Northamptonshire countryside providing an ideal setting for the ten acre garden. Originally laid out in the 1920s by the grandparents of the current owner it comprises a number of smaller gardens, each one distinctive, providing variety and interest throughout the season.

The 17th century manor house acts as a central focus for the garden with the walls supporting unusual climbing roses, clematis and shrubs while the surrounding York stone terraces are populated by numerous pots and containers overflowing with pelargoniums, verbenas, heliotropes, salvias and agapanthus. The rest of the garden slopes down from the house and is landscaped on different levels lending a natural informality. Old yew and holly hedges complement the many luxuriant borders packed with unusual plants (most available in the specialist nursery) and displaying inspirational colour schemes throughout the season. Water is abundant at Coton with natural flowing streams, ponds and fountains everywhere. Beyond the confines of the garden there is a magnificent bluebell wood and established wildflower meadow.

The widely respected Good Gardens Guide says of Coton'This is a beautifully maintained garden of exceptional charm with unexpected vistas at every turn....there is something for everyone here'.

Fact File

Opening times: Tuesday 31st March 2009 and close on Saturday 3rd October 2009. Tues to Sat and Bank Holiday weekends. (Also Sundays in April and May) 12 noon - 5.30pm.

Admission Rates: Adults £5.00, Senior Citizens £4.50, Child £2.00.

Group Rates: Adults £4.50

Facilities: Restaurant available for group bookings. Cafe serving light lunches and teas, Extensive nursery with many unusual plants mostly grown from the garden. Shop.

Disabled Access: Yes (difficult in places) Toilet and parking for disabled on site.

Tours/Events: Tours by appointment (Wednesdays), Hellebore weekends (Mid Feb), Bluebell Wood (late April/early May), Roses (late June).

Coach Parking: Yes.

Length of Visit: 2 - 2 ½ hours

Booking Contact: Sarah Ball,
Coton Manor Garden, Nr Guilsborough, Northampton NN6 8RQ.
Telephone: 01604 740219 Fax: 01604 740838

Email: pasleytyler@cotonmanor.co.uk

Website: www.cotonmanor.co.uk

Location: 9 miles NW of Northampton, between A5199 (formerly A50) and A428.

Please quote this guide when making a booking

Huge 300-year-old cedars set off magnificent double herbaceous borders, pools and lily-ponds, whilst on the south front are formal parterres framing the vista towards the famous 7th century church at Brixworth.

There is a stately Yew Statue Walk and many captivating views over the lake and Park. Here too are pergolas, rose borders and individually planted courtyards. In midsummer, visitors enjoy the splendid array of planters, a sight not to be missed.

The magical Wild Garden is a short walk across the Park and is planted along the course of a stream with its small cascades and arched bridges. Here are the wonderful colours of acers and rhododendrons, with bamboos and gunneras.

A number of distinguished landscape designers have been involved with gardens at Cottesbrooke including, Robert Weir Schultz, Sir Geoffrey Jellicoe, Dame Sylvia Crowe and more recently, James Alexander-Sinclair.

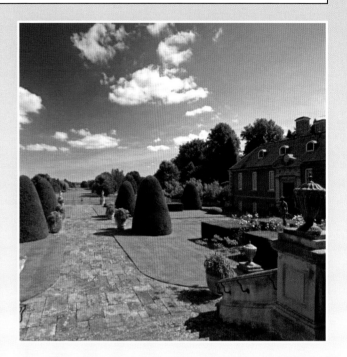

Fact File

Opening Times: May 4th to the end of September. May & June: Wed & Thurs 2pm - 5.30pm, July, Aug & Sept: Thurs 2pm - 5.30pm, Plus Bank Hol Mondays (May-Sept) 2pm - 5.30pm

Admission Rates: House & Gardens: Adults £8.00, Child £3.50. (5 - 14yrs), Concession £6.50
Gardens only: Adults £5.50, Child £2.50 (5 - 14yrs), Concession £4.50

Group Rates: Group and private visit rates on application.

Facilities: Tearoom, Free car park.

Disabled Access: Yes (Gardens only), Toilet and parking for disabled on site.
(Please contact administrator regarding disabled access)

Tours/Events: Guided tour of the house (45 mins), Garden tours by arrangement, groups welcome - please pre book. The Cottesbrooke Hall Plant Finders Fair - 26th, 27th and 28th June 2009. See website for more event details.

Coach Parking: Yes.

Length of Visit: 1 1/2 hours (Garden) 45 mins (House).

Booking Contact: Via the Administrator on 01604 505 808 or Fax on 01604 505 619 or email enquiries@cottesbrooke.co.uk

Email: enquiries@cottesbrooke.co.uk

Website: www.cottesbrookehall.co.uk

Location: Cottesbrooke is situated 10 miles north of Northampton off the A5199.
Easily accessible from the A14 (junction 1 - A5199) and M1/M6.

The Alnwick Garden is one of the great wonders of the contemporary gardening world. The centrepiece is the Grand Cascade, a magnificent tumbling mass of water, ending in an eruption of fountains sending 350 litres of water into the air every second. A computer system synchronises four sensational displays that offer not only a visual treat but also an interactive experience for children who can play in the water jets.

Beyond this lies the Ornamental Garden, a symmetrical, structured garden with a strong European influence containing 16,500 plants. Nestled in a corner of The Garden is the Rose Garden, with pergola lined paths covered in climbing and shrub roses mixed with glorious honeysuckle and clematis. The Garden is also home to one of the largest wooden tree houses in the world with rope bridges and walkways in the sky. There's the Serpent Garden, with a wonderful array of water features and topiary, the Bamboo Labyrinth and the intriguing Poison Garden. New for 2009 is the Cherry Orchard, planted with hundreds of the wonderful great white cherry, Tai Haku.

Designed by the renowned Belgian father and son company, Wirtz international, The Garden is the vision of the Duchess of Northumberland.

Fact File

Opening Times: Open from 10am daily except Christmas Day, closing at 6pm in Summer and 4pm in Winter.

Admission Rates: Adults £10.00, Senior Citizen £7.50, Children 1p (up to 4 children per adult). Prices include an optional donation to The Alnwick Garden Trust. Prices valid to 31st March 2009, see www.alnwickgarden.com for current information.

Groups Rates: Minimum group size: 14. Adults £6.25, Children 1p (up to 4 children per adult). Prices valid to 31st March 2009, see www.alnwickgarden.com for current information.

Facilities: Treehouse restaurant and bar, Pavilion Café, Courtyard Coffee Shop, Gift Shop & Plant Sales.

Disabled Access: Yes. Toilet and parking for disabled on site.

Tours/Events: Please tel 01665 511350 or visit www.alnwickgarden.com for details of tours & special events.

Coach Parking: Yes

Length of Visit: At least 2.5 hours

Booking Contact: The Alnwick Garden, Alnwick, Northumberland, NE66 1YU
Telephone: 01665 511350 Fax: 01665 511351

Email: info@alnwickgarden.com

Website: www.alnwickgarden.com

Location: Leave the A1 North of the town at the junction signposted by the tourist information sign for The Alnwick Garden. The Garden is clearly signposted, approx 1 mile from the A1 junction.

Please quote this guide when making a booking

Clumber Park Walled Kitchen Garden   Nottinghamshire

Located in 3,800 acres of woodland, heathland and historic landscape park, this beautiful four acre walled kitchen garden was built in 1772 to supply the Newcastle family with fruit and vegetables. Today, unusual and old strains of vegetables are grown alongside modern cultivars, the apple orchard consists of local varieties and trained fruit occupies the walls of the upper section. This year a soft fruit garden has been planted.

The double herbaceous borders produce spectacular summer colour and now run the entire 400 feet length of the garden.

The 450 feet Long Range glasshouse consists of 12 sections growing grape vines, peaches, nectarines, figs, annual vegetables and decorative climbers. The Conservatory and Palm House display ornamental plants.

Behind the glasshouse is the Museum of Gardening Tools, whose exhibits include old lawn mowers and hand tools and a re-creation of the gardeners' mess room.

Fact File

Opening Times: 14th March – 28th March, 11.00 - 4.00. 29th March - 27th September 10.00 - 5.00: Monday to Friday, 10.00 - 6.00: Saturday & Sunday, (closing mid afternoon on concert days, 21st, 22nd, 23rd August) 28th September - 1st November 11.00-4.00pm. Last admission 30 mins before closing.

Admission Rates: Clumber Park: £5.00 per vehicle. Coaches, cyclists, pedestrians, NT members: Free
Walled Kitchen Garden: Adults: £3.00*, Senior Citizens: £3.00*, Children/NT Members: Free
*£3.00 includes voluntary 10% gift aid donation towards restoration and upkeep of the property.

Group Rates: Minimum Group Size: 15. Group Rate as above

Facilities: Visitor Centre, Shop, Plant Sales, Restaurant, Teas, Cycle Hire

Disabled Access: Yes, Bookable wheelchair loan available. Toilet and car parking available.

Tours/Events: Yes, please contact estate office for details, Fruit & Veg tastings, Apple Day, demonstrations.

Coach Parking: Yes.

Length of Visit: 2 hours.

Booking Contact: Estate Office,
Clumber Park, Worksop, Nottinghamshire, S8O 3AZ.
Tel: 01909 476592 Fax: 01909 500721

Email: clumberpark@nationaltrust.org.uk

Website: www.nationatrust.org.uk

Location: 4½ miles south-east of Worksop, 1 mile from A1/A57, 11 miles from M1, Exit 30

Please quote this guide when making a booking

The magnificent gardens of Blenheim Palace
On passing through the triumphal arch at the Woodstock entrance to Blenheim Palace, it is clear to see why Lord Randolph Churchill proclaimed 'This is the finest view in England'.

What takes the eye and holds it is the great lake, with Sir John Vanbrugh's Grand Bridge and 'Capability' Brown's hanging beech woods beyond. This awesome view, which appears so effortless and natural, was designed to take the breath away.

The splendour and tranquillity of the 2000 acres of parkland and the 100 acres of Formal Gardens are unrivalled. Visit the Secret Garden with its winding path, streams and water features, or the delicate Rose garden and the Arboretum. From the Water Terraces, designed by Achille Duchêne, to the Rose Garden, Grand Cascade and the magnificent lake, fringed by majestic oaks and maples, beauty abounds. In spring, hosts of bluebells, daffodils and rhododendrons cover the banks.

Fact File

Opening Times: Saturday , 14th Feb to Sunday, 13th December 2009. Closed Mondays & Tuesdays from 4th November to 13th December.
Palace and Gardens open daily from 10.30 a.m. to 5.30 p.m. (last admission 4.45 p.m.) with areas to be vacated by 6.00 p.m. Park open daily from 9.00 a.m. to 4.45 p.m. or dusk.

Admission Rates: Palace, Park & Gardens Ticket (main season 2009): Adult: £17.00, Concessions: £14.00, Child: £10.00 Family: £45.00.

Group Rates: Palace, Park & Gardens Ticket (main season group 2009): Adult: £12.30, Concessions: £10.80, Child: £6.75 Family: n/a

Facilities: Shop, Restaurant, Hampers, Afternoon Teas, Sunday Lunches

Disabled Access: Yes, toilet on site. Buggies, wheelchairs & Mobility Scooters available.

Tours/Events: Yes, Calendar events available from 01993 811091.

Coach Parking: Yes

Length of Visit: At least 2 hours

Booking Contact: Cathy Tuckey, Blenheim Palace, Woodstock, Oxfordshire OX20 1PP
Telephone:01993 811091 Fax: 01993 810570

Email: operations@blenheimpalace.com

Website: www.blenheimpalace.com

Location: Situated in Woostock eight miles north west of Oxford on A44.

Please quote this guide when making a booking

Buscot Park was laid out in the late eighteenth century in the English Landscape style to provide a naturalistic setting for the Palladian style house built between 1780 and 1783.

The famous water garden was added in 1904 by Alexander Henderson, later the first Lord Faringdon, who commissioned the architect and garden designer Harold Peto to create a link between the eighteenth century house and the great lake. Peto was the leading exponent of formal Italianate garden design of his day and this water garden is widely regarded as one of his finest works. It consists essentially of a series of stairways, formal lawns, pools and basins interlinked by a descending canal complete with rills, miniature cascades and a bridge all flanked by box hedges sheltering statuary and stone seats.

The present Lord Faringdon continues to enhance the grounds and has transformed the former eighteenth-century kitchen garden into a beautifully structured ornamental garden.

'I consider Buscot Park to be one of England's most unsung country estates' - Tony Russell, Country Gardener Magazine.

Photo of Peto Water Garden by David Dixon

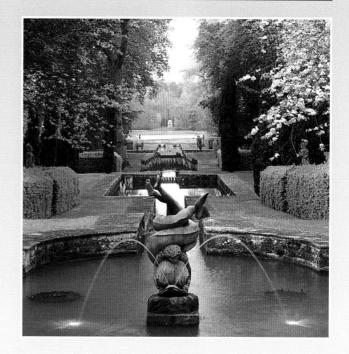

Fact File

Opening Times: 1st April - 30th September
House, Grounds and Tearoom: Wed-Fri, Bank Holidays and the following weekends, 11/12, 25/26 April; 2/3, 9/10, 23/24 May; 13/14, 27/28 June; 11/12, 25/26 July; 8/9, 22/23, 29/30 August; 12/13, 26/27 September, 2-6pm (last admission to House 5pm)
Grounds Only: Mon-Tue, 2-6pm

Admission Rates: Adults £7.50 (House & Gardens) £5.00 (Gardens Only), Child ½ Adult price.

Facilities: Picnic Area, Homemade Teas, Occasional plant sales.

Disabled Access: Partial. Adapted Lavatory. Ramps to tearoom, marquee and garden. Two single seater powered mobility vehicles for use in the grounds can be booked in advance.

Coach Parking: Yes.

Length of Visit: 3 hours

Booking Contact: Estate Office
Buscot Park, Faringdon, Oxfordshire, SN7 8BU.
Telephone: 01367 240786 Fax: 01367 241794

Email: estbuscot@aol.com

Website: www.buscotpark.com

Information Line: 0845 345 3387

Location: Buscot Park is on the A417 between Faringdon and Lechlade. It is marked on most larger scale road maps.

Please quote this guide when making a booking

Always a family favourite with animal lovers the Park has, in more recent times, become an unexpected attraction to gardeners surprised at the rich diversity of plants and planting styles throughout the 160 acre parkland surrounding a Listed Regency Gothic Manor House.

Herbaceous borders and formal parterres are a link with the past whereas the original walled kitchen garden is now adorned with exuberant exotic displays including unique arid borders of cacti; dramatic foliage displays of bananas and cannas and giant water lilies in the open air. The calling of kookaburras and macaws further enhance the exotic atmosphere.

Planting in and around the 270 animal species has become an important feature with particular highlights being the Madagascar exhibit, where you can walk with lemurs, and the Tropical House which combines exotic plants, birds and sloths.

Extensive plantings of ornamental grasses and perennials give a flavour of the savannah around the white rhino paddock. Flowering shrubs, magnificent specimen trees, mixed borders and flower meadows provide year round interest. Elsewhere spring and summer bedding and container displays provide riots of colour well into the autumn.

Fact File

Opening Times: Everyday (except Christmas Day). 10am.
(last admission 3.30pm October - February).

Admission Rates: Adults £10.50, Senior Citizens (over 65) £8.00, Children £8.00, (age 3-16yrs).

Group Rates: Minimum group size: 20
Adults £9.00, Senior Citizens (over 65) £7.00, Children £6.50 (age 3-16 yrs).

Facilities: Shop, Teas, Restaurant.
(Restaurant available for booked lunches and teas, waitress service in Orangery).

Disabled Access: Yes. Parking for disabled on site. Wheelchairs on loan, booking necessary.

Tours/Events: Gardens Special for inclusive charge, talk by Head Gardener or his Deputy in the Drawing room of the Manor House and Cotswold Cream Teas in the Orangery.

Coach Parking: Yes

Length of Visit: 2 ½ - 3 hours

Booking Contact: General Office. Cotswold Wildlife Park, Burford, Oxfordshire, OX18 4JW
Telephone: 01993 823006 Fax: 01993 823807

Email: feedback@cotswoldwildlifepark.co.uk

Website: www.cotswoldwildlifepark.co.uk

Location: On A361 2.5 miles south of A40 at Burford.

Please quote this guide when making a booking

ROUSHAM and its landscape garden should be a place of pilgrimage for students of the work of William Kent (1685 - 1748).

Rousham represents the first phase of English landscape design and remains almost as Kent left it, one of the few gardens of this date to have escaped alteration, with many features which delighted eighteenth century visitors to Rousham still in situ.

The house, built in 1635 by Sir Robert Dormer, is still in the ownership of the same family. Kent added the wings and the stable block. Don't miss the walled garden with their herbaceous borders, small parterre, pigeon house and espalier trees. A fine herd of rare Long-Horn cattle are to be seen in the park.

Rousham is uncommercial and unspoilt with no tea room and no shop. Bring a picnic, wear comfortable shoes and its yours for the day.

Fact File

Opening times:	Every Day All Year
Admission Rates:	Adults £5.00, Senior Citizen £5.00, No Children under 15.
Groups Rates:	None
Facilities:	None
Disabled Access:	Partial, parking for disabled on site.
Tours/Events:	None
Coach Parking:	Yes
Length of Visit:	1 - 2 hours.
Booking Contact:	C Cottrell - Dormer
	Rousham, Nr Steeple Aston, Bicester, Oxon, OX25 4QX.
	Tel: 01869 347110 Fax: 01869 347110
Email:	ccd@rousham.org
Website:	www.rousham.org
Location:	South of B4030, East of A4260.

Stonor Park & Gardens   Oxfordshire

Situated in a beautiful Chiltern Valley, the walled garden rises up behind the ancient house built and lived in by the Stonor family since the twelfth century. The garden today features swathes of daffodils in April. A field of Narcissi "Pheasant Eye" can be seen through iron gates at the top of the garden, while irises bloom inside the walls in May. Old fashioned roses, peonies and lavenders bloom on the seventeenth century terraces in June, flanked by ancient yew trees and clipped box hedges by the lily ponds. Climbing the terrace stages one finds a long mixed border, ending with a Japanese garden house built by the 5th Lord Camoys after his visit to Kyoto in 1906. The jasmine and rose bower offers spectacular views of the house and deer park. This area was the old kitchen garden now converted by Lady Camoys in the 1980's into a pleasure garden. It is divided into six plots as shown in the seventeenth century painting of the house, which can be seen in the drawing room. Irish yews box hedging and old fruit trees delineate the design.

Fact File

Opening times:	Open in 2009 on Sundays (Easter to mid September inclusive), Bank Holiday Mondays and Wednesdays (July and August only)
Admission Rates:	House and Gardens: Adult: £8.00, first child (5-16) £4.00, additional children, under 5's free. Gardens only: Adult £4.00, first child (5-16) £2.00, additional children, under 5's free.
Group Rates:	Minimum Group Size: 20 A private guided tour is available at £9.00 per person on Tuesday to Thursday, April to September.
Facilities:	House, Chapel, Gardens, Shop, Old Hall Tea Room
Disabled Access:	Unsuitable for physically disabled.
Tours:	The house, tea room and shop open at 2.00pm - last entry 4.30pm. Gardens are open on each of the above days between 1.00pm and 5.30pm.
Events:	VW Rally (Sunday 7 June 2009), Classic Concert (Saturday 1 August), Chilterns Craft Fair (Friday 28 August - Monday 31 August)
Coach Parking:	Yes.
Length of Visit:	1 – 4.5 hours.
Booking Contact:	Administrator, Stonor Park, Henley-on-Thames, Oxon RG9 6HF Tel: 01491 638587 Fax: 01491 639348
Email:	administrator@stonor.com
Website:	www.stonor.com
Location:	Five miles north of Henley-on-Thames, on the B480 Henley-on-Thames – Watlington Road.

Sulgrave Manor is a superb example of a 16th century house and home of George Washington's ancestors. The historic garden seen to-day was designed in the 1920s by the leading protagonist of the English formal garden movement, Sir Reginald Blomfield.

With its lawns, knot garden topiary, yew hedges and herbaceous borders of this style, Sulgrave is one of only eight Blomfield gardens which are currently open to the public.

The orchard boasts the oldest apple tree in Northamptonshire and the oldest Loddington in the country.

The garden is a delight to visit at any time and is truly a garden for all seasons.

The house is shown by friendly and informative guides. Garden tours can be arranged for pre-booked groups.

New for 2009: an early Virginian settlers' garden.

Fact File

Opening Times:	Weekends April - October 12.00 - 4.00 last entry. Tuesday, Wednesday, Thursday May - October 2.00 - 4.00 last entry.
Admission Rates:	Adults £6.25, Children (5-16 yrs) £3.00, Family (2 adults + 2 or more children) £17.50. Garden only £3.00, Children free. Prices held since 2007
Group Rates:	Minimum group size: 15.
Facilities:	Gift Shop, Cafe
Disabled Access:	Partial. Toilet for disabled on site.
Tours/Events:	Yes, Please call for details or see website.
Coach Parking:	Yes
Length of Visit:	2 hours
Booking Contact:	Thea Young
	Sulgrave Manor, Sulgrave, Banbury, OX17 2SD
	Telephone: 01295 760205 Fax: 01295 768056
Email:	enquiries@sulgravemanor.org.uk
Website:	www.sulgravemanor.org.uk
Location:	Follow brown tourist signs from A43, M40 or M1

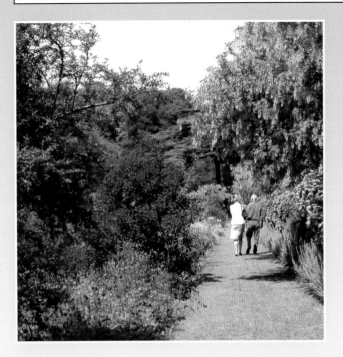

Discover 32 acres of magnificent gardens set in unspoilt countryside on the Warwickshire-Oxfordshire border. Created from two spring-fed valleys on the Edge Hill plateau, the gardens have been in use since the 12th Century, but were largely transformed by Kitty Lloyd-Jones in the 1930's, with the creation of cascading terraces on the valley sides, extensive herbaceous borders, and a rare Bog Garden on the site of medieval fish ponds. The gardens provide today's visitors with a variety of experiences, including large lawns, terraced borders, elegant stone staircases, rose garden, orchards, and a rare kitchen display garden.

A highlight is the National Collection of Aster amellus, Aster cordifolius, and Aster ericoïdes, providing sumptuous colour in early autumn. Also recognised as one of the National Trust's Top 10 gardens for butterflies.

At the heart of the site is the 17th century mansion, extended and remodelled in the 1920s for the 2nd Viscount Bearsted as a weekend retreat, and as a gallery for his incredible art collection regarded as one of the nation's most important private collections of the 20th century. New winter walk for 2009.

Fact File

Opening Times: Spring & Summer: 28th Feb - 1st Nov. Sat-Wed & BHs 11-5pm (Daily in Easter and Summer Holidays) House by guided tour only 11-1pm
Winter: Gardens, Restaurant & Shop: 2nd Nov - 20th Dec, Sat-Wed & 26th Dec-3rd Jan daily. 12-4pm. House (ground floor) 7th Nov-20 Dec, Sat & Sun, 12-4pm.

Admission Rates: House & Gardens: £8.90 (£5.25 Garden Only), Child £4.40 (£2.60), Family £22 (£13.25) Groups £7.00, National Trust Members FREE.

Group Rates: Minimum group size: 15

Facilities: Visitor Centre, Shop, Plant Sales, Restaurant, Teas, Free car parking, Bookable holiday cottage in garden.

Disabled Access: Yes – partial. Toilet and car parking on site. Wheelchair loan available please call to book.

Tours/Events: Jazz concerts, Aster open days, lecture lunches, 1930s days, vintage car meetings, art days Christmas opening, historical re-enactments.

Coach Parking: Yes

Length of Visit: 3 hours

Booking Contact: Jane Scarff, Upton House & Gardens, Upton House, Banbury, Oxfordshire OX15 6HT. Telephone 01295 670266 Fax: 01295 671144

Email: uptonhouse@nationaltrust.org.uk

Website: www.nationaltrust.org.uk

Location: On the A422 between Banbury and Stratford upon Avon. Signposted from Junction 12 M40.

Please quote this guide when making a booking

Waterperry Gardens Oxfordshire

Waterperry gardens are steeped in history, with the famous, purely herbaceous border dating back to the 1930's when Beatrix Havergal established her Ladies Horticultural School. Running more than 200 feet along the length of the old kitchen garden wall, the south facing border provides interest from early May to late September, using early, mid-season and late-flowering herbaceous plants and climbers.

New design elements have been incorporated into the 8 acre gardens over the years, including the colour border, showing how to use flowers, stems, autumn foliage and fruit in design. A formal knot garden reflects planting through the ages from Tudor to modern times and there's also a herb border and spectacular white and lavender wisteria arch. The Mary Rose Gardens show how roses can be used in design and there's a waterlily canal, herbaceous nursery stock beds from which all our cuttings are taken for the plants sold in the walled garden plant centre; island beds designed by nurseryman Alan Bloom; an alpine garden and riverside walk.

As well as an art gallery, small rural life museum and teashop, the garden shop sells a full range of garden sundries, gifts and books. Waterperry is an oasis of calm and beauty within easy reach of Oxford.

Fact File

Opening times:	March to October 10am to 5.30pm. November - February 10am to 5pm.
Admission Rates:	January and February 2009. Adults & concessions £3.50, Children aged 16 & under Free.
	March to October 2009. Adults £5.45, Concessions £4.35, Children aged 10 - 16 £3.65 Children under 10 Free
	November 2009 - February 2010. Adults & concessions £3.85, Children aged 16 & under Free
Group Rates:	January and February 2009 group rate is £3.50 for parties of 20 or more booked in advance.
	March to October 2009 group rate is £4.25 for parties of 20 or more booked in advance.
	November 2009 - February 2010 group rate is £3.85 for parties of 20 or more booked in advance.
Facilities:	Garden shop, Plant centre, Teas, Restaurant, Gallery, Museum
Disabled Access:	Yes. Toilet and parking for disabled on site. Wheelchairs on loan.
Tours/Events:	Tours can be arranged. Waterperry has a full programme of annual events from those with a horticultural theme to outdoor concerts and theatre. There's also a full programme of gardening, arts and crafts classes. Please visit our website www.waterperrygardens.co.uk for more information.
Coach Parking:	Yes. Coach drivers also receive a meal voucher on booking.
Length of Visit:	Approximately 3 – 4 hours.
Booking Contact:	Main Office, Waterperry Gardens, Waterperry, Near Wheatley, Oxfordshire OX33 1JZ. Tel 01844 339254. Fax 01844 339883.
Email:	office@waterperrygardens.co.uk
Website:	www.waterperrygardens.co.uk
Location:	7 miles east of Oxford – junction 8 M40 from London. Follow brown signs. Junction 8a M40 from Birmingham.

Please quote this guide when making a booking

Wollerton Old Hall Garden

Shropshire

Created 20 years ago around a Tudor house (not open), this quality garden has achieved the highest "Good Garden Guide" rating and RHS Partnership status. Designed by the owner, Lesley Jenkins, this outstanding garden combines a strong structure with clever planting combinations using perennials.

The early spring shows of anemones, hellebores and trilliums are followed by tulips, aquilegias and oriental poppies. The summer roses herald the arrival of the delphiniums which in turn give way to the dominance of stately hollyhocks and vibrant phlox. August sees the hot garden ignited which still burns when the asters and euonymus seed capsules arrive in September.

The garden has significant collections of rare perennials, salvias, paniculata phlox and clematis and many of these are available in the Plant Centre. The Tea Room provides excellent lunches, teas and evening meals with all the food being prepared freshly on the premises.

Fact File

Opening Times: Public days – Good Friday, every Friday, Sunday and Bank Holiday until end of September: 12 noon – 5 p.m.

Admission Rates: Adults/Senior Citizens: £5.00 per person, Children 4-15 years: £1.

Group Rates: Garden groups welcome by appointment on Tuesdays and Wednesdays. Minimum 25, Group rate £4.70.

Facilities: Plant Sales, Lunches, Teas, large car park for cars.

Disabled Access: Easy wheelchair access for 80% of the garden. The remainder accessible with helper.

Tours/Events: Guided tours available: topic-specific garden tours with Head Gardener. Lectures by garden personalities. Evening Summer Strolls with candlelit garden and salmon supper.

Coach Parking: Coaches welcome by appointment. Coach parking available on the lane outside the garden.

Length of Visit: 2 – 4 hours, depending upon level of plant interest.

Booking Contact: Diana Oakes. Wollerton Old Hall Garden, Wollerton, Market Drayton, TF9 3NA. Telephone: 01630 685760 Fax: 01630 685583

Email: info@wollertonoldhallgarden.com

Website: www.wollertonoldhallgarden.com

Location: The garden is brown-signed off the A53 between the A41 junction and Hodnet.

Located in an area of outstanding natural beauty, the hilltop site of Claverton Manor, the home of the American Museum, takes full advantage of the spectacular views over the valley of the River Avon. The grounds total some 120 acres of which forty are open to visitors. A unique replica of George Washington's flower garden at Mount Vernon, Virginia is flanked by an Arboretum devoted to American trees and shrubs. Below this has been added the Lewis and Clark trail containing trees and shrubs discovered on the pioneering expedition across the States, now celebrating its 200th anniversary. The parkland, with its majestic old cedars, provides a circular walk through ancient meadows while above the house a path has been created through woodland. A small vegetable garden dye plant area and colonial herb garden give a flavour of early colonial plantings.

Fact File

Opening Times: 14th March - 1st November: Tuesday to Sunday, Bank Holiday and every Monday in August. 12.00noon – 5.00pm

Admission Rates: House & Garden: Adult £8.00, Concession £7.00, Child (5-16) £4.50, Family £21.50. Grounds & Exhibition Gallery only: Adult £5.50, Concession £4.50, Child £3.50.

Group Rates: Pre-booked parties over 15 £6.00 each.

Facilities: Shop. Plant sales. Restaurant. Teas. Museum of American Decorative Art.

Disabled Access: Limited disabled access. Toilet and parking on site.

Tours/Events: Guided tours available. Visit www.americanmuseum.org for details on special events.

Coach Parking: Yes.

Length of Visit: 1½ - 2 hours

Booking Contact: Helen Hayden.
The American Museum in Britain, Claverton Manor, Bath, Somerset, BA2 7BD
Telephone: 01225 460503 Fax: 01225 469160

Email: info@americanmuseum.org

Website: www.americanmuseum.org

Location: Just along from the University of Bath. Signposted from Bath City Centre and A36 Warminster Road. Coaches MUST approach from city centre, up Bathwick Hill.

Please quote this guide when making a booking

Five miles West of Wellington, hidden in the high-banked lanes of Somerset, lies Cothay, built at the end of the Wars of the Roses in 1485. Virtually unchanged in 500 years, this sleeping beauty sits on the banks of the river Tone within its twelve acres of magical Gardens.

The Gardens, laid out in the 1920's, have been re-designed and replanted within the original structure. Many garden rooms, each a garden in itself, are set off a 200 yard yew walk. In addition there is a bog garden with azaleas and drifts of primuli, a cottage garden, a courtyard garden, river walk and fine trees. A truly romantic plantsman's paradise. Two stars in the Good Garden Guide.

Fact File

Opening Times: Easter to September incl. Wed, Thurs, Sun & Bank Holidays - 2pm to 6pm.

Admission Rates: Prices vary - Please visit our website.

Group Rates: Minimum group size: 20+ All groups by appointment. Please contact us for an information pack or download them from our website. Click on Times & Prices.

Facilities: Plant Sales, Cream Teas, (Groups 20+ catering by arrangement).

Disabled Access: Yes (Garden) Partial (House), Toilet and parking for disabled on site.

Tours/Events: Groups only
Guided house tour 1½hrs. The Manor is open to groups throughout the year.

Coach Parking: Yes.

Length of Visit: 1½ - 3½ hours

Booking Contact: The Administrator, Cothay Manor, Greenham, Wellington, Somerset, TA21 0JR
Telephone: 01823 672 283 Fax: 01823 672 345

Email: cothaymanor@btinternet.com

Website: www.cothaymanor.co.uk

Location: From junction 26 M5, direction Wellington, take A38 direction Exeter, 3½ miles turn right to Greenham. From junction 27 M5 take A38 direction Wellington, 3½ miles take 2nd turning left to Greenham.

Please quote this guide when making a booking

Greencombe is intimate and unexpected. Set in woodland on a steep slope, looking north to Porlock Bay and the Severn Sea, it makes its own world of trees, ferns, moss and colour. Come in April for erythronium, early rhododendrons and camellias, in early May for fragrant rhododendrons, and mid to late May for knock-out azalea colour; come in June for roses, July for lilies, clematis and hydrangeas, and much else every time, including a great variety of small woodland plants.

Walking is easy because main paths go with the contours, and it is only 3½ acres.

This is Jo Swift's favourite garden and is among the few selected for his personal top choice by Patrick Taylor, the great garden guru. It is completely organic and has been so for over 40 years. Compost heaps and leaf tips are on show. Come and see.

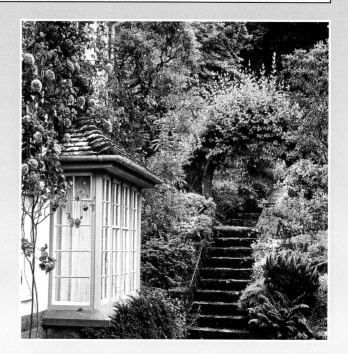

The lovely 'Constance Spry' - one of the many Climbing Roses at Greencombe.

Fact File

Opening Times: 2 – 6 p.m. on Saturdays, Sundays, Mondays, Tuesdays & Wednesdays throughout April, May, June and July

Admission Rates: Adults including Senior Citizens: £6.00, Under 16's: £1.00

Group Rates: Maximum Group Size: 40
Adults including Senior Citizens: £6.00, Under 16's: £1.00

Facilities: Garden Registry open to visitors to refresh themselves and refer to Garden Records, Greencombe plants for sale, Make your own Tea facilities.

Disabled Access: Yes, with car parking on site.

Tours/Events: Owner present for plant talk and answering questions.

Coach Parking: Not here but 1/4 mile away.

Length of Visit: 1-4 hours.

Booking Contact: Joan Loraine
Greencombe Gardens, Greencombe, Porlock, Somerset TA24 8NU
Tel: 01643 862363

Email: none

Website: www.greencombe.org.uk

Location: About ½ a mile west of Porlock, off the B road to Porlock Weir, on the left.

Please quote this guide when making a booking

This is a unique place to visit as you can explore not only the beautiful gardens that have been part of the National Gardens Scheme (and have recently received the royal seal of approval from both Prince Charles and Camilla, Duchess of Cornwall) but also the house that belonged to one of Britain's most popular and respected comedians, Frankie Howerd OBE.

The gardens cover about 1 acre and are in a wonderful setting, at the foot of the Mendips in an Area of Outstanding Natural Beauty. There is a wide mixture of plants: a lovely show of Edwardian plants, over 30 varieties of daffodils, snowdrops, bluebells, gladioli, rhododendrons, the "Winston Churchill fig tree", and over 40 hanging baskets. The recently discovered "tomb" in the front garden – apparently an air-raid shelter for Churchill's Chief of Staff who was a previous owner of the house – may be open for public viewing. Enjoy a cream tea on the sweeping lawns of "Wavering Down House" and admire the house and gardens where Frankie Howerd would learn his lines for a "Carry On …" film or an episode of "Up Pompeii!"

Fact File

Opening times: Sunday 12th & Monday 13th April; Sunday 3rd May; Sunday 2nd August - 10.30am to 4.30pm. Also, Fathers' Day (Sunday 21st June) 2 – 6 pm during open-air, charity concert with top "Abba" tribute band and local performers and artistes.
Tickets for the concert £10 – pig roast available and licensed bar on site.
Private organisations and clubs from 20 to 150 can book throughout the year for a private visit of the house and gardens.

Admission Rates: Adults £5, Child £2.50
(Donated to charities via The Frankie Howerd OBE Trust – registered charity no: 1122850)

Group Rates: None

Facilities: Cream teas. Nearby pubs (The Lamb, The White Hart and The New Inn for meals.)
Plant sales. Plenty of car parking nearby

Disabled access: Partial. Toilets 25 yards away

Tours / Events: Tour of house by owner. Special events – see above, or website

Coach parking: Yes; drop-off outside gardens – parking close-by

Length of visit: About one hour.

Booking contact: Chris Byrne
"Wavering Down House", Webbington Road, Cross, nr. Axbridge, Somerset BS26 2EL
Booking telephone number: 01934 732013

E-mail: secretary@frankiehowerdobetrust.org

Website: www.frankiehowerdobetrust.org

Location: 3 miles from Cheddar Garden Centre and from Sanders Gardenworld; 1/4 mile off A38. Follow signs

Please quote this guide when making a booking

On show in the house are over 4,000 items of Frankie's personal and professional life. Everything is there: from his school reports to his dry cleaning bills, from the gardening medals he won in the 1930s to his first job contract, from many photos with the stars of his time to his famous toupee, along with gifts from Sir Laurence Olivier, Pope John Paul II and the Queen Mother. Chris Byrne (Curator and co-owner of the Wavering Down House Estate) knows all the stories and the anecdotes, and will be pleased to give you a guided tour of the house and gardens and answer any other questions you may have. The gardens have also been the scene for open-air concerts with performances by local bands, singers and groups such as "The Wurzels", "Abba" and "Queen" tribute bands and Tim Pitman. Over the last couple of years, nearly £100,000 has been raised through these concerts and Open Days. The Frankie Howerd OBE Trust has been formed to promote and administer revenue from Wavering Down House, with all its historical, cultural and horticultural interest and to help local individuals and groups – please visit our website.

It is easy to understand how Frankie so loved living here and why the house and gardens have been graced by the presence of so many famous celebrities like Elizabeth Taylor, Richard Burton, Princess Margaret and Bette Davis. Indeed, contemporary stars have also visited, such as Sir Ian McKellen, Richard Wilson and Justin Lee Collins – June Whitfield frequently stays at the house. "Little Britain" star David Walliams and famous actor Rafe Spall spent a day at the house talking to Dennis Heymer (Frankie's life-long partner and manager) for the recently-screened BBC drama, "Frankie Howerd: Rather You Than Me". Dennis himself will be on hand to answer questions about "The Beatles", Princess Grace of Monaco, Elvis and the Queen Mother, and on his amazing life with the stars, politicians and royalty.

Lose yourself in 40 acres of walks, streams and temples, vivid colours, formal terraces, woodland, lakes, cascades and views that take your breath away.

This is Hestercombe: a unique combination of three period gardens. The Georgian landscaped garden was created in the 1750's by Coplestone Warre Bampfylde, whose vision was complemented by the addition of a Victorian terrace and Shrubbery and the stunning Edwardian gardens designed by Sir Edwin Lutyens and Gertrude Jekyll. All once abandoned, now being faithfully restored to their former glory: each garden has its own quality of tranquillity, wonder and inspiration.

Free entry to our fabulous Courtyard Café and excellent shop; conference and business facilities, weddings, parties, year round events.

Fact File

Opening Times:	Open every day 10am - 6pm (last admissions 5pm).
Admission Rates:	Adults £7.90*, Senior Citizen £7.30* (adult & senior citizens include free entry for 2 children). *Includes 10% voluntary donation towards the continuing restoration.
Group Rates:	Groups 20 or more £6.00. Guided tours minimum 20 people £9.00.
Facilities:	Visitor Centre with Courtyard Cafe, Shop, Plant Sales. Function Rooms.
Disabled Access:	Partial. Toilet & parking for disabled on site. Wheelchairs on loan, booking not required.
Tours/Events:	A wide range of events including Themed Fairs, Food Markets, Childrens Trails and many other seasonal events. Walks. Garden tours available for groups.
Coach Parking:	Yes
Length of Visit:	Refreshment stop or part to full day out.
Booking Contact:	Hestercombe Gardens, Cheddon Fitzpaine, Taunton, Somerset, TA2 8LG Telephone 01823 413923 Fax: 01823 413747
Email:	groupbookings@hestercombe.com
Website:	www.hestercombe.com
Location:	4 miles from Taunton, Signposted from all main roads with the Tourist Information Daisy symbol.

Please quote this guide when making a booking

Kilver Court is the secret garden of England, over 150 years old, spanning two centuries of local, garden and industrial history yet never opened to the public!

A nineteenth century viaduct creates a stunning backdrop with glimpses of the Mendips. The 5-acre garden boasts undulating lawns, herbaceous borders, a lake, mill pond, and a Chelsea Gold Medal winning rockery with waterfalls (Designer: Charles Whiteleg 1963).

A garden for all seasons: spring sees flowering shrubs, summer is serenaded by the buzz of insects from the rockery and borders, autumn is a blaze of fiery colours and winter has the crisp, architectural structure of the parterre, designed by Mulberry creator and Kilver Court owner, Roger Saul.

Don't miss Sharpham Park Organic farmshop bringing together the best seasonal, local produce from his estate and from Somerset. The Harlequin café offers morning coffee with yummy Spelt cakes, light lunches and scrumptious English afternoon teas.

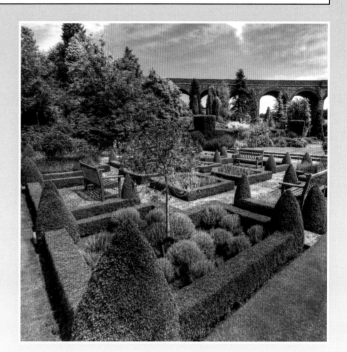

Fact File

Opening Times:	10 a.m. – 4 p.m.
Admission Charges:	Adults £4.00, Senior Citizens: £3.50, Children: Free under 16, if with an adult.
Group Rates:	Minimum Group Size: 8, Adults: £3.50, Senior Citizens: £3.00, Children:
On-Site Facilities:	Organic Farm Shop, Conference Centre, Wellness Centre
Disabled Access:	Yes, wheelchair loan available. Booking required.
Toilets on site:	Yes
Car Parking on site:	Yes
Coach Parking:	Yes
Length of Visit:	1 1/2 hours
Special Events:	Lectures and talks on cooking, baking, complementary health and gardening
Booking Contact:	Cindy, Kilver Court, Kilver Street, Shepton Mallet, Somerset BA4 5NF
	Booking Tel No.01749 340416 Booking Fax No. 01749 340420
Email:	info@kilvercourt.com
Website:	www.kilvercourt.com
Location:	On the main A37 in Shepton Mallet, directly opposite the Gaymer Cider Company factory or 50 m down hill from the Mulberry Factory shop.

One of only four Palladian bridges in the world can be crossed at Prior Park, which was created in the 18th Century by local entrepreneur Ralph Allen with advice from 'Capability' Brown and the poet Alexander Pope. The garden is set in a sweeping valley where visitors can enjoy magnificent views of Bath. Recent restoration of the 'Wilderness' has reinstated the Serpentine Lake, Cascade and Cabinet which are fully accessible to visitors.

A five-minute walk leads to the Bath Skyline, a six-mile circular route encompassing beautiful woodlands and meadows, with spectacular views over the City.

Prior Park is a green tourism site; there is only disabled car parking (please telephone to book). Public transport runs regularly to the garden from the City Centre. Call for a leaflet on how to find us or download a copy from the website.

Fact File

Opening times:	3 Jan - 13 Feb: 11 - dusk, Saturday, Sunday. 14 Feb - 30 Oct: 11 - 5.30, Wednesday - Monday. 31 Oct - 31 Jan 2010: 11 - dusk, Saturday, Sunday
Admission Rates:	Adults: £5.25, Child: £2.95, Family Ticket (2 adults, 2 children): £13.45 NT members free.
Group Rates:	Call for details.
Facilities:	Tea kiosk, February – October open weekends, school holidays and special events.
Disabled Access:	Yes, wilderness and viewpoint only.
Toilets on site:	Yes.
Car Parking on site:	Disabled parking only.
Coach Parking:	No.
Guided Tours:	Yes, booking required.
Length of Visit:	1 ½ hours
Special Events:	See website for details.
Booking Contact:	Katy Smith, The National Trust, Prior Park Landscape Garden, Ralph Allen Drive, Bath BA2 5AH Booking Tel No.01225 833977, Booking Fax No. 01225 838626
Email:	priorpark@nationaltrust.org.uk
Website:	www.nationaltrust.org.uk/priorpark
Location:	The garden is a 30-minute uphill walk from Bath City Centre. Public transport runs regularly. Call for details.

Please quote this guide when making a booking

A new University Botanic Garden has been created in Bristol with four core plant collections illustrating plant evolution, plants from the world's Mediterranean climates, useful plants and rare and threatened native plants. The new garden has a strong evolutionary theme including a sunken dell that charts the most important stages of plant evolution on land from green algae to the diversity of flowering plants and a 'family tree' based on the latest understanding of flowering plant relationships using DNA analysis. New Chinese and European Herb Gardens contain medicinal plants many rare in cultivation and a new Glasshouse complex is home to five climate controlled zones. Each zone is filled with exciting plants from sub-tropical ferns and orchids to exotic bulbs, cacti and succulents. A tropical pool is home to the Giant Amazon Water Lily and many food, spice and medicinal plants are grown. New for 2009 is a large display illustrating the numerous ways in which plants are pollinated and a rocky Mediterranean hillside planting, illustrating the drought tolerant plants of Southern Europe.

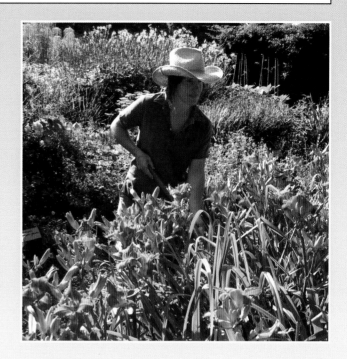

Fact File

Opening Times: Open Wednesday, Thursday, Friday and Sunday 10am - 4.30pm plus special summer Saturday openings, see website for further details.

Admission Rates: There is an administration charge

Group Rates: Minimum Group Size 10. Cost £4.50 per person for guided tour.

Facilities: Visitor Centre, Classroom/Meeting Room.

Disabled Access: Yes. Toilet and car parking on site. Bookable Wheelchairs available.

Tours/Events: Guided tours available at £4.50 per person. Jazz Concert and Theatre in July, educational activities, courses and study days

Coach Parking: Yes

Length of Visit: 1½ - 2 hours

Booking Contact: Zaria Fraser, University of Bristol Botanic Garden
The Holmes, Stoke Park Road, Stoke Bishop, Bristol. BS9 1JB
Tel: 0117 3314906 Fax: 0117 3314909

Email: botanic-gardens@bristol.ac.uk

Website: www.bris.ac.uk/depts/botanicgardens

Location: By car from city centre proceed across the Downs towards Stoke Bishop. Cross the traffic lights at the edge of the Downs, Stoke Park Road is the first turning right off Stoke Hill. The entrance to the Botanic Garden is opposite Churchill Hall.

Please quote this guide when making a booking

Consall Hall Landscape Gardens   Staffordshire

The Consall Hall Landscape Gardens lie on the edge of the beautiful Churnet Valley where four intersecting valleys form an exceptional 70 acre landscape.

Over the last fifty years, William Podmore OBE has developed the gardens to create a series of beautifully composed rural vistas. These have been enhanced by the construction of six lakes, bridges, follies, grottoes and other focal points, set against the enclosing shelter belts planted with swathes of trees and shrubs, to form a colourful background.

The viewing points have been made easily accessible by the construction of four miles of paths at different levels, and the edges screened with trees so that the views are hidden until the vista is revealed on reaching the correct view point, where a seat is provided.

In many cases, the seat is enclosed so the picture is framed to concentrate the attention on the carefully selected composition, and the views can be enjoyed whatever the weather.

Fact File

Opening Times: Wednesday & Sunday & Bank Holiday 10a.m. – 5p.m. from Good Friday to 28th October

Admission Rates: Adults & Senior Citizens £5.50, Children £1.50, Family Ticket £13.00 (2 adults + 3 children).

Group Rates: Minimum Group Size: 25 (1 free entry). Adults & Senior Citizens £5.50, Children £1.50.

Facilities: Shop, Plant Sales, Halcyon Tea Room: light lunches and afternoon teas served during opening hours. Halcyon Function Room: Licensed for marriage ceremonies. Toilet.

Disabled Access: Yes.

Coach Parking: Yes

Tours/Events: Guided tours available. 3 & 5 seater Golf buggy advanced booking recommended.

Length of Visit: 2 – 4 hours

Special Events: Please see website for details

Booking Contact: Allan Booth
Consall Hall Landscape Gardens, Consall, Wetley Rocks, Staffordshire Moorlands, ST9 0AG
Booking Telephone No: 01782 749994 / 551947 Booking Fax No. 01782 749447

Email: info@consallgardens.co.uk

Website: www.consallgardens.co.uk

Location: From the main A52 Stoke – Ashbourne road take the A522
(Wetley Rocks – Cheadle). Follow brown signs 3/4 mile beyond
Consall village, signposted 'No Through Road'.

Please quote this guide when making a booking

After 4 years of major restoration and vast replanting, Trentham has re-established itself amongst Europe's leading heritage attractions.

Set within the finest of English landscapes are the grand Italianate Parterres and the more relaxed pleasure gardens which have been brought back to life with stunning new displays of modern planting by leading garden designers Tom Stuart-Smith and Piet Oudolf.

Hundreds of thousands of plants provide breathtaking displays throughout the year, in a garden that only closes on Christmas day! In truth there is something for everyone - Formal Gardens and Fountains, Wild and Colourful Prairies, 12 Show Gardens, The Woodland Walk with Trails and Hides, a very engaging children's play area, and Britain's first Barefoot Walk.

The 750 acre Trentham Estate is set to become one of Europe's finest visitor destinations offering a range of high quality facilities including the garden and lake, shopping, restaurants and a hotel.

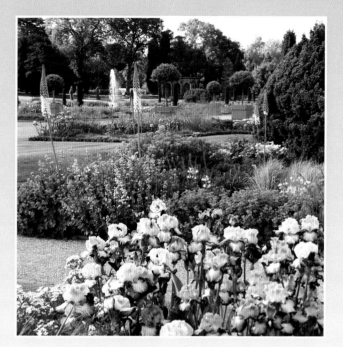

Fact File

Opening Times:	10.00am - 6.00pm during the Summer (tel 01782 646646 to confirm opening times & prices).
Admission Rates:	Adults: £7.00. Senior Citizens: £6.00. Children: £5.50. Family (2+3) £24.00.
	Trentham will be offering a joint garden and monkey forest ticket from 1st April 2009.
Group Rates:	Groups prices start from £4.50 for concessions if pre booked and pre paid.
	Schools £3.00. Supported schools activity inc entry £7.50
	Minimum Group Size: 12. RHS Members Free (only during RHS offer period).
Facilities:	Trentham is a leading tourism destination with a wide range of shops, restaurants and major garden centre. Toilets. (Beautiful NewGarden Room Restaurant open May 2009).
Disabled Access:	Yes, with wheelchair loan available.
Car Parking on site:	Yes
Coach Parking:	Yes
Tours/Events:	Guided tours available. Booking required.
Length of Visit:	Site: 1 day
Special Events:	Family Easter, summer festival and concerts
Booking Contact:	Jackie Grice
	Trentham Leisure Ltd., Stone Road, Trentham, Stoke-on-Trent, Staffordshire, ST4 8AX
	Booking Telephone No: 01782 645223 Booking Fax No: 01782 644536
Email:	jgrice@trentham.co.uk
Website:	www.trentham.co.uk
Location:	5 minutes from Junction 15 M6, Staffordshire

Somerleyton Hall & Gardens Suffolk

Somerleyton Hall was originally a Jacobean manor but was remodelled in 1844 transforming it into a fine example of an early Victorian Hall in Anglo-Italian style. The gardens are renown for their wide variety of splendid specimen trees including giant redwood , Monterey pine and Atlas cedar, with a multitude of shrubs, borders and plants providing colour and contrast throughout the year. In spring a wealth of bulbs, blossoms and early flowering shrubs appear followed by rhododendrons, azaleas and wisteria.

One of the most spectacular features of the garden is the yew hedge maze designed by William Nesfield the celebrated landscape gardener which was planted in 1846. The entrance is through a yew arch and those who successfully find their way to the centre will be rewarded by the sight of an enchanting small pagoda perched on a grassy mound.

There are walled, sunken and vegetable gardens and a notable range of glasshouses and peach-cases designed by Sir Joseph Paxton.

Fact File

Opening times: 5th April – 1st November: Thursday, Sunday, Bank Holidays 19th July - 20 September: Tuesday, Wednesday, Thursday, Sunday & Bank Holidays.

Admission Rates: Adults: £5.00 Senior Citizens: £4.00. Children: £3.00.

Group Rates: Minimum Group Size: 20. Adults: £4.10. Senior Citizens: £3.10. Children: £2.10.

Facilities: Interior of stately home (extra cost). Toilets.

Disabled Access: Yes. Wheelchair loan available.

Car Parking on site: Yes

Coach Parking: Yes

Tours/Events: Guided tours available. Booking required.

Length of Visit: 2 – 3 hours

Special Events: Refer to website

Booking Contact: Cathy Hatt
Somerleyton Hall & Gardens, Somerleyton, Lowestoft, Suffolk NR32 5QQ
Booking Telephone No: 01502 734901 Booking Fax No: 01502 732143

Email: cathy@somerleyton.co.uk

Website: www.somerleyton.co.uk

Location: Four miles north-west of Lowestoft on the B1074.
Coaches follow signs to rear west gate entrance.

Cherkley Court & Gardens Surrey

Set in 400 acres of park and woodlands, Cherkley Court was the home of the press baron and cabinet minister, the 1st Lord Beaverbrook between 1910-1964.

Following a 5 year renovation of the entire estate by the Beaverbrook Foundation, 16 acres of exquisitely landscaped gardens are open to the public.

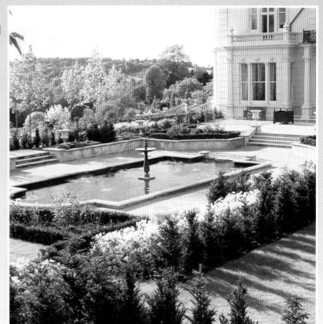

Cherkley Court offers an immaculate mix of formality and intimacy with outstanding views across the Mole Valley. The garden has been designed by Simon Johnson, who specialises in country house work. As well as grand terraces and long herbaceous borders, there are garden pavilions, a shell grotto, and a stunning Italianate garden. There is a wild flower meadow, Mediterranean planting, a potager, vegetable garden and walnut grove.

Short tours of the gardens are available free to visitors, plant guides are on sale and there is a tranquil Orangery Teashop serving lunches, homemade cakes and teas.

Fact File

Opening Times:	1st April – 30th September, Sunday – Thursday 10.30 a.m. – 5 p.m.
Admission Rates:	Adult: £6.00, Senior Citizens: £4.70, Children (5-16): £4.50 (under 5): FOC Family (2 adults, 2 children): £18.00.
Group Rates:	Minimum Group Size: 10 Adults: £5.50, Senior Citizens: £4.00, Children: £4.00.
Facilities:	Restaurant, Plant sales, Retail, Visitor Display.
Disabled Access:	Yes, wheelchair loan available.
Tours/Events:	Guided garden tours available.
Coach Parking:	Yes
Car Parking on site:	Yes
Length of Visit:	2 hours.
Booking Contact:	Lin Ward Cherkley Court & Gardens, Reigate Road, Leatherhead, Surrey KT22 8QX Telephone: 01372 380980 Fax: 01372 376378
Email:	enquiries@cherkleycourt.com
Website:	www.cherkleycourt.com
Location:	Juction 9 of M25, A24 towards Dorking. At 3rd roundabout take B2033 to Headley. Entrance 200m on right.

The flamboyant Henry VIII is most associated with this majestic palace, which he extended and developed in grand style after acquiring it from Cardinal Wolsey in the 1520s. He lavished money on fabulous tapestries and paintings, housed and fed a huge court and pursued a succession of wives, political power and domination over Rome.

The first Privy Garden at Hampton Court Palace was laid out between 1530 and 1538 for Henry VIII. The palace now boasts over 60 acres of formal gardens and 750 acres of royal parkland, 8,000 trees in the gardens and estates, the longest herbaceous border in Britain, a tender exotics section and the National Collection of helitropus arborescens, attended to by a team of 38 gardeners and specialists.

Exceptional features of the gardens include the world famous Maze, the pond gardens, the Privy Garden – restored to its 1702 state under William III – and the Great vine – the world's oldest and largest known vine. The grounds also include the Wilderness and Home Park, 750 acres of unspoilt land providing a rich habitat for wildlife including 300 fallow deer, horses and 30 to 40 ring-necked parakeets.

Fact File

Opening times: 1st April 2009 - 30th September 2009, 10.00 – 18.00 (last admission 17.00)
1st October 2009 - 30th March 2010, 10.00 – 16.30 (last admission 15.30)

Admission Rates: Palace & Gardens: Adults £13.30, Concessions £10.80, Child £6.65, Family £37.00
Prices and dates are corrrect at time of printing however are subject to change at any time.
Gardens only tickets are also available please call 0844 482 7777

Group Rates: For group rates and bookings, please call 0203 166 6311

Facilities: Visitor centre, shops, restaurant and coffee shop

Disabled Access: Yes, toilets and car parking on site. Bookable wheelchair loan available

Tours/Events: Guided tours

Coach Parking: Yes

Length of Visit: 3 hours+

Booking Contact: Hampton Court Palace, East Molesey, Surrey, KT8 9AU
Tel: 0844 482 7777

Email: hamptoncourt@hrp.org.uk

Website: www.hrp.org.uk

Location: Car: from the M25 take either exit 10 and the A307 or exit 12 and the A308
From central London take A3 to the Hook underpass and then the A309.
Train: 30 minutes direct from London Waterloo, 24 minutes from
Clapham Junction and 6 minutes from Surbiton.
Alternatively take the train to Kingston and catch a bus.

Please quote this guide when making a booking

Loseley Park Surrey

Part of the magnificent grounds of Loseley Park, the original two and a half acre Walled Garden is largely based on a design by Gertrude Jekyll.

The Walled Garden features five exquisite gardens, each with its own theme and character. The award-winning Rose Garden is planted with over one thousand bushes, mainly old-fashioned varieties. The extensive Herb Garden contains four separate sections devoted to culinary, medicinal, household and ornamental. The Fruit and Flower Garden is designed to provide interest and bold fiery colour throughout the season. The White Garden, in total contrast, is planted with white, cream and silver plants, with two water features, creating an idyllic and tranquil area. The Organic Vegetable Garden is spectacular with a huge variety and the wild flower meadow is an attractive display during the summer months. Other features include the magnificent vine walk, mulberry tree, ancient wisteria and moat which runs almost the entire length of the Walled Garden and is abundant with wildlife and pond plants.

Fact File

Opening times: Gardens open: May - September, Tuesday - Sunday 11am - 5pm.
Loseley House open (guided tours only): May - August, Tues - Thurs & Sun, 1pm - 5pm.
May and August Bank Holidays.

Admission Rates: Gardens only: Adults £4.50, Senior Citizens £4.00, Child £2.25.
House & Gardens: Adults £8.00, Senior Citizen £7.50, Child £4.00.

Groups Rates: Minimum group size: 10. Adults £7.00, Child £3.50.

Facilities: Courtyard Tea Room & light snacks, Gift shop, Plant Sales.

Disabled Access: Yes. Toilet and parking for disabled on site. Wheelchair on loan.

Tours/Events: House tours and garden tours for groups by arrangement.

Coach Parking: Yes

Length of Visit: 4 hours

Booking Contact: Group Co-Ordinator
Loseley Park, Estate Office, Guildford, Surrey, GU3 1HS
Telephone: 01483 405112   Fax: 01483 302036 General Information: 01483 304440

Email: groups@loseley-park.com

Website: www.loseley-park.com

Location: 3 miles south of Guildford via A3 and B3000.

Please quote this guide when making a booking

Step into a 'living picture of paradise' and discover a Georgian landscape, created by the Hon. Charles Hamilton between 1738 and 1773 as a Living Work of Art... Enjoy 158 acres of award-winning authentically restored 18th century parkland complete with 14 acre lake, spectacular views across Surrey, an amazing crystal Grotto plus many more interesting and unusual follies.

From snowdrops to Autumn colour the pleasure grounds and plantings have something to offer the visitor throughout the year. Enjoy exploring the American Roots exhibition which tells an amazing story of the 18th century craze for new and exciting exotic plants from outside the British Isles and discover the NCCPG John Bartram Heritage Plant Collection of North American Trees and Shrubs.

Guided tours for pre-booked groups give a fascinating insight into Hamilton's vision and it's a great way to discover the pleasure grounds. We hold entertaining events and interesting talks throughout the year covering a wide range of subjects and sell Painshill Honey and Wine from the Vineyard.

Fact File

Opening Times: Open all year. (Closed Christmas Day and Boxing Day) March - October 10.30am – 6pm or dusk if earlier (last entry 4.30pm) November – February 10.30am – 4pm or dusk if earlier (last entry 3pm). The Grotto has limited opening hours. Opened for groups by appointment.

Admission Rates: Adults: £6.60. Concessions: £5.80. Children (5 – 16): £3.85, under 5's: Free. Carer of Disabled Person: Free. Family Ticket (2A & 4C): £22.00. Dogs on a lead welcome.

Group Rates: Pre-Booked Adult Groups of 10+: £5.80 plus £1.00 per person for a Guided Tour. Free Entry & Refreshments for Group Organiser and Coach Driver.

Facilities: Visitor Centre & Gift shop, Licensed Tea Room (Group Menu available), Picnic Area, Education Visits, Classrooms, Meeting Room, Permanent Marquee (Weddings & Corporate).

Disabled Access: Yes. Accessible Route. Toilet and Parking on site. Free of charge pre-booked Wheelchair loan & Buggy Tours (Capacity Max. 3) available for disabled persons.

Tours/Events: Guided Tours/Introductory Talks for pre-booked Groups. Events throughout year, telephone or visit website for details. American Roots Exhibition and NCCPG Plant Collection.

Coach Parking: Yes. No Charge.

Length of Visit: 2 – 4 hours.

Booking Contact: Visitor Manager. Painshill Park Trust, Portsmouth Road, Cobham, Surrey KT11 1JE Telephone: 01932 868113 Fax: 01932 868001

Email: Info@painshill.co.uk **Website:** www.painshill.co.uk

Location: Just off M25/J10/A3 to London. Exit A245 towards Cobham. Entrance in Between Streets, 200m East of A245/A307 roundabout. Nearest Station Cobham/Stoke d'Abernon. The Surrey Parks & Gardens Explorer Bus Route 515/515A.

Please quote this guide when making a booking

Ramster is famous for its stunning collection of rhododendrons and azaleas, which flourish under the mature woodland canopy. Established in the 1900s by Gauntlett Nurseries of Chiddingfold, with influences from the Japanese gardens, it now stretches over twenty acres. April heralds the arrival of many varieties of daffodils, complementing the camellias, the early flowering rhododendrons and the stunning magnolias. The carpets of scented bluebells contrast exquisitely with the fiery display of azaleas and rhododendrons in May and the warmth of June brings forth the Mediterranean grasses, and the subtle pink climbing roses. In the bog garden a mass of colourful primulas cascade down the rill, and stepping-stones weave a path under the leaves of the giant gunnera.
Always peaceful and beautiful the changing colours are reflected in the pond and lake. Wildlife abounds throughout the season, including kingfishers, herons, ducks, geese and moorhens.

Fact File

Opening times:	4th April – 21st June 2009: 10.00 a.m. – 5.00 p.m.
Admission Rates:	Adults: £5.00, OAP £4.50, Children: Under 16 – free.
Group Rates:	Minimum Groups Size: 10
	Group Adults: £4.50, Children: Under 16 – free.
Facilities:	Plant sales, homemade teas, sandwiches and snacks.
Disabled Access:	Yes. Toilet and car parking on site.
Tours/Events:	Guided tours available for groups of over 20, please book.
	Special Event: Ramster Embroidery and Textile Art Exhibition, open 17th-28th April 2009, 10am-5pm. Over 250 pieces of work are for sale in the Long Hall.
	26th April, Charity Plant and Local Food Fair 11.00 a.m. - 4.00 p.m.
Coach Parking:	Yes.
Length of Visit:	Between 2-4 hours.
Booking Contact:	Ramster Gardens, Petworth Road, Chiddingfold, Surrey GU8 4SN
	Telephone: 01428 654167 Fax: 01428 642481
Email:	info@ramsterweddings.co.uk
Website:	www.ramsterweddings.co.uk
Location:	1½ miles south of Chiddingfold on the A283

Please quote this guide when making a booking

Titsey Place Gardens   Surrey

The Trustees are delighted to welcome visitors to Titsey Place and Gardens. The House which dates back to the 17th Century is home to four stunning Canaletto paintings, superb collection of porcelain and objets d'arts belonging to the Leveson Gower and Gresham families who have owned this beautiful mansion house in the North Downs. The gardens extend to some 15 acres and are a mix of formal lawns and rose gardens to informal walks around the two lakes. There is a modern Etruscan temple, walled kitchen garden and four miles of woodland walks.
For further information visit www.titsey.org or telephone 01273 715359.

Fact File

Opening Times: 1 p.m. – 5 p.m. Mid-May to End September on Wednesdays and Sundays.
Additionally open summer bank holidays. The garden only open on Easter Monday.

Admission Rates: Adults: £7.00, Senior Citizens: £7.00, Garden only: £4.50.

Group Rates: Please telephone for details
Adults/Senior Citizens/Children: £8.50

Facilities: Picnic Area and Tea Room.

Disabled Access: Yes, but garden only and not very easy. Toilet and parking on site.

Tours/Events: Guided tours of house & garden by arrangement.

Coach Parking: Yes. By arrangement only.

Length of Visit: 1 hour garden/ 45 minutes house.

Booking Contact: Karen Kilshaw
Titsey Place Gardens, Titsey Place, Oxted, Surrey RH8 0JD
Telephone: 01273 715362 Fax: 01273 779783

Email: karen.kilshaw@struttandparker.com

Website: www.titsey.org

Location: From the A25 between Oxted & Westerham turn left onto B629 and at the end of Limpsfield High Street turn left & follow signs to visitors car park.

Please quote this guide when making a booking

Great Dixter House & Gardens East Sussex

Great Dixter was the birthplace and home of gardening writer Christopher Lloyd. Built c1450 it boasts the largest surviving timber-framed hall in the country which was restored and enhanced by Sir Edwin Lutyens.
The magnificent gardens are now the hallmark of Christopher who devoted his lifetime to creating one of the most experimental gardens in the country, including flower meadows, ponds and the famous Long Border and Exotic Garden. Great Dixter Nurseries offer a wide range of rare and interesting plants that can be seen in the fabric of the garden. Head Gardener Fergus Garrett will lead a number of educational Study Days during the year, please see website for details.

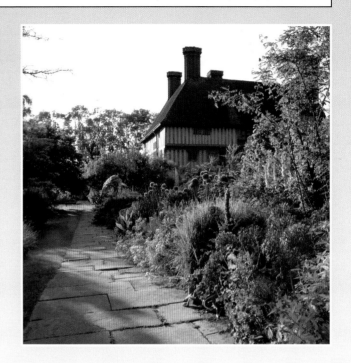

Fact File

Opening Times:	April – October Tuesday – Sunday and Bank Holiday Mondays
	House: 2 – 5 p.m., Garden: 11.00 – 5 p.m.
Admission Rates:	Adults House & Garden: £8.00, Children House & Garden: £3.50.
	Adults Garden Only: £6.50, Children Garden Only: £3.00.
Group Rates:	Min Group Size: 25, Adults: £7.00, Seniors: £7.00, Children: £3.00. Annual tickets available.
Facilities:	Shop, Plant sales, Light Refreshments.
Disabled Access:	Limited. Bookable wheelchair loan available.
Toilets on site:	Yes.
Tours/Events:	Guided tours available, booking required. Study Days, (Horticultural Lectures)
Coach Parking:	Yes.
Car Parking on site:	Yes.
Length of Visit:	2 hours.
Booking Contact:	Isabelle Sambrook
	Great Dixter House & Gardens, Great Dixter, Northiam, Rye, East Sussex TN31 6PH
	Telephone: 01797 252878 Ext 2
	Fax: 01797 252879
Email:	groupbookings@greatdixter.co.uk
Website:	www.greatdixter.co.uk
Location:	Signposted from the centre of Northiam on the A28.

Gardens & Grounds of Herstmonceux Castle — East Sussex

Herstmonceux is renowned for its magnificent moated castle, set in beautiful parkland and superb Elizabethan Gardens. Built originally as a country home in the mid 15th century, Herstmonceux Castle embodies the history of medieval England and the romance of renaissance Europe. Set among carefully maintained Elizabethan Gardens and parkland, your experience begins with your first sight of the castle as it breaks into view.

In the grounds you will find the formal gardens including a walled garden dating from before 1570, a herb garden, the Shakespeare Garden, woodland sculptures, the Pyramid, the water lily filled moat and the Georgian style folly.

The Woodland walks will take you to the remains of three hundred year old sweet chestnut avenue, the rhododendron garden from the Lowther/Latham period, the waterfall (dependent on rainfall), and the 39 steps leading you through a woodland glade.

Fact File

Opening Times: 11th April - 1st November, open daily.
Admission Rates: Adults £6.00, Senior Citizen £4.95, Child £3.00 (5-15yrs).
Group Rates: Minimum group size: 15
Adults £4.50, Senior Citizen £4.00, Child/Students £2.00 (5-15yrs).
Facilities: Visitor Centre, Gift Shop, Tea Room, Nature Trail, Children's Woodland Play Area.
Disabled Access: Limited. Toilet and parking for disabled on site. 1 Wheelchair on loan. booking essential.
Tours/Events: Guided Tours are conducted at an extra charge and subject to availablity.
Please telephone for confirmation of tours before you visit.
Coach Parking: Yes
Length of Visit: 2 - 4 hours
Booking Contact: Caroline Cullip
Herstmonceux Castle, Hailsham, East Sussex, BN27 1RN
Telephone: 01323 834457 Fax: 01323 834499
Email: c_cullip@isc-queensu.ac.uk
Website: www.herstmonceux-castle.com
Location: Located just outside the village of Herstmonceux on the A271, entrance is on Wartling Road.

Please quote this guide when making a booking

Legend has it that King John II, who became King of France in 1350, was held hostage in this house for some years. King John's Lodge is a listed Jacobean house surrounded by a garden for all seasons. Snowdrops and hellebores precede spring bulbs, wild orchids, primroses and violets. This exceptionally romantic garden is noted for its roses, especially those cascading over apple trees in the wild garden. The borders around the formal garden are planted with softly-coloured roses and clematis and herbaceous plants. The year ends with carpets of pink and white cyclamen. The five acre garden is surrounded by meadows with fine trees, grazing sheep and panoramic views. There are a number of water features including a lily pond and fountain in the formal garden, a wild pond and a secret pond in the woodland area. A propagation nursery and shop has now opened selling a wide range of unusual perennials and shrubs, statuary and iron work as well as a range of interesting garden equipment and gifts.

Fact File

Opening Times:	10.00am – 4.00pm. Daily, closed from 24 December – 31 January
Admission Rates:	Adults: £3.50, Children (0-16yrs): Free
Group Rates:	Minimum Groups Size: 10 for concession price
	Adults: £3.00 Between Oct to May 09 spend £20 at the Nursery and receive one complimentary visit to the garden
Facilities:	Shop, plant sales, teas, lunch by arrangement, B&B and holiday accommodation
Disabled Access:	Car parking on site and garden access
Coach Parking:	Yes
Length of Visit:	1 hour
Booking Contact:	Jill Cunningham
	King John's Lodge, Sheepstreet Lane, Etchingham, East Sussex TN19 7AZ
	Telephone: 01580 819232 Nursery: 01580 819220
Email:	kingjohnslodge@aol.com or kingjohnsnursery@btconnect.com
Website:	www.kingjohnslodge.co.uk
Location:	2 miles west of Hurst Green. A265 Burwash to Etchingham. Turn left before Etchingham Church into Church Lane which leads into Sheepstreet Lane after 1/2 mile. On the left after 1 mile, the entrance and parking is at King John's Nursery.

Please quote this guide when making a booking

A garden not be missed - Merriments Garden at Hurst Green offers everything for the "Garden Lover's" day out.

Set in 4 acres of gently sloping Weald farmland, this is a garden of richly and imaginatively planted deep curved borders, colour themed and planted in the great tradition of English gardening. These borders use a rich mix of trees, shrubs, perennials, grasses and many unusual annuals which ensure an arresting display of colour, freshness and vitality in the garden right through to its closing in autumn. Also in the garden are two large ponds, dry scree area, bog and wilder areas of garden planted only using plants suited for naturalising and colonising their environment. It delights all who visit.

The extensive Nursery offers a wide choice of unusual and interesting plants for sale many of which can be seen growing in the garden.

Fact File

Opening times:	Easter to 30th September.
Admission Rates:	Adults £4.50, Senior Citizens £4.50, Child £2.00.
Group Rates:	Minimum group size: 15 (£4.00 per Adult)
Facilities:	Gift Shop, Plant Sales, Restaurant, Wild Bird Centre.
Disabled Access:	Yes. Toilet and parking for disabled on site, Wheelchairs on loan booking advisable.
Tours/Events:	None
Coach Parking:	Yes
Length of Visit:	2 - 3 hours
Booking Contact:	Taryn Murrells
	Hawkhurst Road, Hurst Green, East Sussex. TN19 7RA.
	Telephone: 01580 860666 Fax: 01580 860324
Email:	info@merriments.co,uk
Website:	www.merriments.co.uk
Location:	15 miles north of Hastings just off the A21 at Hurst Green.

Please quote this
guide when
making a booking

Michelham Priory & Gardens

Magical Michelham, set on an island approached through a 14th century gatehouse in the beautiful Cuckmere Valley. It is surrounded by the longest water-filled medieval moat in England.

The historic buildings include part of an Augustinian priory that over 800 years evolved into a splendid country house (reputedly haunted) surrounded by spacious gardens. The property also includes a fully restored watermill and a stunning Elizabethan Barn. Exhibitions, exciting events plus a working forge and rope museum are all part of what makes Michelham a fascinating day out for all family members. The various planting areas appeal to many as well, from the gentle Moat Walk around the island, to the Physic, Cloister and Kitchen Gardens and medieval Stew Pond filled with historically accurate plants.

The licensed restaurant serving hot meals and home-baked cakes, outside picnic and area and plenty of free parking make Michelham Priory a place you'll want to return to again and again.

Fact File

Opening Times: 1 Mar-1 Nov: Tues-Sun from 10.30am Closed Mondays except on Bank Holidays and in August Closing Times: Mar & Oct - 4.30pm, April-July & Sept, 5pm, August, 5.30pm Last admission 45 minutes before closing time.

Admission Rates: Adults £6.50, Student £5.50, OAP £5.50, Child £3.40, Disabled/Carer £3.40 each, Family (2+2) £16.60. Game Fair: Adults £8.00, Student £6.00, OAP £6.00, Child £5.00, Disabled/Carer £5.00 each, Family (2+2) £23.50

Groups Rates: Adults £5.00, Student £5.00, OAP £5.00, Child £3.15, Disabled/Carer £3.40 each. Game Fair: Adults £6.00, Student £5.20, OAP £5.20, Child £3.50, Disabled/Carer £5.00 each.

Facilities: Gift Shop, Restaurant, Plant Sales, Weddings.

Disabled Access: Yes. Toilet and parking for disabled on site. Loan wheelchairs available.

Tours/Events: Spring Garden Fair-April, Iron Age & Roman Event-May, Food Fair-June, Game & Country Fair-July, Crafts in Action; Sussex Guild-August, Medieval Weekend & Early Music Fair-September, Hallow'een-October

Coach Parking: Yes. Free meal voucher for Coach Drivers.

Length of Visit: 3 - 4 hours

Booking Contact: Michelham Priory, Upper Dicker, Nr Hailsham, East Sussex, BN27 3QS Telephone: 01323 844224   Fax: 01323 844030

Email: adminmich@sussexpast.co.uk

Website: www.sussexpast.co.uk/michelham

Location: 2 miles west of Hailsham & 8 miles north west of Eastbourne. Signposted from A22 & A27. (OS map 198 TQ558 093).

Please quote this guide when making a booking

The de Passele family built a moated Manor in 1262 and held the estate until 1453, when it was sold to the forebears of Anne Boleyn. It is possible that Anne, second wife of Henry VIII, stayed here during her childhood. In 1543 the estate was sold to Sir Thomas May, who built the Tudor house you see today, the fine Georgian Facade was added in 1720.

The Gardens offer a sumptuous blend of romantic landscaping, imaginative plantings and fine old trees, fountains, springs and large ponds. This is a quintessential English Garden of a very individual character, with exceptional views to the surrounding valleyed fields. Many eras of English history are reflected here, typifying the tradition of the English Country House and its Garden.

Pashley, a winner of the HHA/Christie's Garden of the Year Award, holds a Tulip Festival in late April/May, Sculpture Fortnight middle to end of May, Special June Rose Weekend, Kitchen Garden Weekend 3rd-5th July and Lily Time mid July/mid August, The Sussex Guild Craft Show and an exhibition and sale of sculpture and botanical art lasting throughout the season.

Fact File

Opening Times: 2nd April - 30th September, Tuesday, Wednesday, Thursday, Saturday, Bank Holiday and Special Event Days 11am - 5pm.
Admission Rates: Adults £7.50, Children £5.00.
Groups Rates: Minimum group size 15, Adults £7.00. Tulip Festival £8.00 no concessions.
Facilities: Gift Shop, Plant Sales, Licensed Café, Light Lunches and Afternoon Teas.
Disabled Access: Limited. Toilet and parking for disabled on site. Wheelchairs on loan, booking necessary.
Tours/Events: Pre-booked tours of garden available. Please call for special event details.
Coach Parking: Yes
Length of Visit: 2 1/2 hours - half day.
Booking Contact: Pashley Manor Gardens, Ticehurst, East Sussex, TN5 7HE
Tel: 01580 200888 Fax: 01580 200102
Email: info@pashleymanorgardens.com
Website: www.pashleymanorgardens.com
Location: On the B2099 between the A21 and Ticehurst village (Tourist brown-signed).

Please quote this guide when making a booking

The National Trust Sheffield Park Garden — East Sussex

This magnificent informal landscape garden was laid out in the 18th century by 'Capability' Brown and further developed in the early years of the 20th century by its owner Arthur G. Soames. The original four lakes form the centrepiece. There are dramatic shows of daffodils and bluebells in spring, and the rhododendrons and azaleas are spectacular in early summer. Autumn brings stunning colours from the many rare trees and shrubs, and winter walks can be enjoyed in this garden for all seasons. Don't forget to visit our newly acquired parkland – perfect for a good walk with stunning views.

Whatever the season, Sheffield Park Garden offers a fantastic visit for all!

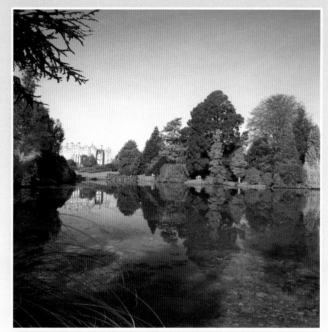

Fact File

Opening times:	Open all year, please telephone or check website for details.
Admission Rates:	Adults: *GAOE £7.70, Senior Citizens: *GAOE £3.85, Family: *GAOE £19.25
	*Including a voluntary 10% donation; visitors can, however, choose to pay the standard admission prices which are displayed at the property and at www.nationaltrust.org.uk.
	NT members free. RHS members free, (individual members only)
Group Rates:	(pre-booked), Minimum Group Size: 15, Adults: £6.50, Children: £3.25
Guided tour:	£2.00 pp (inc. NT members), (Must be pre-booked)
Facilities:	Visitor Centre, Shop, Plant Sales, Restaurant (not NT)
Disabled Access:	Yes. Wheelchair loan available. PMV Loan, Yes booking required, book on 01825 790302
Toilets on site:	Yes
Car Parking on site:	Yes
Coach Parking:	Yes
Guided Tours:	Yes, booking required.
Length of Visit:	2 hours garden 2 hours parkland
Special Events:	Throughout the year - check website for details.
Booking Contact:	Jill Reeves, The National Trust Sheffield Park Garden, Sheffield Park, East Sussex TN22 3QX
	Booking Tel No.01825 790231, Booking Fax No. 01825 971264
Email:	sheffieldpark.groups@nationaltrust.org.uk
Website:	www.nationaltrust.org.uk/sheffieldpark
Location:	5 miles NW of Uckfield, on east side of A275 (between A272 and A22).

Please quote this guide when making a booking

Borde Hill, a beautiful and botanically rich Grade II* listed heritage garden in the heart of the Sussex High Weald, was created in the era of the Great Plant Hunters – a legacy that, today, provides interest and wonder for every horticultural enthusiast.

The 17-acre formal garden has distinctive, linked 'rooms' each with their own unique style, offering a variety of seasonal colours. Early spring-flowering bulbs, magnolias, camellias, rhododendrons and azaleas, give way to exuberant summer borders of roses and herbaceous plants and the vivid blaze of autumnal colour. These plantings extend into 200 acres of traditional woodland and parkland, where the variety of micro-climates has contributed to the best collection of the tallest and largest girth 'champion' trees on privately-owned land in Britain.

Other highlights include the Azalea Ring and the tranquil Garden of Allah, a Mediterranean Garden, our fragrant Rose Garden and the Long Dell, planted with a Sino-Himalayan theme.

Fact File

Opening times:	10 a.m. – 6 p.m. 20 March – 13 September 2009 and 24 October -1 November 2009
Admission Rates:	Adults: £7.50, Senior Citizens: £6.50, Children: £4.00
Facilities:	Shop, Plant Sales, Restaurant, Teas, children's adventure playground, coarse fishing
Disabled Access:	Yes, wheelchair loan available (booking required)
Toilets on site:	Yes
Car Parking on site:	Yes
Coach Parking:	Yes
Guided Tours:	Yes, booking required
Length of Visit:	1-4 hours
Special Events:	Full programme – see website for details
Booking Contact:	Borde Hill Garden, Balcombe Road, Haywards Heath, W. Sussex RH16 1XP Booking Tel No.01444 450326 Booking Fax No. 01444 440427
Email:	info@bordehill.co.uk
Website:	www.bordehill.co.uk

Please quote this guide when making a booking

Denmans Garden West Sussex

A beautiful garden designed for year-round interest – through use of form, colour and texture. Nearly 4 acres in size and owned by John Brookes MBE, renowned garden designer and writer and Michael Neve, it is a garden full of ideas to be interpreted within smaller home spaces.

Gravel is used extensively in the garden both to walk on and as a growing medium so that you walk through the plantings rather than past them. A dry gravel 'stream' meanders down to a large natural looking pond. There is a walled garden, conservatory and a glass area for tender plants.

There is a fully licensed Les Routiers award winning Garden Café which serves a selection of light lunches, coffees, teas and a variety of delicious cakes and a beautiful Plant Centre which stocks around 1500 varieties of perennials and shrubs.

Fact File

Opening Times:	Daily all year round 9am - 5pm. (Except 25th, 26th Dec & 1st Jan)
Admission Rates:	Adults £4.95, Senior Citizens £4.75, Child (4-16 years) £3.95.
Group Rates:	Minimum group size: 15 (by appointment only)
	Adults £4.50, Senior Citizens £4.50.
Facilities:	Plant Centre, Café, Gift Shops.
Disabled Access:	Yes, Wheelchairs on loan, booking advisable.
Tours/Events:	Guided Tours and introductory talks by appointment only.
Coach Parking:	Yes.
Length of Visit:	2 - 3 hours
Booking Contact:	Claudia Murphy,
	Denmans Garden, Denmans Lane, Fontwell, West Sussex BN18 0SU.
	Telephone: 01243 542 808 Fax: 01243 544 064
Email:	denmans@denmans-garden.co.uk
Website:	www.denmans-garden.co.uk
Location:	Situated off A27 (westbound) between Chichester 6 mls and Arundel 5 mls adjacent to Fontwell Racecourse. The nearest railway station in Barnham 3 mls.

Please quote this guide when making a booking

Especially colourful in spring and autumn, High Beeches is a romantic landscape, changing with the seasons. Discover 27 acres of beautiful and historic woodland and water gardens full of rare and unusual plants and trees. Wander down the winding paths, through open sunlit glades, enjoy stunning vistas and sit by tranquil ponds.

In spring enjoy daffodils along with camellias and many different magnolias, followed by bluebells throughout the woodland glades. The gardens are spectacular in May and early June, carpeted with amazing colour and fragrance from azaleas and magnificent rhododendrons.

The old wildflower meadow is full of wild orchids, cowslips, oxeye daisies and many other wildflowers throughout June and The National Collection of Stewartia flower at the end of June. In August the wonderful azure blue Willow Gentians bloom throughout the glades – High Beeches is the only site in the UK where these have naturalised.

In autumn the views alter again as the varied foliage changes to a splendid crescendo of crimson, copper, gold and green with one of the finest displays of autumnal colour in the country.

Fact File

Opening times:	1 – 5 p.m. every day except Wednesday, 21 March – 31 October
Admission Rates:	Adults: £6.00, Senior Citizens: £6.00, Children: Under 14 – Free
Group Rates:	Minimum Group Size: 20. Adults: £5.50, Senior Citizens: £5.50, Children: Under 14 – Free
Facilities:	Restaurant, Teas
Disabled Access:	Limited – tearoom yes
Toilets on site:	Yes
Car Parking on site:	Yes
Coach Parking:	Yes
Guided Tours:	Yes, booking required.
Length of Visit:	2 hours
Special Events:	See website.
Booking Contact:	Sarah Bray, High Beeches Gardens, Handcross, West Sussex RH17 6HQ Booking Tel No. 01444 400589. Booking Fax No. 01444 401543
Email:	gardens@highbeeches.com
Website:	www.highbeeches.com
Location:	1 mile east of the A223 at Handcross on the south side of the B2110 in mid-Sussex.

Please quote this guide when making a booking

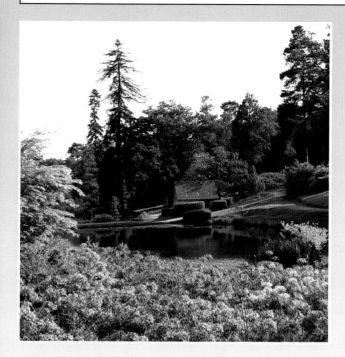

Leonardslee is home to one of the most magnificent displays of rhododendron and azaleas and the fascinating miniature 1/12 scale model exhibition "Beyond the Doll's House". The gardens which nestle in a romantic valley with walks around seven beautiful lakes is one of the finest in Europe when the sumptuous rhododendrons overhang paths fringed with bluebells, making an earthly paradise full of fragrances. The Rock Garden is a kaleidoscope of colour with azaleas of every hue. "Beyond the Doll's House", an exhibition of Victorian life, is one of the most detailed examples in the world with a frontage of around 140ft. Discover the wildlife: wallabies, wildfowl and much more. Enjoy hot food in our licensed self-service restaurant and visit the gift shop and plant sale.

Fact File

Opening Times:	1st April - 31st October 9.30am-6pm (last admission 4.30pm)
Admission Rates:	May (Weekends & Bank Holidays) £9.00; May (Weekdays) £8.00
	April and 1st June - 31st October £6.50; Children aged 5-15 (Anytime) £4.00
Groups Rates:	May (Weekends & Bank Holidays) £8.00; May (Weekdays) £7.00
	April and 1st June - 31st October £5.50; Children aged 5-15 (Anytime) £3.50
Facilities:	Shop, Licensed Self-service Restaurant, Plant Sales.
Disabled Access:	No
Tours/Events:	-
Coach Parking:	Yes (Free)
Length of Visit:	4 - 5 hours
Booking Contact:	The Secretary, Leonardslee Gardens, Lower Beeding, Horsham, West Sussex, RH13 6PP
	Telephone: 01403 891212 Fax: 01403 891305
Email:	info@leonardsleegardens.com
Website:	www.leonardsleegardens.com
Location:	4 miles from Handcross at bottom of M23 via B2110, entrance is at junction of B2110 and A281, between Handcross and Cowfold.

Please quote this guide when making a booking

One of the top twenty in Simon Jenkins' book "England's Thousand Best Houses", Parham is one of England's finest Elizabethan examples. Set in the heart of a deer park, with its dark   fallow deer first recorded in 1628, the house sits below a completely unspoilt stretch of the South Downs. Its Pleasure Grounds, laid out in the 18th century, encompass specimen trees and a brick and turf maze built in 1991, and lead down to a peaceful lake overlooked by a summer house.

The spectacular four-acre walled garden, cultivated for many centuries, contains herbaceous and mixed borders of Edwardian opulence. Vibrant with colour, it is run on organic principles and designed for a long season, peaking in summer and in late autumn. With its herbs, vegetables, lavender, roses and fruit trees, the garden is a series of interlocking pictures, woven into each other with a tapestry-like effect in the English romantic tradition.

The Wendy House, built into the old garden wall, with its balcony, fireplace and parquet floor, was built in 1928 for the daughters of the Hon. Clive and Alicia Pearson, who bought the estate in 1922.

Parham is justly famous for its long tradition of flower arrangements which decorate every room in the house. Everything is cut from the garden, which won the HHA/Christie's Garden of the Year Award in 1990.

Fact File

Opening Times:	House: Easter Sunday - end of September, Wednesdays, Thursdays, Sundays & Bank Holiday Mondays, also Tuesdays & Fridays in August 2pm - 5pm. Gardens: Tuesday to Friday incl, Sundays & Bank Holiday Mondays 12 noon - 5pm.
Admission Rates:	(2009 rates) Gardens only: Adult £6.00, Senior Citizen/Disabled £5.00 Carer free. House & Gardens: Adult £8.00, Senior Citizen/Disabled £7.00 Carer free.
Group Rates:	Discounted rates for group advanced bookings.
Facilities:	Restaurant, Gift Shop, Picnic Area, Plant Sales, Shop, Brick & Turf Maze, Wendy House.
Disabled Access:	Yes. Toilet and parking for disabled on site.
Tours/Events:	Parham Garden Weekend, 11th, 12th July 2009.
Coach Parking:	Yes. No Charge.
Length of Visit:	2 - 3 hours
Booking Contact:	Parham House & Gardens, Storrington, Pulborough, West Sussex, RH20 4HS. Telephone: 01903 742021 or 744888 (information line) Fax: 01903 746557.
Email:	bookings@parhaminsussex.co.uk
Website:	www.parhaminsussex.co.uk
Location:	Parham is located on the A283 midway between Storrington and Pulborough, Equidistant from the A24 or A29.

Please quote this guide when making a booking

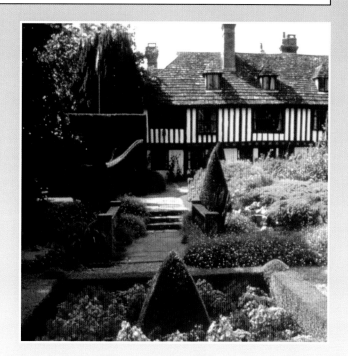

Listed by 'The Independent' as one of Britain's ten best gardens with literary connections.

A short lime avenue leads to the Topiary Garden with its amusing animals and birds in clipped box and yew. Beyond the stone balustraded bridge a riot of hollyhocks can be seen in high summer in front of the fifteenth-century timber-framed house. The yew tunnel through the stone arch leads to the mysterious ivy-clad Monks' Walk. The upper lawn is enclosed by herbaceous borders, while the lower lawn has clipped yew hedges and roses, with an exceptional example of the prehistoric tree Ginkgo Biloba and, further down, a colourful bog garden and tidal stream.

The five acres of gardens include the Victorian 'Secret' Garden, with its 40-metre fruit wall, original heated pineapple pits and stove house. The Rose Garden was planted to commemorate the Queen's Golden Jubilee. The Terracotta Garden has been planted with box parterres, complemented by colourful herbaceous borders, and in the English Poetry Garden there is an inner circle of yew, joining a long curved pergola. The Victorian Boulton and Paul potting shed now houses a Rural Museum of horticultural implements from the family farms.

Fact File

Opening Times:	May to end of September (House and Gardens).
	Public open afternoons Suns, Thurs, BH Mondays 2-6pm (last entry 5pm).
	Groups at other times by appointment.
Admission Rates:	Adults £7.00, Senior Citizen £6.50, Child £3.00.
Group Rates:	Groups (of 25 or more).
	Adults £6.50, Child £3.00.
Facilities:	Gift Shop, Teas, Car Park.
Disabled Access:	Partial.
Tours/Events:	Guided tours of House and Gardens for groups.
Coach Parking:	Yes.
Length of Visit:	2 - 3 hours.
Booking Contact:	Jean Whitaker
	St Mary's House, Bramber, West Sussex, BN44 3WE.
	Tel: 01903 816205 Fax: 01903 816205
Email:	info@stmarysbramber.co.uk
Website:	www.stmarysbramber.co.uk
Location:	8 miles NE of Worthing off A283 in Bramber Village, 1 mile east of Steyning.

Please quote this guide when making a booking

Created over the last decade the gardens are mature and varied. Visitors can enjoy the delights within the different areas: The Courtyard with Elizabethan Knot Garden, The Walled Garden, The Courtyard, The Bog Garden, Riverside and Lake Walks amongst others.

Opened in 1996 the Walled Garden is a splendid example of individual 'garden rooms'. One of the most spectacular is the Rose Labyrinth, celebrated during the annual Rose Festival in June when it becomes rich with colour and perfume. In 2006, this garden was given an "Award of Garden Excellence" by the World Federation of Rose Societies, the first time ever it has been awarded in the UK. There are beautiful 'hot' and 'cold' herbaceous borders containing plants, nurtured at Coughton Court, which are also on sale to visitors.

Thanks to the enthusiasm of the Throckmorton family, who have lived at Coughton Court for 600 years, the gardens are now considered to be some of the finest in the country.

Fact File

Opening Times:	Please call our info line on 01789 762542 or visit our website www.coughtoncourt.co.uk for details.
Admission Rates:	Please call to confirm 2009 admission prices or visit our website.
Group Rates:	Minimum group size: 15 (paying visitors) House & Gardens: £7.20, Gardens only: £5.00
Facilities:	Shop, Plant Sales, Teas, Restaurant, Gunpowder Plot Exhibition.
Disabled Access:	Yes (Gardens only), Toilet and parking for disabled on site.
Tours/Events:	There is a programme of events from April to October (see website).
Parking:	All Cars Free of Charge. Coaches by prior arrangement.
Length of Visit:	3 hours
Booking Contact:	Coughton Court, Alcester, Warwickshire, B49 5JA. Telephone: 01789 400777 Fax: 01789 764369
Email:	office@throckmortons.co.uk
Website:	www.coughtoncourt.co.uk
Location:	Take the A435 from Alcester towards Birmingham, the House is signposted from the road.

Please quote this guide when making a booking

Ragley Hall Warwickshire

Although Ragley's 400 acres of parkland were designed by Lancelot 'Capability' Brown during the 18th century, little is known about the gardens prior to 1873, when Victorian garden designer, Robert Marnock created a formal flower garden intended to show off plants discovered in the New World.

The management and maintenance of the gardens now aims to optimise habitat and food resources for insects, birds and small mammals. The result is a garden in which traditional horticultural features incorporate, and exist alongside, valuable wildlife habitat.

The success of this naturalistic approach demonstrates that it is possible to maintain the horticultural interest and aesthetic appeal of a garden, without compromising native flora and fauna or limiting bio diversity.

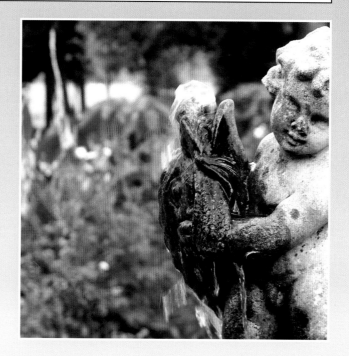

Fact File

Opening times:	10 a.m. – 6 p.m. weekends and school holidays
Admission Rates:	(2008), Adults: £8.50, Senior Citizens: £7.00, Children: £5.00
Group Rates:	Minimum Group Size: 20, Adults: £7.50, Senior Citizens: £6.00, Children: £4.50
Facilities:	Shop, Restaurant, Teas
Disabled Access:	Yes. Wheelchair loan available – booking required
Toilets on site:	Yes
Car Parking on site:	Yes
Coach Parking:	Yes
Guided Tours:	Yes, booking required.
Length of Visit:	2 hours for gardens, plus further 2 hours to visit woodland walk and house
Booking Contact:	Sabrina Davey, Ragley Hall, Alcester Warwickshire, B48 5NJ
	Booking Tel No.01789 762090, Booking Fax No. 01789 768691
Email:	ragley@ragleyhall.com
Website:	www.ragleyhall.com
Location:	Ragley is situated 2 miles southwest of Alcester, off the A435/A46

Garden Organic Ryton is home to the UK's leading organic growing charity showcasing ten acres of stunning organic display gardens. These demonstrate all aspects of domestic horticulture including herbs, roses, lawns, shrubberies, herbaceous planting and vegetable and fruit growing.

The gardens are full of information for gardeners on organic techniques including composting and pest and disease control. The grounds also boast a large conservation area with native trees and wild flowers, a bee garden, living willow structures and the world's first public biodynamic garden.

The Vegetable Kingdom, an interactive visitor centre, houses Garden Organic's world renowned Heritage Seed Library which conserves hundreds of threatened vegetable varieties.

The site is also home to an award winning restaurant and shop where organic, local and sustainable produce, including delicious home cooked food, gifts and products, are available to buy.

Fact File

Opening Times: 9am - 6pm in summer, 9am - 5pm in winter. Open 7 days a week.

Admission Rates: Adults £6.00 (admits 1 child free), Concessions £5.50, £3.00 for additional child, members go free.

Facilities: Visitor centre, award winning shop & restaurant, garden café, plant sales, picnic area, large car park.

Disabled Access: Disabled toilet and parking facilities. Mobility scooters available – booking necessary. Braille Guidebook.

Tours/Events: Annual programme of events. Garden tours and group visits available to book.

Coach Parking: Yes.

Length of Visit: Half a day

Booking Contact: Garden Organic Ryton, Wolston Lane, Coventry, CV8 3LG. Telephone: 02476 303517 Fax: 02476 639229

Email: enquiry@gardenorganic.org.uk

Website: www.gardenorganic.org.uk

Location: Just off the A45 on the road to Wolston, five miles south east of Coventry.

Please quote this guide when making a booking

The Shakespeare Gardens Warwickshire

The Shakespeare Gardens contain many of the plants and herbs mentioned in Shakespeare's writing and are immaculately maintained by a dedicated team of gardeners.

Each garden has its own unique character and reflects traditional gardening styles and practices from the 16th Century to the present day. Features include The Cottage Garden, Orchard, Sculpture Garden, romantic willow cabin and a new Woodland Walk at Anne Hathaway's Cottage; an Elizabethan-style Knot Garden and historic Great Garden at Nash's House & New Place and a herbal bed and ancient mulberry tree at Hall's Croft.

Garden Tours: Groups can enjoy a fully escorted tour of the gardens of their choice with our award winning Head Gardener. Choose from:

The Town Gardens – Nash's House & New Place gardens include an Elizabethan-style knot garden a pleached alley and the historic Great Garden whilst Hall's Croft's tranquil walled garden encloses a formal herbal bed, glorious herbaceous borders and a rose garden.

Anne Hathaway's Cottage boasts an award-winning Victorian cottage garden, an orchard, a pretty woodland walk, a gardens-themed exhibition and a growing willow cabin.

Fact File

Opening times:	Opening times vary, please see website for details. The Shakespeare Houses & Gardens are open all year except December 25 and 26
Admission Rates:	Prices vary – please see website for details. RHS Members Free
Facilities:	Visitor Centre, Shop, Plant Sales, Restaurant,Teas
Disabled Access:	Yes – limited. Wheelchair loan available.
Toilets on site:	Yes
Car Parking on site:	Yes, only at AHC and Mary Arden's Farm
Coach Parking:	Yes – at AHC, Birthplace and Mary Arden's Farm.
Length of Visit:	Each house varies – approximately 1 – 2 hours
Guided Tours:	Yes
Special Events:	Please see website for details
Booking Contact:	The Shakespeare Houses, The Shakespeare Centre, Henley Street, Stratford-upon-Avon, CV37 6QW Booking Tel No.01789 201806. Booking Fax No. 01789 263138
Email:	groups@shakespeare.org.uk
Website:	www.shakespeare.org.uk

Please quote this guide when making a booking

Beside the Abbey Church in Malmesbury and straddling the River Avon, this truly spectacular 5 acre garden has brought praise from around the world.

These are just some of the comments from our visitors' book:

"I thought I'd seen all the best gardens in the world – until now!"
"The loveliest truly English garden on the planet!"
"This garden alone made my visit to the UK worthwhile"

With over 1000 years of history, burial place of an English King, knot gardens, herb gardens, river walk, monastic fishponds, waterfall over 2000 different roses (largest collection in the UK) over 100,000 tulips, 10,000 different plants with constant colour from March to November, these 5 acres are a must see garden and history experience with approx. half an hour drive from Bath.

p.s. you can even get married here!

Fact File

Opening Times:	11am - 5.30pm 21st March - 31st October
Admission Rates:	Adults £6.50, Concessions £5.75, Children £2.50
Group Rates:	Minimum Group Size: 20. £5.50 per person.
Facilities:	Plant Sales, Teas.
Disabled Access:	Yes.
Tours/Events:	Plays, Demonstrations, Sculpture and Exhibitions. Also licensed for Civil Marriage/Partnerships, See website for additional information.
Coach Parking:	Yes.
Length of Visit:	2 hours minimum
Booking Contact:	Geraldine Wilkins. Abbey House Gardens, Market Cross, Malmesbury, Wiltshire, SN16 9AS Tel: 01666 827650, Fax: 01666 822782
Email:	info@abbeyhousegardens.co.uk
Website:	www.abbeyhousegardens.co.uk
Location:	In Malmesbury town centre. Off A429 between M4 junction 17 (5miles) and Cirencester (12 miles). Coaches drop passengers in centre of town, 3 minute level walk from garden. Cars follow signs for long stay car park from Malmesbury town centre. Garden is 5 min walk across the bridge, up the Abbey steps and entered left of Cloister Garden.

Please quote this guide when making a booking

Bowood Rhododendron Woodland Garden　　　Wiltshire

The Bowood Rhododendron Woodland Garden is a sixty acre Aladdin's cave of ericaceous plants. It lies on a seam of greensand fed by multiple springs. The peak flowering season is from April, through to early June. In late April, the under storey is carpeted with bluebells. Towering above are magnificent scented Loderi and Kewensis with huge pink trusses, followed in May and June, by the earliest known hardy hybrids introduced in 1854, many of which are unique to this garden. Plants thrive in this microclimate. A group of Lacteum brought back as seed by Mr. Roy Lancaster in 1979 are now eight feet high, and flower profusely.

The rides through this woodland garden cover approximately four miles. Visitors should allow at least two hours to explore this paradise. Also visit Bowood House, Gardens and Arboretum, which are reached by a separate access and car park. So why not make it a day out?

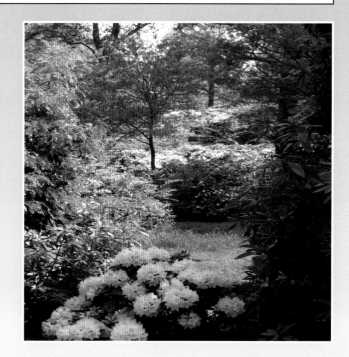

Fact File

Opening times: 11.00 – 18.00 Mid April – early June
Admission Rates: Adults: £5.60, Senior Citizens: £5.10, Children: FOC
Facilities: Toilets.
Disabled Access: Limited, bookable wheelchair loan available.
Tours/Events: None.
Coach Parking: Yes
Length of Visit: Minimum of 2 hours
Booking Contact: Mrs. Jane Meadows
　　　　　　　　　　Bowood House, Calne Wiltshire SN11 0LZ
　　　　　　　　　　Telephone:01249 812102
　　　　　　　　　　Fax: 01249 821757
Email: houseandgardens@bowood.org
Website: www.bowood.org
Location: Off A342 between Derry Hill and Sandy Lane. 8 miles south of Junction 17, M4.

Great Chalfield Manor & Gardens Wiltshire

Alfred Parsons designed Arts and Crafts gardens to complement restoration of the manor in 1905-1912. He kept the large lawn but designed terraces, walls, flagged paths, topiary pavilions beside a lily pond, and cedar over a gazebo with swept roof in local stone: creating subtle frameworks for the future.

Snowdrops and aconites sparkle around the springfed lower moat; daffodils, tulips and Queen Anne's lace follow in the orchard. A charming rill is fed from the upper moat or mill pond. Roses flourish: Caroline Testout and Bennetts' Seedling in the forecourt, Old Blush China in the churchyard, Natalie Nyples surrounds the well, Rambling Rector and Sanders White climb in apples, and The Fairy tumbles in profusion to the lower moat.

In autumn asters flower below the terrace, Virginia creeper then willows flame at the entrance. Robert Fuller gave his Manor to the National Trust in 1943, it is now home to his grandson's family who have replanted the gardens. The house and garden feature in the new film 'The Other Boleyn Girl'.

Fact File

Opening Times:	Garden open Tuesday, Wednesdays, Thursday, 11am - 5pm. Manor Admission by guided tour Tuesday – Thursday 11, 12, 2, 3 & 4 Sunday: Garden open 2pm – 5pm. Manor tours at 2, 3 & 4.
Admission Rates:	Adults: £6.70 (Garden only: £4.40) Senior Citizens: N/A, Children: £3.40 (Garden only: £2.20), Family: £16.80
Group Rates:	Minimum Group Size: 15 Adults: £5.70, Senior Citizens: N/A, Children: £2.90
Disabled Access:	No – photo album available. Garden partly accessible. Car parking and toilet on site.
Tours/Events:	Yes.
Coach Parking:	Drop-off point
Length of Visit:	Whole visit: 1 hour, 30 minutes.
Booking Contact:	Mrs. R. Floyd Great Chalfield Manor & Garden. Nr. Melksham, Wiltshire SN12 8NH Tel: 01225 782239
Email:	greatchalfieldmanor@nationaltrust.org.uk
Website:	www.nationaltrust.org.uk/greatchalfieldmanor
Location:	3 miles south-west of Melksham, off B3107, via Broughton Gifford Common.

Please quote this guide when making a booking

Romantically sited overlooking the valley of the River Frome, close to Bradford-on-Avon, Iford Manor is built into the hillside below a hanging beechwood and fine garden terraces. The house was owned during the first part of the last century by Harold Peto, the architect and landscape designer who taught Lutyens, and who expressed his passion for classical Italian architecture and landscaping in an English setting, After many visits to Italy he acquired statues and architectural marbles. He planted phillyrea and cypress trees and other Mediterranean species to add to the plantings of the eighteenth century and to enhance the Italian character of the garden.

The great terrace is bounded on one side by an elegant colonnade and commands lovely views out over the orchard and the surrounding countryside. Paths wander through the Woodland and garden to the summerhouse, the cloister and the casita and amongst the water features.

Fact File

Opening Times:	2pm - 5pm Sundays April and October. 2pm - 5pm Tuesdays - Thursdays, Saturday, Sunday and Bank Holiday Mondays, May to September. Mornings and Mondays and Fridays reserved for group visits by Appointment.
Admission Rates:	Adults £4.50, Senior Citizen £4.00, Child over 10 yrs £4.00.
Group Rates:	Minimum group size: 8 Adults £5.00, Senior Citizen £5.00, Child over 10 yrs £5.00 for visits outside normal hours.
Facilities:	House Keeper Teas - May to August at weekends, Mini teas weekdays.
Disabled Access:	Yes, Toilet and parking for disabled on site.
Tours/Events:	By appointment
Coach Parking:	Yes.
Length of Visit:	1-1½ hours
Booking Contact:	Mrs Elizabeth Cartwright-Hignett Iford Manor, Bradford on Avon, Wiltshire BA15 2BA Telephone:01225 863146 Fax: 01225 862364
Website:	www.ifordmanor.co.uk
Location:	Follow brown tourist signs to Iford Manor:- 7 miles south of Bath on A36 Warminster Road and ½ mile south of Bradford on Avon on B3109.

Please quote this guide when making a booking

Often referred to as "Paradise", Stourhead is an exquisite example of an English landscape garden. It was once described by Horace Walpole as 'one of the most picturesque scenes in the world'.

Visitors can discover the inspiration behind Henry Hoare II's world famous garden, laid out between 1741 and 1780 and enjoy breathtaking views all year round.

The garden is dotted with Classical temples including the Pantheon and the Temple of Apollo, which provide a dramatic backdrop to the majestic lake, secluded valley and magnificent trees.

Stourhead House, an 18th century Palladian Mansion, is situated at the top of the gardens surrounded by lawns and parkland.

The Stourhead Estate extends east to King Alfred's Tower, a 160 foot folly 2½ miles from the House which affords stunning views across three counties, and is the perfect place for picnics. Visitors can also enjoy breathtaking walks across Whitesheet Hill's chalk downs, and explore the mature woodland packed with an exciting range of trees, and a rich array of native wildlife.

Fact File

Opening Times: Garden open all year daily 9am-7pm.. House open Friday-Tuesday 14th March-1st November, 11am-5pm, last entry 4.30pm
King Alfred's Tower open daily, 14th March-1st November, 11am-5pm, last entry 4.30pm.

Admission Rates: Garden & House: Adults £12.30*, Child £6.10*. Garden or House: Adults £7.40*, Child £4*. National Trust members free.
Includes a voluntary donation but visitors can choose to pay the standard prices displayed at the property and on the website.

Group Rates: Minimum group size 15: Garden & House £10.40, Garden or House £6.30, NT members free.

Facilities: Visitor Centre, Shop, Plant Centre, Self-service Restaurant, Farm Shop, Spread Eagle Inn, Art Gallery, Ice Cream Parlour, Licensed Civil Ceremony venue.

Disabled Access: Toilets, parking. Shuttle Bus March to October. Sympathetic hearing scheme. Assistance dogs welcome. Wheelchairs, Self-drive mobility vehicle, Stair-climber available advance booking.

Tours/Events: See our fascinating exhibition and film 'Servants' in the basement of the House. Opportunity to see conservation in action while the Temple of Apollo undergoes restoration.

Coach Parking: Yes.

Length of Visit: Minimum 2 hours.

Booking Contact: Georgina Mead. Stourhead Estate Office, Stourton, Nr Mere, Warminster, Wiltshire BA12 6QD Tel: 01747 841152 Fax: 01747 842005

Email: stourhead@nationaltrust.org.uk

Website: www.nationaltrust.org.uk/stourhead

Location: Stourhead is in the village of Stourton, off the B3092, 3 miles north west of Mere (A303). It is 8 miles south of Frome (A361).

Please quote this guide when making a booking

Come and enjoy the beautiful landscape of Croome Park, 'Capability' Brown's first complete design. Brown's work was commissioned by the 6th Earl of Coventry and established the principles of the 'English Landscape Style' – an idealised vision of nature.

Visitors can stroll through winding shrubberies to discover temples, grottos and a lakeside garden. There are walks through the meadows to the newly restored Park Seat where you can marvel at the views across the landscape as you relax.

You can learn about the secret work of RAF Defford in a restored WWII building, or simply relax and enjoy a slice of cake in the 1940s-style canteen.

Why not come and experience one of Worcestershire's most enchanting landscapes for yourself? Now in its 13th year of restoration, Croome gives you a unique opportunity to see a landscape in the making.

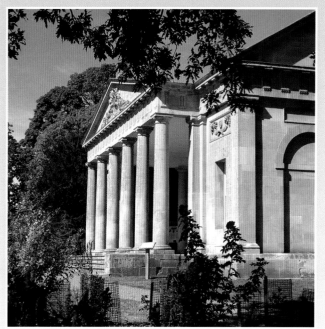

Fact File

Opening Times: Jan & Feb, Saturday & Sunday 10am - 4pm.
4th - 29th March & 2nd Sept - 1st Nov, Wed - Sun 10am - 5.30pm.
30th March - 31st Aug, daily 10am - 5.30pm.
7th Nov - 20th Dec, Sat & Sun 10am - 4pm.
26th Dec - 3rd Jan, Daily 10.00am - 4.00pm.

Admission Rates: Adults £5.00, Child (6-16) £2.50. Family £12.60. NT Members and under 5's Free

Group Rates: Minimum Groups Size: 15 Adults: £4.25

Facilities: 1940's style canteen, 1940's exhibition.

Disabled Access: Yes. Toilet and parking on site. Wheelchair Loan and powered mobility vehicles available.

Tours/Events: Guided tours available at £8.50 each. Full programme of events. Please call for information.

Coach Parking: Yes.

Length of Visit: 2 hours

Booking Contact: Amy Fox. Croome Park, NT Estate Office, Builders Yard, High Green, Severn Stoke, Worcestershire WR8 9JS
Telephone: 01905 371006 Fax: 01905 371090
For information on the opening of Croome Court please contact 01905 371006

Email: croomepark@nationaltrust.org.uk

Website: www.nationaltrust.org.uk/croomepark

Location: 9 Miles south of Worcester. Signposted on A38 and B4084.

Please quote this guide when making a booking

Hanbury Hall was completed in 1701 by Thomas Vernon and is a fine example of a William and Mary-style house which is surrounded by 20 acres of a stunning recreated George London garden and 400 acres of park.

Keen to have an up to date and fashionable garden, Thomas employed the pre-eminent garden designer of the day, George London, to create such a garden which was to include all the elements associated with the formal style of gardening; a Parterre, Fruit Garden, Wilderness, Grove and Bowling Green. The garden remained as such until the 1770's when it was swept away as the fashions changed from the very formal to the natural landscape style.

In the mid 1990's with help from generous bequests and a European Union grant, the garden was carefully restored using the distinguished surveyor, James Dougherty's, 1731-1733 garden survey, the original plan and archaeological work to confirm the garden design accuracy. Today the gardens are truly spectacular; from the beautiful intricately laid out formal parterre, fruit garden and grove to the bowling green, a visit to Hanbury Hall's garden is unforgettable.

Fact File

Opening times:	28 February 2009 – 1 November 2009: 11.00 – 5.30; November 09 – February 2010: 11.00 – 4.00. 28 February – 15 March: weekends only. 16 March – 1 November: Saturday – Wednesday. 7 November – 20 February 2010 weekends only (house closed January & February 2010) Garden, park, café and shop open 7 days a week during local school holidays and July & August.
Admission Rates:	(park, garden, shop, tearoom, café): Adults: £5.00 + house: £2.60 Senior Citizens: £5.00+ house: £2.60, Child: £2.50 + house: £1.30
Group Rates:	Minimum Group Size for house & garden 15. Adults: £6.30, Senior Citizens: £6.30, Child: No group rate for children. NT members free.
Facilities:	Visitor Centre, Shop, Plant Sales, Restaurant, Teas, children's play area.
Disabled Access:	Yes. Wheelchair loan – booking required.
Toilets on site:	Yes
Car Parking on site:	Yes
Coach Parking:	Yes
Guided Tours:	Yes, booking required.
Length of visit:	3 hours
Special Events:	Various throughout the year – check website for details.
Booking Contact:	Emily Knight, Hanbury Hall, School Road, Hanbury, Droitwich Spa, Worcestershire WR9 7EA Booking Tel No.01527 822102 Booking Fax No. 01527 821251
Email:	hanburyhall@nationaltrust.org.uk
Website:	www.nationaltrust.org/hanburyhall
Location:	From M5 exit follow A38 to Droitwich. From Droitwich, 4.5 miles along B4090.

Please quote this guide when making a booking

Spetchley Park Gardens

This lovely 30 acre garden is owned by the Berkeley family, whose other home is historic 12th Century Berkeley Castle in Gloucestershire.

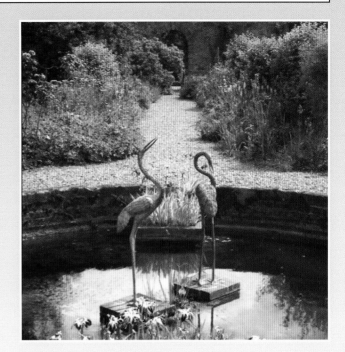

At Spetchley you will find most aspects of gardening, the formal and informal, woodland and herbaceous. A Garden full of secrets, every corner reveals some new vista, some new treasure of the plant world, whether it be tree, shrub or plant. The exuberant planting and the peaceful walks make this an oasis of peace and quiet. Many of the vast collection of plants are rarely found outside the major botanical gardens. The wonderful display of spring bulbs in April and May, together with flowering trees and shrubs, are followed in June and July by the large selection of roses, whilst July, August and September reveal the great herbaceous borders in all their glory. This is indeed a garden for all seasons.

Fact File

Opening times: 21st March - 30th September. Wednesday - Sunday 11am - 6pm, 1st - 31st October. Saturdays and Sundays 11am - 4pm. Bank Holiday Mondays 11am - 6pm. Last admissions one hour before closing.

Admission Rates: Adults £6.00, Senior Citizen £5.50, Under 16s free. Adults Season Tickets £25.00

Group Rates: Minimum group size: 25 Adults £5.00, Senior Citizen £5.00, Child £1.90.

Facilities: Tea Room

Disabled Access: Partial. Parking for disabled on site, Booking necessary for parties. (Access restricted, please telephone contact details below for advice).

Tours/Events: See website for details.

Coach Parking: Yes.

Length of Visit: 2 hours minimum.

Booking Contact: Berkeley Estate Office, Ham, Berkeley, Gloucestershire GL13 9QL. Tel: 01453 810303 Fax: 01453 511915

Email: hb@spetchleygardens.co.uk

Website: www.spetchleygardens.co.uk

Location: 2 miles east of Worcester on A44, leave M5 at either junctions 6 or 7

Please quote this guide when making a booking

Stone House Cottage Garden   Worcestershire

A ¾ acre garden created in the last thirty years. James Arbuthnott has embellished the existing red brick Victorian walls of the garden with an eclectic collection of follies and towers while Louisa has covered both with an equally eclectic collection of unusual climbers. Within the walls the garden has been skilfully divided into a series of 'rooms' by hedges of differing sorts. In these she grows and maintains a staggering array of plants from the ordinary to the weird and wonderful. From spring until late summer this acclaimed garden has plenty of botanical delights to interest the enthusiastic plants person as well as colour and fragrance to charm the casual visitor.

A very personal and ever changing collection of plants reflects the owner's tastes making this an intimate, unusual and very English garden. It also serves as shop window for the renowned adjoining nursery.

Fact File

Opening Times: Mid march to Mid September (March 18th - September 12th):
Admission Rates: Adults: £3.00, Senior Citizens: £3.00
Group Rates: Adults: As above, Senior Citizens: As above
Facilities: Large nursery stocked with rare plants.
Disabled Access: Partial. Toilet and parking on site.
Tours/Events: Pre-arranged evening visits welcomed (minimum 15) £4.00 with a glass of wine.
Coach Parking: No (nearby)
Length of Visit: 1½ - 2 hours
Booking Contact: Stone House Cottage Garden, Stone, Nr. Kidderminster, Worcestershire DY10 4BG
Tel: 01562 69902
Email: louisa@shcn.co.uk
Website: www.shcn.co.uk
Location: 2 miles out of Kidderminster on A448 (Bromsgrove Road).
The drive next to the church leads to the garden.

Please quote this guide when making a booking

Winners of 2005 HHA Christies Garden of the Year Award

Burton Agnes is a magnificent Elizabethan Hall surrounded by lawns, topiary yew bushes and beautiful award winning gardens. The eastern aspect of the house showcases a classical pond with beautiful fountains and a newly created pebble mosaic. To the right of the house lies an Elizabethan walled garden, home to over 3,000 different plants , a potager of herbs and vegetables, fruit beds, herbaceous borders, a jungle garden and even a maze! Contained within the walled garden is also a National Collection of campanulas, a fantastic knot garden with coloured themed gardens and giant board games.

Fact File

Opening Times:	Snowdrop Opening 7th Feb to 1st March.
	Christmas Opening 14th November to 20th December
Admission Rates:	Adults: £4.00, Senior Citizens: £3.50, Children: £2.50.
Facilities:	Shops, Plant Sales, Café.
Disabled Access:	Yes. Toilet and car parking on site. Wheelchair loan available please book.
Tours/Events:	Guided tours available. Introductory talks if requested for groups.
	Orchid Weekend 7th and 8th March.
	Everything open 1st April to 31st October.
	Easter Egg Weekend 12th and 13th April.
	Gardeners Fair 6th and 7th June.
	Michaelmas Fair 24th and 25th October
	Contact the booking office for details.
Coach Parking:	Yes
Length of Visit:	1 hour.
Booking Contact:	Natasha Taylor
	Burton Agnes Hall & Gardens, Burton Agnes, Driffield YO25 4NB.
	Telephone 01262 490324 Fax: 01262 490513
Email:	office@burtonagnes.com
Website:	www.burtonagnes.com
Location:	On A614 between Driffield and Bridlington.

The early 18th Century green gardens of 35 acres (14ha) have been described as "the supreme masterpiece of the art of the landscape gardener". Peace and tranquillity reign supreme in this classical English setting – a rare survivor of a style of gardening using the natural landscape.

The designer is unknown although it has been suggested that either Switzer or Bridgeman, or both, may have been involved. The parterres to the North and South of the house were added in the middle of the 19th Century and along with the conservatory are the only additions that have been made to the garden since it was landscaped in the middle of the 18th Century. Explore at leisure the great lawn and level terraces, temples, yew tree walk, woodland walks and the scented 'secret garden' around the conservatory.

Fact File

Opening Times:	Sunday 12th April – Sunday 25th October, Sunday – Thursday. Closed 24th, 25th & 29th June. Parkland Centre: 11.00a.m. – 5.30p.m. Garden: 11.00a.m. – 5.30p.m., Last Admission 4.30p.m. House – by Guided Tour only. Tours: 12.30p.m., 1.30p.m., 2.30p.m. & 3.30p.m.
Admission Rates:	House & Gardens: Adult: £8.25, Concession: £6.25, Child 10-16 yrs: £3.75 (under 5's Free) Family (2 adults & 2 children 5-16 yrs): £17.00, E.H. Members: £4.50. Gardens & Parkland: Adult: £5.00, Child 10-16 yrs: £2.00 (under 5's Free). Parkland: Adult: £3.00, Concession: £4.50, Child 5-16 yrs: £3.00 (under 10's Free). Season Ticket: Family (2 adults & 2 children 5-16 yrs) £35.00, Adult: £20.00
Group Rates:	House & Gardens (15 or more): £5.75. Gardens & Parkland (15 or more): £4.00 or Group Guided Tour £5.00
Facilities:	Visitor Centre, Shop, Restaurant, Teas.
Disabled Access:	No, only partial to the garden. Bookable wheelchair loan available.
Toilets on site:	Yes.
Tours/Events:	Guided tours available, booking required.
Coach Parking:	Yes.
Car Parking on site:	Yes.
Length of Visit:	3 hours.
Booking Contact:	Mrs. E M Williams, House Manager, Duncombe Park, Helmsley, York, YO62 5EB Telephone: 01439 772625 Fax: 01439 772114
Email:	liz@duncombepark.com
Website:	www.duncombepark.com
Location:	1 mile from A170 entrance in the centre of Helmsley.

Please quote this guide when making a booking

Fountains Abbey and Studley Royal Water Garden North Yorkshire

Yorkshire's first World Heritage site is a truly remarkable place encompassing nearly 900 years of history.

Once wild and wooded, this landscape was transformed into one of England's most spectacular Georgian water gardens by the Aislabie family. Conserved to look much as it would in the 18th century, this elegant ornamental garden is adorned with neo-classical statues, temples and follies which appear reflected in long mirror-like stretches of water. Take in the formal geometric design with beautifully contrived vistas, majestic sweeping avenues and breathtaking surprise views. Let yourself be transported to another era where peace and tranquillity reign.

The perfect complement to the garden is 12th century Fountains Abbey, landscaped into the garden as the ultimate surprise view. Lose yourself in the passages, staircases and towers of the largest, best-preserved monastic ruins in the country, and marvel at a unique relic of ancient craftsmanship.

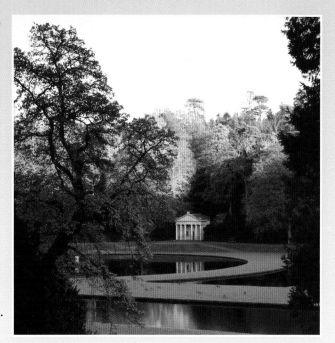

Fact File

Opening Times: March - October 10am - 5pm, November - February 10am - 4pm.
Closed Fridays in November - January and closed 24th and 25th December.

Admission Rates: Adults £8.25, Child £4.40, Family's £22.00,
NT/EH Members Free. Under 5's Free.

Groups Rates: Group discounts and bespoke tours available, call the Group Visits Organiser on 01765 643197.

Facilities: Shop, Tea Room, Restaurant, Kiosk and Play Area.

Disabled Access: Yes. Toilet and parking for disabled on site.
Personal Mobility Vehicles on loan, booking necessary.

Tours/Events: Guided Tours for groups, must be pre booked, telephone 01765 643197.
Annual events programme, please enqire for details.

Coach Parking: Yes

Length of Visit: 1½ hours minimum.

Booking Contact: Fountains Abbey, Ripon, Yorkshire, HG4 3DY
Telephone: 01765 608888   Fax: 01765 601002

Email: fountainsenquiries@nationaltrust.org.uk

Website: www.fountainsabbey.org.uk   www.nationaltrust.org.uk

Location: 4 miles west of Ripon of B6265 to Pateley Bridge, signposted from A1,
10 miles north of Harrogate A61.

Please quote this guide when making a booking

Wander through tranquil surroundings in this stunning 58 acre garden and pick up the latest tips and techniques for your own borders...or simply relax with family and friends on a leisurely stroll.

Find inspiration in the innovative Main Borders with their creative combinations of mixed perennials, grasses and roses, beautifully combined with sustainable practices and admire the dramatic Rose Revolution Borders - planting with a contemporary twist! Meander through 200 years of gardening history in the Gardens through Time, take practical ideas from the raised beds in the extensive Kitchen Garden, enjoy the beautiful Streamside Garden and the enticing Scented Garden.
The garden offers interest for all seasons from spring bulb displays, through rich summer & autumn colour to the frosted silhouettes of winter.

Year-round events include activities for all the family - outdoor theatre, guided walks, workshops, demonstrations. Visit the extensive RHS Shop & Plant Centre, and linger over delicious goodies in Bettys Café Tea Rooms.

Fact File

Opening Times: 9.30am - 6pm (4pm Nov - Feb incl.) with last entry 1 hour before closing.
Admission Rates: (2009 prices) Adults £7.00, Child (6-16yrs) £2.50 (under 6 Free).
Groups Rates: Minimum group size 10, Adults £6.00.
Facilities: Largest Gardening Bookshop in the north, Bettys Cafe Tea Rooms, RHS Gift Shop & Plant Centre, Library.
Disabled Access: Yes. Toilet and parking for disabled on site. Wheelchairs on loan, booking necessary.
On The Website: A full programme of events is available from the gardens or from the website.
Coach Parking: Yes
Length of Visit: 2 hours
Booking Contact: The Admin Department
RHS Garden Harlow Carr, Crag Lane, Harrogate, HG3 1QB
Tel: 01423 565418 Fax: 01423 530663
Email: harlowcarr@rhs.org.uk
Website: www.rhs.org.uk/harlowcarr
Location: Take the B6162 Otley Road out of Harrogate towards Beckwithshaw.
Harlow Carr is 1.5 miles on the right.

Please quote this guide when making a booking

Newby Hall was built between 1691-1695, shortly afterwards the owner, Sir Edward Blackett, commissioned Peter Aram to lay out formal gardens in keeping with the period. Very little of Aram's layout for Newby remains today and the present design is largely attributable to the present owner's grandfather, the late Major Edward Compton, who inherited in 1921. Influenced by Lawrence Johnston's Hidcote Manor in Gloucestershire, he created a main axis for the garden running from the south front of the house down to the River Ure. The axis consisted of double herbaceous borders flanked by yew hedges. Either side of the borders are numerous compartmented gardens such as the Rose Garden, the Autumn Garden, the Rock Garden, the Laburnum pergola walk, a Water Garden and even a Tropical Garden here in North Yorkshire - truly a 'Garden for all Seasons'. Newby also holds the National Collection of CORNUS.

Fact File

Opening Times:	1st April - 27th September 2008, 11am - 5.30pm, Tuesday - Sunday & Bank Holidays, and Mondays in July and August.
Admission Rates:	(2008 Rates). Adults £10.20, Senior Citizen £9.20, Child £7.80. (House & Garden Ticket)
Groups Rates:	Minimum group size 15
	Adults £8.50, Senior Citizen £8.50, Child £6.50. (House & Garden Ticket)
Facilities:	Visitor Centre, Shop, Plant Sales, Teas, Restaurant.
Disabled Access:	Yes. Toilet and parking for disabled on site. Wheelchairs on loan, booking necessary.
Tours/Events:	Tours on request with pre-booking essential.
Coach Parking:	Yes
Length of Visit:	2 hours minimum
Booking Contact:	Rosemary Triffit
	Newby Hall, Ripon, North Yorkshire, HG4 5AE
	Tel: 01423 322583 Fax: 01423 324452
Email:	info@newbyhall.com
Website:	www.newbyhall.com
Location:	2 miles from A1M at Ripon exit - junction 48.

Please quote this guide when making a booking

These substantial walled gardens and wooded pleasure grounds, recently restored and much improved, are well worth visiting in all seasons: massive herbaceous borders, Victorian Kitchen garden with rare vegetable collection, the National Hyacinth Collection, herb and shade borders, extensive hothouses and thousands of snowdrops, bluebells, daffodils and narcissi. A stroll around the lake takes you through the deer park, where fallow deer graze beneath the boughs of living oak trees, now believed to be over a thousand years old. This walk also offers the best views of the 14th century castle. Children will have fun spotting the faces on several of our older trees.

Guided tours of the castle give you a chance to view the civil war armour, secret priests hiding hole and splendid furnishings. On site facilities include ample free parking, wc's (including disabled), tea room, historic inn with beer garden and gift shop selling plants.

Fact File

Opening Times: Daily - Throughout the year 9am - 5pm (dusk in the winter months).
Admission Rates: Gardens, Adults £5.00, Senior Citizen £4.50, Child £3.50. (under 5 yrs Free)
Group Rates: Minimum group size 15 people
Gardens, Adults £4.50, Senior Citizen £4.50, Child £3.50.
Facilities: Gift Shop, Plant Sales, Tea Rooms, Restaurant, Children's play area.
Disabled Access: Yes. Toilet and parking for diabled on site. Wheelchairs on loan, booking necessary.
Tours/Events: Guided tours of gardens by prior arrangement only.
Coach Parking: Yes
Booking Contact: Jenny Carter
Ripley Castle Gardens, Ripley, Nr Harrogate, North Yorkshire, HG3 3AY
Telephone: 01423 770152 Fax: 01423 771745
Email: groups@ripleycastle.co.uk
Website: www.ripleycastle.co.uk
Location: Three miles north of Harrogate on the A61.

Please quote this guide when making a booking

The Walled Garden at Scampston

Set within the 18th century walls of the original kitchen garden for Scampston Hall, the 4¹/₂-acre Walled Garden has been completely redesigned by internationally acclaimed plantsman, Piet Oudolf, to produce a stunning garden with an unashamedly contemporary feel. Amongst nine contrasting garden rooms is a striking perennial meadow and a reflective silent garden. The 400m border walk contains many spring and autumn flowering shrubs and bulbs.

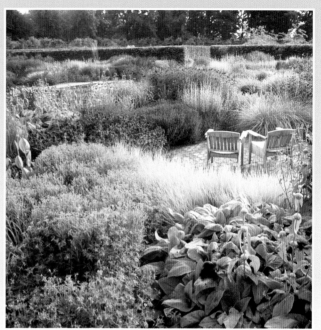

The plant sales area specialises in unusual species and, along with an excellent on-site restaurant, helps to make this a modern plantsman's paradise. 'It's bold and beautiful – a must if you are heading to Yorkshire' – Toparius

A self-guided Woodland Walk provides visitors with the opportunity to visit the traditional gardens around the Hall, including a splendid 19th century Rock Garden and 'Capability' Brown lakes and park.

Scampston Hall, open for a short period during the spring, is home to a superb collection of paintings, porcelain and furniture including pieces by Gainsborough, Scott and Chippendale.

Fact File

Opening Times:	10th April – 1st November: 10 a.m. – 5 p.m.
Admission Rates:	Walled Garden: Adults: £5.00, Children (12 – 16): £3.00. Under 12: free.
	RHS Members free except June - September.
	Woodland Walk: Adults £3.00, Children (12-16): £1.50. Under 12: free.
Group Rates:	Minimum Group Size: 20, Cost (Walled Garden): £4.50 including a free plant list.
Facilities:	Restaurant/teas, shop, plant sales, toilets.
Disabled Access:	Yes. Bookable wheelchair loan available
Car Parking on site:	Yes
Coach Parking:	Yes
Tours/Events:	Introductory talk available for pre-booked groups of 20+.
Length of Visit:	1¹/₂ - 2 hours
Special Events:	Spring Plant Fair Sunday 31st May 2009
	Annual events programme. Please enquire or see website for details.
Booking Contact:	The Administrator
	The Walled Garden at Scampston, Scampston Hall, Malton, North Yorkshire YO17 8NG
	Booking Telephone No. 01944 759111 Booking Fax No. 01944 758700
Email:	info@scampston.co.uk
Website:	www.scampston.co.uk
Location:	5 miles east of Malton on the north side of the A64.
	Just east of the village of Rillington.

Stillingfleet Lodge Garden & Nursery — Yorkshire

Walking around Stillingfleet Lodge Garden and Nurseries is a journey through one woman's passion for plants. Vanessa Cook, who is usually on hand to offer planting advice, held the National Collection of Pulmonaria and now turns her attention to trees as well as unusual perennials and climbers. She has created a charming country garden that combines cottage garden planting with traditional herbaceous borders. Abundant displays of shady planting and inspiring plant combinations with the emphasis on texture and shape, weave throughout a series of gardens creating a haven of peace. Interest continues around every corner with a wildflower meadow, wildlife pond, rare breeds of poultry and a contemporary rill garden which is a tranquil delight. Homemade cakes and refreshments are available in the converted barn. Complete your trip with a visit to the well-stocked nursery.

Fact File

Opening times: April 4th 2009 - Sept 30th 2009, Wednesday and Friday 1.00 p.m. – 5.00 p.m.
1st and 3rd Saturdays of each month 1.00 p.m. – 5.00 p.m.

Admission Rates: Adults: £4.00, Senior Citizens: £4.00, Children: 5 – 16 years: £0.50
RHS Members Free – on Wednesday afternoons

Group Rates: Minimum Group Size: 15
Adults: £4.00, Senior Citizens: £4.00, Children: 5 – 16 years: £0.50

Facilities: Visitor Centre, Plant Sales, Teas

Disabled Access: Yes

Toilets on site: Yes

Car Parking on site: Yes

Coach Parking: Yes – 200 yards away

Length of Visit: 1½ - 2 hours

Special Events: Courses for RHS and listed on the website.

Booking Contact: Vanessa Cook, Stillingfleet Lodge Garden and Nursery, Stewart Lane, Stillingfleet, York YO19 6HP
Booking Tel No. 01904 728506. Booking Fax No. 01904 728506

Email: vanessa.cook@stillingfleetlodgenurseries.co.uk

Website: www.stillingfleetlodgenurseries.co.uk

Location: 6 miles south of York on B1222. Brown sign opposite the church.

Please quote this guide when making a booking

Sutton Park Yorkshire

A wonderful and romantic garden located in the vale of York, not too far from most of the stunning areas of North Yorkshire countryside.

The garden has beautiful terraces, an exotic bamboo border, Edwardian fernery and overlooks the parkland which is bordered by a Woodland Walk. In the late spring the bluebells add to the attraction and from the Woodland Walk you can enter the garden under a tunnel of yellow provided by the Laburnum Walk.

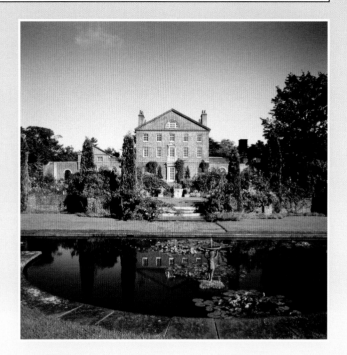

As we progress into summer old fashioned shrub roses and the herbaceous borders burst into colour. Other highlights include a fine old Ice House and magnificent specimen trees, an Austrian Pine being just one of many to note. A small but really interesting museum is crammed with many exhibits.

A visit to Sutton Park is an ideal way to relax and unwind.

Fact File

Opening times:	April – September: daily 11 a.m. – 5 p.m.
Admission Rates:	Adults: £3.50, Senior Citizens: £3.00, Children: £1.50
Facilities:	Shop, Plant Sales, Teas
Disabled Access:	Yes. Wheelchair loan available – booking required.
Toilets on site:	Yes
Car Parking on site:	Yes
Coach Parking:	Yes
Guided Tours:	Yes, booking required.
Length of Visit:	1 - 1.5 hours
Booking Contact:	Elaine Ellis, Sutton Park, Sutton on the Forest, York YO61 1DP Booking Tel No. 01347 810249, Booking Fax No. 01347 811251
Email:	suttonpark@statelyhome.co.uk
Website:	www.statelyhome.co.uk
Location:	8 miles north of York on B1363 in the village of Sutton on the Forest

Torosay Castle & Gardens - Isle of Mull

Scotland

'What a desolate place would be the world without a flower!
It would be a face without a smile, a feast without a welcome.

A.J. Balfour

Alongside such stunning castle garden landscapes as
Castle Kennedy, Cawdor and Torosay, we have this year for the first
time included in Gardens to Visit all four of the Scottish botanic gardens
for your visiting pleasure – Edinburgh, Logan, Benmore and Dawyck.
Between them they provide some of the most diverse garden landscapes
and plant collections to be found anywhere in the British Isles.

Armadale Castle Gardens & Museum of the Isles — Isle of Skye

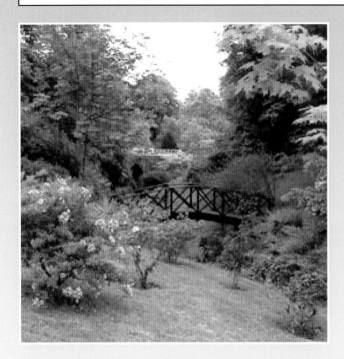

Armadale Castle Gardens & Museum of the Isles has a spectacular setting within the Sleat Peninsula of the Isle of Skye called the 'Garden of Skye'.

The forty acre Garden is set around the ruins of Armadale Castle. The warm, generally frost free climate of the west coast of Scotland - a result of the Gulf Stream - allows these sheltered gardens, dating back to the 17th Century, to flourish.

Wander over the expanses of lawn leading from the ruined Armadale Castle to viewpoints overlooking the hills of Knoydart. Terraced walks and landscaped ponds contrasting with wildflower meadows bring the natural and formal side by side. The Nature Trails provide another dimension to this garden experience. In May during the bluebell season, a carpet of blue around the Arboretum creates a visual and fragrance sensation that is so prevalent around the gardens at that time of year.

Fact File

Opening Times:	9.30am - 5.00pm (last entry 5pm), 7 days Easter Friday to 31st October.
Admission Rates:	Adults £6.00, Concessions £4.40, Child £4.40, Family £18.00.
Groups Rates:	Minimum group size: 8. £4.00.
Facilities:	40 Acres of Woodland Garden and mature Trails, Museum of the Isles, Restaurant, 3 Shops.
Disabled Access:	Yes, Toilet and Parking for disabled on site. Electric Wheelchairs on loan, booking necessary.
Tours/Events:	Guided walks on request. Audio tour available in Museum Of The Isles - French, German, Italian, Spanish, English and Gaelic, also available, a visually impaired tour in English.
Coach Parking:	Yes
Length of Visit:	2 hours
Booking Contact:	Mags MacDonald
	Armadale Castle, Armadale, Sleat, Isle of Skye, IV45 8RS
	Telephone: 01471 844305 Fax: 01471 844275
Email:	office@clandonald.com
Website:	www.clandonald.com
Location:	2 minutes from Armadale/Mallaig Ferry. 20 miles from Skyebridge on A851.

Please quote this guide when making a booking

Benmore Botanic Garden Argyll

Benmore with its magnificent mountainside setting is a joy to behold. Its 120 acres boast a world-famous collection of flowering trees and shrubs including over 300 species of rhododendron and over one third of the world's hardy conifer species plus fine collections from North and South America, the Orient and the Himalaya.

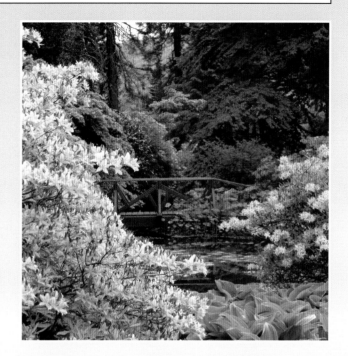

Visitors are welcomed by an impressive avenue of Giant Redwoods, arguably one of the finest entrances to any botanic garden in the world. Established in 1863, these majestic giants now stand over 50 metres high.

The Garden is glorious throughout the seasons, from the vibrant blooms of rhododendrons and azaleas in early spring, striking Eucryphias of late summer and breathtaking displays of rich autumn fruit and foliage.

Trails throughout the Garden lead to beautiful spots such as the Formal Garden with its distinctive Puck's Hut and hillside woodlands to a dramatic viewpoint at 450 feet (140m) overlooking the surrounding mountains and Holy Loch.

Fact File

Opening times:	Open daily from 10 a.m. 1 March – 31 October. Closing: 5 p.m. (March and October) and 6 p.m. (April – September).
Admission Rates:	Adult: 4.00, Senior Citizens: £3.50, Children: £1.00
Group Rates:	Minimum Group size: 11. Adults: £3.60, Senior Citizens: £3.15, Children: £0.90
Facilities:	Shop, Plant Sales, Restaurant/Teas, Courtyard gallery hosting events & exhibitions, audio tours
Disabled Access:	Yes, partial
Toilets on site:	Yes
Car Parking:	Yes
Coach Parking:	Yes
Wheelchair Loan:	Yes, No Booking Required for Wheelchairs
Guided Tours:	Yes, every Tuesday/Wednesday/Thursday/Sunday at 2 p.m., no booking required
Length of Visit:	
Special Events:	Restored Victorian fernery – due to open summer 2009
Booking Contact:	Benmore Botanic Garden, Dunoon, Argyll PA23 8QU Booking Tel No. 01369 706261. Booking Fax No. 01369 706369
Email:	benmore@rbge.org.uk
Website:	www.rbge.org.uk/benmore
Location:	Dramatically set within the Loch Lomond and The Trossachs National Park and the Argyll Forest Park, on the A815 seven miles north of Dunoon on the Cowal Peninsula.

North facing and steep, Bolfracks is a challenge to garden. There has been a graden here for 200 years. Owned by the same family since the 1920's, each generation has made their changes to it.

As you arrive you sweep up a long drive that in spring is just a stream of golden daffodils. An enticement to visit!

The garden is divided into a wild garden and a formal rose and herbaceous garden. The Wild garden follows a burn up, where you see marvellous spring bulbs, Hellebores, Azaleas, Rhododendrons, Meconopsis, Gunnera, Lysichiton, Primula and then wonderful autumn colours from the collection of specimem trees. We are now proud owners of a Wollemi Pine! There are wonderful views across the Tay Valley.

The formal garden has a good selection of roses, clematis, specimem trees and a new herbaceous border and peony beds. There is a wonderful Peony delavyii and a well established Prunus pissardi hedge.

Bolfracks is a graden planted with love by the current owner's uncle. Recent years have seen some much needed changes and renovation. As always, this is an ongoing process

Fact File

Opening times:	April – October, Daily 10 a.m. – 6 p.m.
Admission Rates:	Adults: £4.00, Child free.
Facilities:	Toilet facilities, plants for sale, catering possibilities for groups.
Disabled Access:	Limited
Tours/Events:	None
Coach Parking:	Yes Please call for details.
Length of Visit:	2 hours
Booking Contact:	Mr & Mrs R. A. Price
	Bolfracks Estate Office, Aberfeldy, Perthshire PH15 2EX
	Telephone: 01887 820344, Fax: 01887 829522
Email:	info@bolfracks.fsnet.co.uk
Website:	www.bolfracks.com
Location:	2 miles west of Aberfeldy on A827 towards Loch Tay

Please quote this guide when making a booking

Located in beautiful scenery between two large natural lochs, the Gardens extend to seventy five acres of landscaped terraces and avenues. With the romantic and ruined 16th century Castle Kennedy over looking a walled garden, at one end, and Lochinch Castle at the other, these world famous gardens are uniquely outstanding.

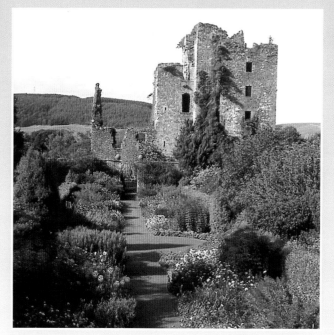

In close proximity to the sea on two sides, the Gardens are greatly influenced by the Gulf Stream, and contain many fine specimens of trees, Rhododendrons and tender exotic plants. Originally designed in 1722 by the 2nd Earl of Stair, Field Marshal and Ambassador to France, who was greatly influenced by the gardens of Versailles, the gardens are full of adventure and history.

Four carefully planned walks of different lengths and interest have been designed for visitors. These reveal the full garden experience throughout the seasons including the Daffodils, Magnolias and Rhododendrons early in the year to the beautiful herbaceous borders later in the summer, as well as many woodland and loch-side walks.

Fact File

Opening Times:	Weekends February & March, 1st April - 30th September, seven days a week, 10am- 5pm. Rest of the year by appointment.
Admission Rates:	Adults £4.00, Senior Citizen £3.00, Child £1.00
Groups Rates:	Minimum group size 20. 10% discount on normal admission rates.
Facilities:	Gift Shop, Tea room, Plant Sales
Disabled Access:	Partial. Toilet and parking for disabled on site.
Tours/Events:	Tours by special appointment. Please telephone for details of events.
Coach Parking:	Yes
Length of Visit:	1 - 4 hours
Booking Contact:	Castle Kennedy Gardens, Stair Estates, Rephad, Stranraer, Dumfries & Galloway, DG9 8BX Gardens Tel: 01581 400225 Telephone: 01776 702024 Fax: 01776 706248
Email:	info@castlekennedygardens.co.uk
Website:	www.castlekennedygardens.co.uk
Location:	Approximately 5 miles east of Stranraer on A75.

Please quote this guide when making a booking

Cawdor Castle, the most romantic Castle in the Highlands, dating from the 14th century is fortunate to have 3 gardens: the walled garden is the oldest and dates from circa 1600. It was planted in 1981 with a series of symbolic gardens: a holly maze that depicts the Minotaur's Labyrinth at Knossos in Crete; a Paradise Garden, where the sound of water and the smell of flowers create peace; a Knot Garden, whose plants were used for medicinal, culinary or still room preparations in the Middle Ages; and a Garden of Eden planted with old Scottish apple trees. The flower garden, south of the Castle, was laid out in the 18th century with rose beds edged with lavender, great herbaceous borders– yet there is still a family feel and plants are chosen out of affection, not affectation. The Auchindoune Garden, which is open on Tuesdays and Thursdays in May, June and July or by appointment, has an organic vegetable garden growing a variety of heritage vegetables; and a Tibetan Garden along the banks of the burn, which was planted with specimens brought back by Jack Cawdor from his travels with Kingdon Ward to the Tsangpo Gorges in 1924

Fact File

Opening Times:	1st May to 11th October, 10.00 a.m to 5.30 pm, last admission 5pm.
Admission Rates:	Castle, garden & grounds - Adult £8.00, OAP £7.10, Child £5.00, Gardens & grounds only - £4.50
	Auchindoune Gardens - £3.00 (Honesty Box - Closes 4pm)
Group Rates:	Minimum Groups Size: 20
	Castle, gardens and grounds - £6.75 Gardens and grounds only - £4.50
Facilities:	Three beautiful gardens, nature trails, 9 hole golf course, putting green, gift shop, book shop, & wool shop, restaurant and snack bar.
Disabled Access:	Access to gardens, grounds, restaurant, shops and toilet facilities. Access to castle limited.
Tours/Events:	Guided tours of gardens by Head Gardener by arrangement.
	Special Gardens Weekends – 6th/7th June, 29th/30th August
Coach Parking:	Yes.
Length of Visit:	Approximately 2 hours.
Booking Contact:	Secretary, Cawdor Castle and Gardens, Nairn, IV12 5RD
	Telephone: 01667 404401 Fax: 01667 404674
Email:	info@cawdorcastle.com
Website:	www.cawdorcastle.com
Location:	Situated between Inverness (15 miles) and Nairn (5 miles) on the B9090 off the A96.

Please quote this guide when making a booking

Dawyck Botanic Garden Scottish Borders

With over 300 years of tree planting Dawyck is truly one of the worlds finest arboreta, boasting some of the tallest trees in Britain, as well as exotic conifers and the unique Dawyck Beech. Set amidst a picturesque glen in the heart of the Scottish borders, these majestic trees form a splendid back-drop to the abundance of native and exotic plants on display.

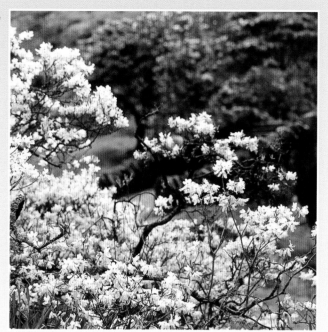

The Garden is a magical place throughout the year, from swathes of snowdrops and daffodils in early spring to breathtaking displays of azaleas, rhododendrons and pools of blue Himalayan poppies in early summer.

In autumn the foliage bursts into vivid hues of red, orange and gold and provides a magnificent backdrop of colour.

Dawyck's new state-of-the-art visitor centre greatly enhances the visitor experience at this renowned botanic garden.

Fact File

Opening times:	Open daily from 10 a.m. 1 February – 30 November.
	Closes 4 p.m. February & November; 5 p.m. March & October; 6 p.m. April – September.
Admission Rates:	Adults: £4.00, Senior Citizens: £3.50, Children: £1.00
Group Rates:	Minimum Group Size 10. Adults: £3.60, Senior Citizens: £3.15, Children: £0.90
Facilities:	Visitor Centre, Shop, Plant sales, Restaurant Teas, studio for exhibitions and events
Disabled Access:	Yes. Wheelchair loan available.
Toilets on site:	Yes
Car Parking on site:	Yes
Coach Parking:	Yes
Booking Contact:	Vicky Brunt, Dawyck Botanic Garden, Stobo, Near Peebles, Scottish Borders, EH45 9JU
	Booking Tel No.01721 760254 Booking Fax No. 01721 760214
Email:	dawyck@rbge.org.uk
Website:	www.rbge.org.uk/dawyck
Location:	28 miles south of Edinburgh on the B712, 8 miles southwest of Peebles in the Scottish Borders.

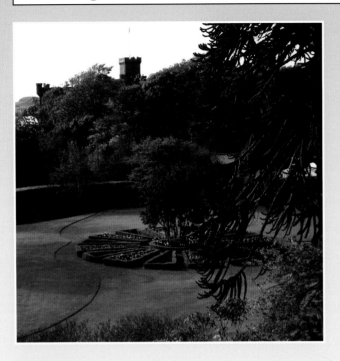

Set in the stunning scenery of the Isle of Skye, Dunvegan Castle & Gardens is the oldest continuously inhabited castle in Scotland and has been the stronghold of the Chiefs of MacLeod for nearly 800 years.

Dunvegan Castle's 5 acres of formal gardens began life in the 18th century. Its development suffered numerous setbacks until John MacLeod of MacLeod (29th Chief of clan MacLeod) decided to restore the gardens to their former glory in the late 1960s. In stark contrast to the barren moorland and mountains that dominate Skye's landscape, the gardens are like a hidden oasis featuring an eclectic mix of plants as you make your way through woodland glades, past shimmering pools fed by cascading waterfalls and burns flowing down to the sea.

For more information about opening times and our annual Friends of Dunvegan Castle & Gardens Membership scheme, please visit www.dunvegancastle.com.

Fact File

Opening times:	1 April – 15 October 10 a.m. – 5.30 p.m. 16 October – 31 March: open by appointment
Admission Rates:	Garden: Adults: £5.50, Senior Citizens/Students: £4.50, Children: £3.00
Group Rates:	Garden: Minimum Group Size: 10. Adults: £4.50, Senior Citizens: £4.50, Children: £3.00
Facilities:	Shop, Café, seal boat trips, fishing and loch cruises, Dunvegan Castle
Disabled Access:	Yes.
Toilets on site:	Yes
Car Parking on site:	Yes
Coach Parking:	Yes
Special Events:	Homecomng 2009
Booking Contact:	Macleod Estate Office, Dunvegan Castle & Gardens, Dunvegan, Isle of Skye, Scotland, IV55 8WF Booking Tel No.01470 521206. Booking Fax No. 01470 521205
Email:	info@dunvegancastle.com
Website:	www.dunvegancastle.com
Location:	1 mile north of Dunvegan on the northwest corner of Skye.

Please quote this guide when making a booking

This exotic Garden, justifiably described as a plantsman's paradise, is home to a spectacular collection of bizarre and beautiful plants. This majestic corner of Scotland is warmed by the Gulf Stream and the climate provides perfect growing conditions for southern hemisphere plants.

Famed for its tender collections, Logan's Walled Garden is a showcase for colourful blooms throughout the season. Adding to the summer colour are Osteospermums, gazanias and diascias – all half-hardy perennials from southern Africa. The Woodland Garden is a haven for the weird and wonderful, from the groves of eucalyptus to the Gunnera Bog and the evocative Tasmanian Creek planting. Visitors who venture to the highest point of the Garden will be rewarded with magnificent views over the Rhins to the Galloway Hills and beyond.

Over 1,800 different plant species, including around 120 that are threatened in the wild, can be seen thriving within Logan's 24-acre site.

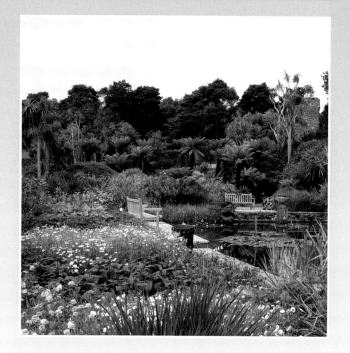

Fact File

Opening times:	Open daily from 10 a.m. 1st March - 31st October. (Sundays only in February 4 p.m.) March & October 5 p.m. April - September 6 p.m. (Sundays only in February), 5 p.m. March & October; 6 p.m. April – September
Admission Rates:	Adults: £4.00, Senior Citizens: £3.50, Children: £1.00
Group Rates:	Minimum Group Size: 11. Adults: £3.60, Senior Citizens: £3.15, Children: £0.90
Facilities:	Visitor Centre, Shop, Plant Sales, Restaurant, Teas, Audio guides
Disabled Access:	Yes
Toilets on site:	Yes
Car Parking on site:	Yes
Coach Parking:	Yes
Guided Tours:	Yes, 10.30a.m. every second Tuesday of the month (April – September) pre-booked tours available.
Booking Contact:	Richard Baines, Logan Botanic Gardens, Port Logan, Stranraer, Dumfries & Galloway DG9 9ND Booking Tel No.01776 860231. Booking Fax No. 01776 860333
Email:	logan@rbge.org.uk
Website:	www.rbge.org.uk/logan
Location:	14 miles south of Stranraer in the Rhins of Galloway, off the B7065.

Please quote this guide when making a booking

Established in 1670, the Royal Botanic Garden Edinburgh has developed into a world leading centre of horticultural excellence and its 70 magnificent acres are home to seven per cent of all known plants.

At the heart of the Garden stands the iconic Palm House - the tallest of its kind in Britain. Within the Glasshouses you will enjoy a fascinating journey through the tropical and temperate regions of the globe as you wander through ten distinct climatic zones.

Reflecting the international research and conservation work of RBGE, the Garden is home to the largest collection of wild-origin Chinese plants outside China. See, too, the Scottish Heath Garden, recreating the plantings and landscape of the Scottish highlands; the world-famous Rock Garden; the stunning 165-long Herbaceous Border, backed by an outstanding century-old Beech Hedge and don't miss the Queen Mother's Memorial Garden – an inspirational tribute to a much-loved royal.

Fact File

Opening times:	Open daily from 10 a.m. (except 25 December and 31 January), closing 4 p.m. November – February; 6 p.m. March & October; 7 p.m. April to September
Admission Rates:	Adults: Free, Senior Citizens: Free, Children: Free. A charge applies to the glasshouses
Disabled Access:	Yes. Wheelchair loan available – booking required.
Toilets on site:	Yes
Car Parking on site:	Yes
Coach Parking:	Yes
Guided Tours:	Yes.
Length of Visit:	Guided tours depart daily at 11 a.m. & 2 p.m., April – September. Booked tours for groups available throughout the year
Special Events:	The John Hope Gateway Biodiversity and Information Centre opens summer 2009.
Booking Contact:	To book guided tours, please contact The Education Department. Booking Tel No.0131248 2937. Booking Fax No. 0131 248 2901
Email:	education@rbge.org.uk
Website:	www.rbge.org.uk
Location:	One mile north of Princes Street on the A092, with entrances on Inverleith Row and Inverleith Place.

Torosay Castle & Gardens Isle of Mull

Torosay Castle, completed in 1858 in the Scottish Baronial style by the eminent architect David Bryce, is one of the finer examples of his work, resulting in a combination of elegance and informality, grandeur and homeliness.

A unique combination of formal terraces and dramatic West Highland scenery makes Torosay a spectacular setting, which, together with a mild climate results in superb specimens of rare, unusual and beautiful plants.

A large collection of Statuary and many niche gardens makes Torosay a joy to explore and provides many peaceful corners in which to relax.

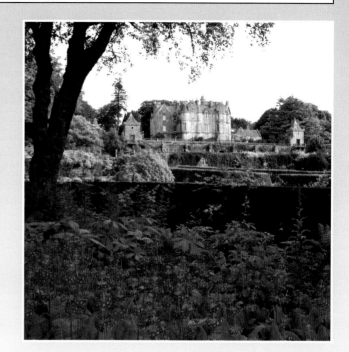

Fact File

Opening Times:	1st April - 31st October, 10.30am - 5.00pm.
	Gardens: Open all year, 9.00am - 7.00pm or dusk if earlier.
Admission Rates:	Adults £6.50, Concessions £5.50, Child £3.75. Discounts for gardens only.
Group Rates:	Minimum group size: 10.
	Adults £5.50, Concessions £5.50, Child £3.50. Guided Tour rate £10.00.
Facilities:	Shop, Plant Sales, Children's Play Area, Tea Room, Holiday Cottages, Parking on site.
Disabled Access:	Yes to gardens only. Toilet and parking for disabled on site.
Tours/Events:	Tours available to groups by arrangement at a cost of £9.00 per person.
	Concerts, plays etc advertised seperately.
Coach Parking:	Yes
Length of Visit:	2 hours minimum.
Booking Contact:	Christopher James
	Torosay Castle, Craignure, Isle of Mull PA65 6AY
	Telephone: 01680 812421 Fax: 01680 812470
Email:	torosay@aol.com
Website:	www.torosay.com
Location:	1 1/2 miles from Craignure (ferry terminal) on A849/on foot by forest walk or by narrow gauge railway.

The National Botanic Garden of Wales - Carmarthenshire

Wales

'Once I saw two flowers blossom in a garden 'neath the hill,
One a lily fair and handsome, and one a rose with crimson frill;
Erect the rose would lift its pennon and survey the garden round,
While the lily-lovely minion meekly rested on a mound.'

Reverend Daniel Evans

From Cardiff Bay to the mountains of Snowdonia, Wales is a country
of contrasts and this can be clearly seen through the diversity of its gardens.
Historic garden restorations such as at Aberglasney, modern garden
creations like the stunning National Botanic Garden of Wales, Dewstow
with its caves and grottoes and the sub-tropical paradise which is
Portmeirion are just some of those to be enjoyed within this book.

Aberglasney Gardens   Carmarthenshire

Aberglasney is one of the finest gardens in Wales. The Gardens have wonderful horticultural qualities and a mysterious history. Within the ten acres of garden are six different garden spaces including three walled gardens. At its heart is a unique and fully restored Elizabethan /Jacobean Cloister Garden and a parapet walk, which is the only example that survived in the UK. The Garden contains a magnificent collection of rare and unusual plants which are seldom seen elsewhere in the country.

The Mansion and Garden will continually be improved over the years, the result is a world renowned Garden set in the beautiful landscape of the Tywi Valley. There is a Café in the grounds, which serves delectable light lunches and snacks. In the summer, tea can be taken on the terrace overlooking the Pool Garden. There is also a shop and plant sales area. The creation of a winter garden in 2005 called the Ninfarium (after the mediaeval garden near Rome) is situated in the ruinous central courtyard of the Mansion. It provides a unique garden environment, displaying a wonderful range of exotic sub-tropical plants.

Fact File

Opening times:	Summer: 10am - 6pm (last entry at 5pm).
	Winter: 10.30am - 4pm (last entry at 3pm).
Admission Rates:	Adult/OAP £7.00, Child £4.00, Family £18.00.
Groups Rates:	Groups 10+
	Adult/OAP £6.50.
Facilities:	Shop, Plant Sales, Cafe.
Disabled Access:	Yes. Toilet and parking for disabled on site. Wheelchairs on loan, booking necessary.
Tours/Events:	Guided tours on request.
Coach Parking:	Yes
Length of Visit:	2 - 4 hours
Booking Contact:	Bookings Department.
	Aberglasney Gardens, Llangathen, Carmarthenshire, SA32 8QH
	Telephone: 01558 668998 Fax: 01558 668998
Email:	info@aberglasney.org.uk
Website:	www.aberglasney.org
Location:	Four miles outside Llandeilo off the A40.

Please quote this guide when making a booking

Bodnant Garden Conwy

Bodnant Garden is one of the finest gardens in the country not only known for its magnificent collections of rhododendrons, camellias and magnolias but also for its idyllic setting above the River Conwy with extensive views of the Snowdonia range.

Visit in early Spring (March and April) and be rewarded by the sight of carpets of golden daffodils and other spring bulbs, as well as the beautiful blooms of the magnolias, camellias and flowering cherries. The spectacular rhododendrons and azaleas will delight from mid April until late May, whilst the famous original Laburnum Arch is an overwhelming mass of yellow blooms from mid-may to mid-June. The herbaceous borders, roses, hydrangeos, clematis and water liles flower from the middle of June until September.

All these, together with the outstanding October autumn colours make Bodnant truly a garden offering interest for all the seasons.

Fact File

Opening Times:	28th February - 15th November 2009
Admission Rates:	Adults £7.50, Child £3.75 (5-16yrs)
Groups Rates:	Minimum group size 15. Adults £6.45.
Facilities:	Tearoom, Car & Coach Park. Garden Centre, Art & Craft Studios (Not NT).
Disabled Access:	Yes. Toilet and parking for disabled on site. Wheelchairs on loan.
Tours/Events:	Phone for details
Coach Parking:	Yes
Length of Visit:	2 hours +
Booking Contact:	Ann Smith Bodnant Garden, Tal Y cafn, Nr Colwyn Bay, Conwy. LL28 5RE Telephone: 01492 650460 Fax: 01492 650448
Email:	ann.smith@nationaltrust.org.uk
Website:	www.bodnant-garden.co.uk
Location:	8 miles south of Llandudno and Colwyn Bay just off A470, signposted from the A55, exit at junction 19.

THE secret is out . . . Dewstow's Hidden Gardens and Grottoes are rapidly becoming one of the most fascinating tourist attractions in South Wales. Situated just a few miles from the M4 motorway and the two Severn Bridges, the Dewstow estate offers a magical oasis of calm, set in the magnificent Monmouthshire countryside.

The "lost" gardens, which date back to the late 1890s, became buried by tons of soil around the time of the Second World War but were rediscovered by new owners in 2000. Now, due to a painstaking and meticulous renovation programme, Dewstow's buried treasure has been unveiled once again and is being viewed and enjoyed by a long line of enchanted visitors.

Dewstow, now Grade One listed, features a stunning series of gardens, pools, water features and ornamental areas just waiting to be explored at your leisure. Don't miss the chance to take a fascinating journey back in time in this subterranean wonderland before relaxing with some refreshments in our delightful tea room.

Fact File

Opening Times: Daily from 20th March until 18th October 2009 10.00 – 4.30 p.m.
Admission Rates: Adults: £6.00, Senior Citizens: £5.00, Children: £3.50.
Group Rates: Minimum Group Size 15, Adults: £5.00, Senior Citizens: £5.00, Children: £3.50.
Facilities: Plant sales, teas.
Disabled Access: No.
Toilets on site: Yes.
Tours/Events: Guided tours available, booking required.
Coach Parking: Yes.
Car Parking on site: Yes.
Length of Visit: 2 hours approximately.
Booking Contact: Liz, Dewstow Gardens, Caerwent, Monmouthshire NP26 5AH
Telephone: 01291 430444
Fax: 01291 425816
Email: gardens@dewstow.co.uk
Website: www.dewstow.co.uk/gardens.htm

Please quote this guide when making a booking

The Dingle garden is set in the heart of glorious mid-Wales. The four acre garden is mostly the work of Barbara Joseph who over the years, created a secluded and beautiful area which serves to inspire garden lovers everywhere.

The R.H.S. partner garden is south-facing with paths that wind down the slope to a lake and small waterfall. The beds are colour themed to look good all year round. Spectacular autumn foliage, including many unusual trees, shrubs and acers, along with an acre primrose wood in spring are special features. This peaceful haven, teeming with wildlife is the ideal spot for a relaxing wander at any time of year.

The Dingle Nursery runs alongside the garden and offers for sale a huge variety of common and rare plants and trees, many of which grow there.

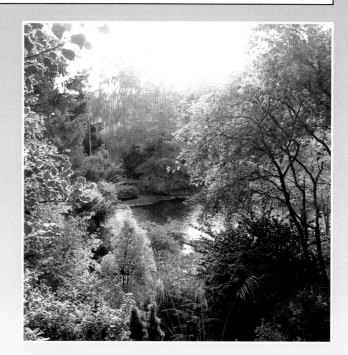

Fact File

Opening Times:	9 – 5 every day. Only closed for one week at Christmas
Admission Rates:	Adults: £3.00, Senior Citizens: £3.00, Children: Free, R.H.S. members free.
Group Rates:	No reduction for groups (free tea and coffee included in the price)
Facilities:	Small shop with free tea and coffee available.
Disabled Access:	Very limited. 1 wheelchair available for booking. Car Parking and toilet on site.
Tours/Events:	No guided tours. Talk for groups.
Coach Parking:	Yes.
Length of Visit:	1 – 3 hours.
Booking Contact:	Jill Rock, The Dingle Garden, Frochas, Nr. Welshpool, Powys. SY21 9JD
	Tel: 01938 555145 Fax: 01938 555778
Email:	info@dinglenurseryandgarden.co.uk
Website:	www.dinglenurseryandgarden.co.uk
Location:	2 miles north of Welshpool, off the A490.

Set in the heart of the Vale of Glamorgan countryside, Dyffryn is one of Wales' largest and most important Edwardian Gardens. The impressive 55 acres are a result of the unique collaboration of landscape architect Thomas Mawson and avid plant collector Reginald Cory.

Dyffryn boasts a magnificent double herbaceous border, a Victorian fernery, a rose garden, a stumpery, a rockery and also an extensive tree collection in the arboretum. As you stroll the beautiful grounds you will also discover a series of intimate garden rooms, such as the Pompeian Garden, Lavender Court and the Reflecting pool.

This outstanding garden has been undergoing considerable restoration works with assistance from the Heritage Lottery Fund. The extensive project is due to conclude this year with the exciting revival of the walled garden and the reinstatement of the magnificent glasshouses.

Fact File

Opening Times: Site open throughout the year. 1st March – 31st October 10am – 6pm.
1st November – 28th February 10am - 4pm.

Admission Rate: 1st March – 31st October Adults £6.50, Concession £4.50, Child £2.50, Family £17.00.
1st November – 29th February Adult £3.50, Concession £2.50, Child £1.50, Family £8.50.

Group Rates: Discount on groups of 15 and over, please contact for more details.

Facilities: Visitor centre, Tearooms, Play area and plant sales all before the pay barrier

Disabled Access: Majority of gardens is wheelchair friendly.
Wheelchairs available to loan, advanced booking is preferable.

Tours/Events: Tours available to groups by prior arrangement at an additional charge. Tours with Head Gardener held throughout the year, please contact for more details.
Varied programme of seasonal events and activities held throughout the year.

Coach Parking: Yes

Length of Visit: 2 – 3 hours

Booking Contact: Dyffryn Gardens, St Nicholas, Vale of Glamorgan, CF5 6SU.
Tel: 029 2059 3328, Fax: 029 2059 1966

Email: dyffryn@valeofglamorgan.gov.uk

Website: www.dyffryngardens.org.uk or www.visitthevale.com

Location: Exit M4 at J33 to A4232(signposted Barry). At roundabout take 1st exit (A4232). At junction with A48/A4050 exit the A4232 at Culverhouse Cross Take 4th exit A48 (signposted Cowbridge). Turn left at lights in St Nicholas.
Dyffryn is on right after approx. 1½ miles.

Please quote this guide when making a booking

Glansevern Hall was built, in Greek Revival style, by Sir Arthur Davies Owen at the turn of the 18th/19th Century.

It looks down on the River Severn from an enclosure of gardens set in wider parkland. Near the house are fine lawns studded with herbaceous and rose beds and a wide border backed by brick walls. A Victorian orangery and a large fountain face each other across the lawns. The large walled garden has been ingeniously divided into compartments separated by hornbeam hedges and ornamental ironwork. There is a rock garden of exceptional size, built of limestone and tufa, which creates a walk-through grotto. A little further afield, woodland walks are laid out around the 4 acre lake and pass through a water garden which, especially in May and June, presents a riot of growth and colour.

Glansevern is noted for its collection of unusual trees.

Fact File

Opening times:	May to September every Thursday, Friday, Saturday and Bank Holiday Monday 12.00 noon - 5.00 pm. Groups on any other day, booking necessary.
Admission Rates:	Adult £5.00, Seniors £4.00, Children under sixteen Free.
Facilities:	Tea Room & Light Lunches (all Homemade), Plant Sales, Art Gallery.
Disabled Access:	Yes. Toilet and parking for disabled on site.
Tours/Events:	Guided walk indentifying the large number of unusual trees.
Coach Parking:	Yes
Length of Visit:	1 ½ hours
Booking Contact:	Neville Thomas Glansevern Hall Gardens, Berriew, Welshpool, Powys, SY21 8AH Telephone: 01686 640644 Fax: 01686 640829
Email:	glansevern@yahoo.co.uk
Website:	www.glansevern.co.uk
Location:	Signposted at Berriew on A483 between Welshpool and Newtown, North Powys, 4 miles S W of Powis Castle.

Within a setting of breathtaking beauty, the Grade 11* listed, 52 roomed Gothic Revival Hall and its seperately listed 12 acres of landscaped grounds overlook the church and the ruins of the 12th century Cistercian "Abbey of The Long Valley", containing the monk's pond, and the grave of Llewellyn The Last..

Following 9 years of restoration, Paul and Victoria Humpherston offer tours conducted by themselves of all 52 rooms, and/or full access to the gardens. The house tours combine viewing fine architectural features with stunning interior designs in all rooms, and thousands of items from a lifetime of collecting.

The gardens are open April to October inclusive. Features include a unique 1.5 acre walled garden; sweeping lawns, terraces and courtyards; a lake and waterfall; and splendid mixed woodland containing a quarter of a mile of pathways below some of Radnorshires' tallest trees. The grounds give wonderful views along "The Long Valley".

Fact File

Opening Times: Daily (except Xmas day) for pre-booked tours of the house commencing at 10.30am, 2pm or 7pm. Tours include full access to the gardens during start April/end October inclusive. Alternatively, visits to the gardens only are available during April/October inclusive.

Admission Rates: House (and gardens); £13 per person. £11 for repeat visitors. £5 per child. Gardens only; £5 per person. Children free.

Groups Rates: Groups defined as 10 + persons pre-booking. House (and gardens); £11 per person.

Facilities: Refreshments, bar and toilets available in The Garden Room. Meals available in Garden Room for pre-booked Group tours. Car parking available.

Disabled Access: Yes, but limited within the house.

Tours/Events: All tours of the house (and gardens) are pre-booked and guided by the owners. All 52 rooms are decorated for Christmas from mid November each year.

Coach Parking: Yes.

Length of Visit: Guided tour of house (all 52 rooms) takes c.2 hours. No time restrictions on garden visits.

Booking Contact: Paul Humpherston, The Hall at Abbey-Cwm-Hir, Abbey-Cwm-Hir, nr. Llandrindod Wells,Powys, LD1 6PH
Telephone: 01597 851727

Email: info@abbeycwmhir.com

Website: www.abbeycwmhir.com

Location: 7 miles NW of Llandrindod Wells / 5 miles East of Rhayader. Take the A44/A483 to Crossgates. The turn for Abbey-Cwm-Hir is 1 mile north on the A 483.

Please quote this guide when making a booking

National Botanic Garden Of Wales — Carmarthenshire

The remarkable National Botanic Garden of Wales is a very special place. The largest single-span glasshouse in the world designed by Norman Foster, poised in the landscape like a giant raindrop is home to some of the most endangered plants on the planet from six Mediterranean climate regions, Western Australia, Chile, the Canaries, California, southern Africa and the Mediterranean basin. It helps protect and conserve what is considered to be the best collection of its kind in the world. The Tropical House located in the unique and historic double-walled garden is bursting with palms, pineapples, coconuts, cardamom and scores of orchids. The Garden lies on land that was once a magnificent Regency water park, many of the original features having been restored. Discover lakes, ponds, walks; theatre; licensed restaurant; shop; gallery; bog garden, apiary; Physicians of Myddfai Exhibition and Apothecaries' Garden; children's play area and discovery centre. Land surrounding the Garden has been designated a National Nature Reserve.

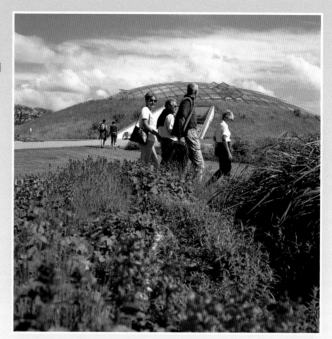

Fact File

Opening times: 10 a.m. – 6 p.m. BST/10 a.m. – 4.30 p.m. BWT. (Closed Christmas Day)

Admission Rates: Adults: £8.00, Senior Citizens: £6.50, Children: Under 16: £4.00, Under 5s: Free

Group Rates: Minimum Group Size: 10. Adults: £7.00, Senior Citizens: £5.50, Children: £3.00
NT members free. RHS members free – between 1st October and 31st March

Facilities: Visitor Centre, Shop, Plant Sales, Licensed Restaurant, Teas, Café, 360 degree Multimedia Theatre, Conference Centre, Children's Activity Centre.

Disabled Access: Yes. Wheelchair loan available FOC, booking advisable.

Toilets on site: Yes

Car Parking on site: Yes

Coach Parking: Yes

Guided Tours: Yes, booking required.

Length of Visit: 4 hours

Special Events: Full events programme

Booking Contact: National Botanic Garden of Wales, Llanarthne, Carmarthenshire, SA32 8HG
Booking Tel No. 01558 668768. Booking Fax No. 01558 668933

Email: info@gardenofwales.org.uk

Website: www.gardenofwales.org.uk

Location: One hour's drive from Cardiff, two hours from Bristol.
Just off the A48 which links directly to the M4 and on to the M5.

Please quote this guide when making a booking

Soak up a special magic as you walk beneath some of the largest and oldest trees in West Wales. The 40 acres of walled and woodland gardens around Picton Castle include a tree fern glade, a restored dew pond and the new jungle garden planted with gingers, banana trees and other vibrant exotics. Unique to Picton are Rhododendrons bred here, plus rare species like Embothrium, Eucryphia and an avenue of myrtles.

Massive Redwoods and oaks dominate the Avenues. Around them, rare trees and flowering shrubs include the largest Rhododendron 'Old Port' in existence, a particularly fine Dawn Redwood (a conifer presumed extinct until rediscovered in remote Chinese valley in 1941) and numerous rare conifers from all over the globe.

Scent and colour rule the Walled Garden, where a vast collection of border plants create riotous summer colour. Equally tantalising is Maria's Mediterranean Restaurant, in the Victorian courtyard.

Fact File

Opening times: Easter – 30th September: Daily 10.30 a.m. – 5.00 p.m. Tuesday to Sunday, and Bank Holiday Mondays. Entrance to the Castle by guided tour only 11.30 a.m. – 3.30 p.m. Winter opening - see website for details.

Admission Rates: Gardens & Gallery: Adults: £4.95, Senior Citizens: £4.75, Children 5 – 16: £2.50
Castle tour with Gardens & Gallery: Adults: £5.95, Seniors: £5.75, Children: £3.00

Group Rates: Reductions on Castle tours for pre-booked groups of 20 or more. RHS Members Free from April – September

Facilities: Shop, plant sales, restaurant, teas, art galleries, castle tours, children's play area, picnic area, toilets.

Disabled Access: Yes. Wheelchair loan available.

Car Parking on site: Yes

Coach Parking: Yes

Tours/Events: Guided tours to Castle only. Booking only required for large groups on Castle tours

Length of Visit: 2 hours for castle tour and Walled Garden, plus 2 hours for 40 acres of woodland gardens.

Special Events: See website for information.

Booking Contact: David Pryse Lloyd
Picton Castle Gardens & Gallery, Picton Castle, Haverfordwest, Pembrokeshire SA62 4AS
Telephone & Fax No. 01437 751326.

Email: info@pictoncastle.co.uk   Website www.pictoncaste.co.uk

Location: OS Ref: SN011 135; two miles south of the A40. Follow brown tourist signs located on the A40 about 3 miles east of Haverfordwest,

> Please quote this guide when making a booking

Portmeirion   Gwynedd

The Italianate village of Portmeirion is surrounded by 70 acres of sub-tropical woodlands known as Y Gwyllt "the wild place"- it was once an area of rough pasture and gorse) with its Victorian shelters, temples and dogs' cemetery. From the 1840s successive tenants landscaped and planted the area with a variety of native and exotic trees. From the early 1900s the Gwyllt was developed by Caton Haig as an exotic woodland garden until his death in 1941 when the garden was bought by Clough Williams-Ellis and incorporated into his Portmeirion estate.

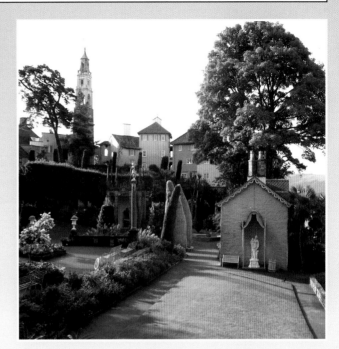

A tree trail has recently been established giving access to some of the most important trees in the garden including one hundred year old rhododendrons, gigantic Californian coast redwoods, the papauma or New Zealand 'dancing tree', the UK's largest Japanese cedar 'elegans' and tallest Chilean maiten tree, the ginkgo or maidenhair tree and many others.

Fact File

Opening Times:	All Year 9.30 - 17.30
Admission Rates:	Adult £7.50, Senior Citizen £6.00, Child £4.00 Family (2+2) £17.00
Group Rates:	Minimum group size: 12
	Adult £5.50, Senior Citizen £4.00, Child £3.00
Facilities:	Gift Shop, Teas, Restaurant, Pizza Parlour Audio Visual, Hotel, 7 Shops, Tree Trail, Beach.
Disabled Access:	Yes. Toilet and parking for disabled on site. Wheelchair on loan, booking advisable.
Tours/Events:	None
Coach Parking:	Yes
Length of Visit:	3 hours
Booking Contact:	Terry Williams. Toll Gate Manager
	Portmerion, Gwynedd, LL48 6ET.
	Telephone: 01766 772311 Fax: 01766 771331
Email:	info@portmeirion-village.com
Website:	www.portmeirion-village.com
Location:	Signposted off A487 at Minffordd between Penrhyndeudraeth and Porthmadog.

Please quote this guide when making a booking

Samares Manor Gardens

Jersey, Channel Islands

These exceptional gardens were originally designed and constructed in the 1920s by wealthy shipping line owner, Sir James Knott. Inspired by an enthusiasm for plants and a special interest in the Orient, he created a rich diversity of planting which included many rare and special plants: a Japanese Garden, rock and water gardens, formal gardens, large ponds with islands and camellia plantations are the result of his passion.

In recent years there has been a programme of restoration, development and diversification. This included the introduction of the internationally renowned herb garden, the inspiration of designer, John Brookes. Sited in the south facing walled garden it contains hundreds of culinary, medicinal and fragrant plants. Manor activities include daily talks on herbs, a plant trail that highlights seasonal specialities and children's competitions. The manor house and the rural life museum are also open to the public.

Fact File

Opening Times: 4th April – 10th October 2009: 9.30 a.m. – 5 p.m.
Admission Rates: Adults: £6.50, O.A.P: £5.95, Children over 5/Student: £2.35.
Group Rates: Minimum Group Size: 10
Adults: £5.85, O.A.P: £5.50, Children over 5 / Student: £2.25.
Facilities: Shop, plant sales, restaurant, Jersey Rural Life and Carriage Museum, Toilets.
Disabled Access: Yes. Bookable wheelchair loan available (1 only)
Car Parking on site: Yes
Coach Parking: Yes
Tours/Events: Guided tours available. Booking required.
Length of Visit: 3 hours minimum
Special Events: Summer Festival and Jersey Rose Show: 20th & 21st June 2009.
Booking Contact: Sally Fleming, Samarès Manor, St. Clements, Jersey JE2 6QW
Booking Telephone No. 01534 870551 Booking Fax No. 01534 768949
Email: enquiries@samaresmanor.com
Website: www.samaresmanor.com
Location: From St. Helier, drive to Georgetown crossroads and follow road signs to St. Clements (A4, A5). Pass New Veterinary Hospital, bear right and turn left at traffic lights St. Clements' inner road. Pass the Roman Catholic Church on the right. Entrance to Samarès Manor is 500 yards on the left. Watch for the flags.

Ireland

'Autumn is over the long leaves that loves us
and over the mice in the barley sheaves;
Yellow the leaves of the rowan above us
And yellow the wet-wild strawberry leaves'.

The falling of the leaves - William Butler Yeats.

The weather is soft in Ireland, seldom offering extremes of heat or cold,
just copious gifts of gently falling rain and mild airstreams enabling every
landscape, plant and garden to green and grow. Irish gardens are like no
other; they too are soft and gentle, full of atmosphere and a fecundity
of foliage. The following pages provide just a little taster of some of the finest
Irish gardens to be found in and around the beautiful city of Dublin.

Cashel House Hotel & Gardens Co Galway

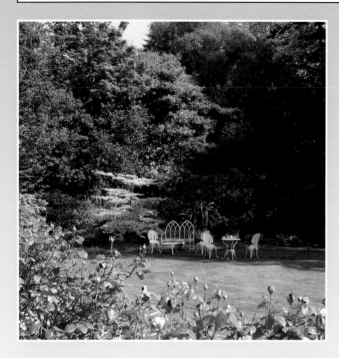

Cashel house is a gracious country house owned by the McEvilly family. The gardens are an informal country house style based on a number of woodland glades. The garden contains profusion of roses both old fashioned and modern along with many herbaceous plants with naturalised day lilies, astilbes and primulas. Also camellias, magnolias, azaleas, eucryphia and many more. Our own herb and fruit gardens, stud farm and garden school are also on site.

Fact File

Opening times:	10.30 – 5 p.m. each day from 12 February – 1 December.
Admission Rates:	Adults: £5.00, Senior Citizens: £3.00, Children and students: £3.00
	RHS members free
Group Rates:	Minimum Group Size: Adults: 40/50, Senior Citizens: 30/40, Children: 8/10
Facilities:	Plant Sales, Restaurant, Teas, Garden, Courses
Disabled Access:	Part of the garden, all of the house, booking required for wheelchairs
Toilets on site:	Yes
Car Parking on site:	Yes
Coach Parking:	Yes, for small coaches 20 – 60 persons
Guided Tours:	Yes, booking required
Special Events:	Garden courses, 2 or 3 days or one day, see leaflet attached
Booking Contact:	Kay McEvilly, Cashel House Hotel & Gardens, Cashel, Connamara, Co. Galway
	Booking Tel No. 353 95 31001. Booking Fax No. 353 95 81077
Email:	res@cashel-house-hotel.com
Website:	www.cashel-house-hotel.com
Location:	West coast of Ireland, 40 miles from Galway, 8 from Roundstone,
	8 from Carna, 12 from Clifden

Please quote this guide when making a booking

The Dublin Garden Group Dublin

The Dublin garden group (DGG) consists of Ireland's most distinguished private gardens in the greater Dublin area. The very mild and temperate climate in Ireland makes it a plants man's joy and allows a wide variety of plants from all over the world, to exist side by side.
The owners of these private gardens, most of which are not open to the public, would like to welcome groups to share their enthusiasm and knowledge.
DGG exists to assist group organisers by suggesting itineraries and, when agreed, booking the individual gardens for them. Gardens that are not in the group can be included in your itineraries. Advice on gardens to visit in the rest of Ireland is also available.

GARDENS IN THE GROUP
The Dillon Garden (www.dillongarden.com), Carysford Lodge, Knockrose, Corke Lodge (www.corkelodge.com), Warble Bank, Primrose Hill, Mount Usher (www.mount-usher-gardens.com), Rathmichael Lodge, Knockmore, Carmel Duignan's Garden, Hunting Brook Gardens (www.huntingbrook.com), June Blake's Garden and Nursery.

Fact File

Opening Times:	For details of individual gardens see www.dublingardens.com
Admission Rates:	see www.dublingardens.com
Group Rates:	see www.dublingardens.com
Facilities:	Look up specific gardens for details. Tea/ coffee/ lunch by arrangement.
Disabled Access:	Look up specific gardens for details.
Car Parking on site:	Yes
Coach Parking:	Yes
Tours/Events:	Guided tours available. Booking required.
Length of Visit:	see www.dublingardens.com
Special Events:	see www.dublingardens.com
Booking Contact:	John Beatty
	Dublin Garden Group
	Waltham Terrace, Black Rock, Co Dublin, Ireland.
	Booking Telephone No. 00353 1 2369796
	Booking Fax No. 00353 1 2369796
Email:	dgg@oceanfree.net
Website:	www.dublingardens.com
Location:	All gardens are located in Dublin or in Wicklow.

Please quote this guide when making a booking

Hunting Brook Gardens   Co Wicklow

Hunting Brook is Ireland's most exciting new garden located 10 miles from Dublin in the foot hills of the Wicklow mountains. The gardens cover 10 acres with woodland walks through the glaciated glen, through to the extensive contemporary borders in a modern fusion of prairie and tropical planting with an incredible plant collection from around the world. Many of the plants are new to cultivation and were collected by the owner Jimi Blake on plant expeditions.

Hunting Brook was featured in Gardens Illustrated in Sept 2008 issue & the English Garden in Nov 2008 issue. New woodland walks through the valley will be open for 2009. If you have a plant collecting obsession like Jimi you have to visit Hunting Brook and bring along a picnic.

Pre booked teas and/or lunches are available in the log cabin at Hunting Brook located in the centre of the garden

Fact File

Opening Times:	Sat 23rd & Sun 24th May/Sat 13th & Sun 14th June/Saturday 10th & Sun 11th July/Sat 8th & Sun 9th August/Sat 12th & Sun 13th September 12 p.m. – 5.30 p.m. Working in the Garden most days, please feel free to visit any time, but phone ahead to check we are in.
Admission Rates:	Adults: 6.00, Children: 2.00
Group Rates:	(One-hour guided tour + tea & biscuits) Adults: 10.00 per person.
Facilities:	Teas/lunch by arrangement for groups, toilets.
Disabled Access:	No Wheelchair - sorry.
Car Parking on site:	Yes
Coach Parking:	Yes – large coaches park down the road
Tours/Events:	Guided tours available. Booking required.
Length of Visit:	Group tours 1 hour guided or as long as you want unguided.
Special Events:	30 courses and evening opening throughout the year in gardening/cookery, art & craft. Check out the website.
Booking Contact:	Jimi Blake Hunting Brook Gardens, Lamb Hill, Blessington, Co. Wicklow Booking Telephone No. 0035 3872 856601
Email:	jimi@huntingbrook.com
Website:	www.huntingbrook.com
Location:	Please see web site. 15 miles from Dublin City Centre.

Please quote this guide when making a booking

June Blake is a passionate plantswoman who runs a remarkable garden and small rare plants nursery from her home, an early Victorian, steward's cottage. The gardens extend over approximately three acres and contain an eclectic collection of plants from around the world.
The garden includes areas of exciting, bold herbaceous planting and serene stillness including a sublime shade garden of ferns, grasses and bamboos punctuated by enormous granite boulders. There is a shallow, linear reflecting pool with an austere sheet of motionless water set amidst exuberant tropical and prairie planting.
The garden's strong skeleton of wide gravel paths leads the eyes along lush borders with ever-changing combinations of hardy and tender herbaceous and woody plants in huge beds of hot colours and shady retreats retained by dry stone walls. There is an allee of 2.5m Dicksonia squarrosa, to give views of architectural, scultpural, horticultural and pastoral elements within the gardens.

Fact File

Opening times:	Fridays, Saturdays, Sundays and bank holidays from mid-May to Mid-September; other times by appointment
Admission Charges:	Adults: 5.00, Senior Citizens: 5.00, Children: Under 12 free
Group Rates:	(Groups can visit any day of the week by arrangement) Minimum Group Size: None Adults: 5.00, Senior Citizens: 5.00, Children: Under 12 free
On-Site Facilities:	Plant sales, picnic facilities available
Disabled Access:	No
Toilets on site:	Yes
Car Parking on site:	Yes
Coach Parking:	Yes
Guided Tours:	Yes, booking required
Length of Visit:	1 hour
Booking Contact:	June Blake, June Blake's Garden and Nursery, Tinode, Blessington, Co. Wicklow, Ireland Booking Tel No.087 277 0299. Garden Tel No. 087 277 0399
Email:	info@juneblake.ie
Website:	www.juneblake.ie
Location:	By car: between Brittas, Co. Dublin and Blessington, Co. Wicklow on the N81; signposted on the right one half mile past turn for Sally Gap/ Kilbride. By bus: Take Dublin Bus number 65 from Eden Quay to one stop past Tramway Treasures Antique Shop opposite the turn for Manor Kilbride; lane to gardens is on the right beside the bus stop.

Please quote this guide when making a booking

Index

Index

Thanks go to the Gardens, Garden Clubs and Garden Visitors who have provided
feedback on the information they would like to see within this publication.

Visit www.gardenstovisit.net for further information on your garden visits.

ISBN: 978-0-9551833-3-1

If you would like to order additional copies of Gardens to Visit 2009
please contact the address below.

Gardens to Visit 2009 is specially published by
Publicity Works • PO Box 32 • Tetbury • Gloucestershire • GL8 8BF
Telephone: 01453 836730 Fax: 01453 835285
Email: mail@publicity-works.org